A Cognitive Pragmatic Analysis of Nominal Tautologies

Hituzi Linguistics in English

No.5	Communicating Skills of Intention	Tsutomu Sakamoto
No.6	A Pragmatic Approach to the Generation and Gender Gap in Japanese Politeness Strategies	Toshihiko Suzuki
No.7	Japanese Women's Listening Behavior in Face-to-face Conversation	Sachie Miyazaki
No.8	An Enterprise in the Cognitive Science of Language	Tetsuya Sano et al.
No.9	Syntactic Structure and Silence	Hisao Tokizaki
No.10	The Development of the Nominal Plural Forms in Early Middle English	Ryuichi Hotta
No.11	Chunking and Instruction	Takayuki Nakamori
No.12	Detecting and Sharing Perspectives Using Causals in Japanese	Ryoko Uno
No.13	Discourse Representation of Temporal Relations in the So-Called Head-Internal Relatives	Kuniyoshi Ishikawa
No.14	Features and Roles of Filled Pauses in Speech Communication	Michiko Watanabe
No.15	Japanese Loanword Phonology	Masahiko Mutsukawa
No.16	Derivational Linearization at the Syntax-Prosody Interface	Kayono Shiobara
No.17	Polysemy and Compositionality	Tatsuya Isono
No.18	fMRI Study of Japanese Phrasal Segmentation	Hideki Oshima
No.19	Typological Studies on Languages in Thailand and Japan	Tadao Miyamoto et al.
No.20	Repetition, Regularity, Redundancy	Yasuyo Moriya
No.21	A Cognitive Pragmatic Analysis of Nominal Tautologies	Naoko Yamamoto
No.22	A Contrastive Study of Responsibility for Understanding Utterances between Japanese and Korean	Sumi Yoon

Hituzi Linguistics in English No.21

A Cognitive Pragmatic Analysis of Nominal Tautologies

Naoko Yamamoto

Hituzi Syobo Publishing

Copyright © Naoko Yamamoto 2014
First published 2014

Author: Naoko Yamamoto

All rights reserved. Except for the quotation of short passages for the purposes of criticism and review, no part of this publication may be reproduced, stored in a retrieval system, or transmitted in any form or by any means, electronic, mechanical, photocopying, recording or otherwise, without the written prior permission of the publisher.
In case of photocopying and electronic copying and retrieval from network personally, permission will be given on receipts of payment and making inquiries. For details please contact us through e-mail. Our e-mail address is given below.

Hituzi Syobo Publishing
Yamato bldg. 2F, 2-1-2 Sengoku Bunkyo-ku Tokyo, Japan
112-0011

phone +81-3-5319-4916 fax +81-3-5319-4917
e-mail: toiawase@hituzi.co.jp
http://www.hituzi.co.jp/
postal transfer 00120-8-142852

ISBN 978-4-89476-684-6
Printed in Japan

Contents

Acknowledgments — ix

Chapter 1 Introduction — 1

Chapter 2 Concepts of Tautology — 7

2.1 What is *Tautology*? — 7
2.2 Tautology in Logic — 8
2.3 Tautology in Natural Language — 10
2.4 Data in This Study — 12

Chapter 3 Previous Studies of Tautology — 15

3.1 Introduction — 15
3.2 Radical Pragmatic Approach — 16
   3.2.1 Grice (1975, 1989) — 16
   3.2.2 Levinson (1983) — 16
   3.2.3 Ward and Hirschberg (1991) — 18
3.3 Radical Semantic Approach — 21
3.4 Non-Radical Approach — 25
3.5 Cognitive Linguistic Approach — 27
   3.5.1 Mizuta (1995, 1996) — 27
   3.5.2 Series of Studies Initiated by Sakahara's Analysis — 30
      3.5.2.1 Sakahara (1993, 2002) — 30
      3.5.2.2 Koya (2002, 2003) — 34
      3.5.2.3 Furumaki (2009a, 2009b) — 36
      3.5.2.4 Sakai (2006b, 2008a) — 39
3.6 Relevance Theoretic Approach — 41

Chapter 4 *A wa A da* 51

    4.1 Introduction 51
    4.2 Previous Studies 52
        4.2.1 Tsujimoto (1996) 52
        4.2.2 Nakamura (2000) 55
    4.3 Tautology and Negation 58
    4.4 Theoretical Background 61
        4.4.1 Essence of Relevance Theory 61
        4.4.2 Four Pragmatic Processes in Explicature Derivation 64
        4.4.3 Conceptual Encoding and Procedural Encoding 68
    4.5 *A wa A da* Data 72
    4.6 Stipulating the Meaning of *A wa A da* 75
        4.6.1 The Need for a Contrastive Assumption 75
        4.6.2 The Cognitive Structure of Negation 76
        4.6.3 The Definition of Q and R 78
    4.7 Validating the Hypothesis that *A wa A da* Has a Specific Meaning 82
    4.8 Summary 86

Chapter 5 *A ga A da* 89

    5.1 Introduction 89
    5.2 Previous Studies 91
        5.2.1 Moriyama (1989) 91
        5.2.2 Okamoto (1993) 94
    5.3 *A ga A da* Data 98
    5.4 Stipulating the Meaning of *A ga A da* 102
    5.5 Validating the Hypothesis that *A ga A da* Has a Specific Meaning 106
    5.6 Summary 111

Chapter 6 *A mo A da* 113

    6.1 Introduction 113
    6.2 Previous Studies 114
        6.2.1 Moriyama (1989) 114
        6.2.2 Okamoto (1993) 115

    6.2.3 *A mo A da* on which Moriyama (1989) and
          Okamoto (1993) Focus   116
        6.2.3.1 What is *A mo A da*?   116
        6.2.3.2 What is the Meaning of *A mo A da*?   120
        6.2.3.3 Applicability to Data not Included in
                Moriyama (1989) and Okamoto (1993)   121
6.3 *A mo A da* Data   126
6.4 Stipulating the Meaning of *A mo A da*   129
6.5 Validating the Hypothesis that *A mo A da* Has a Specific Meaning   134
6.6 Summary   139

Chapter 7 The Phenomenon of Nominal Tautology in Japanese   141

7.1 Introduction   141
7.2 Characteristics of Japanese Nominal Tautology   142
    7.2.1 Contradiction or not?   143
    7.2.2 Explanation or not?   147
7.3 Characteristics of English Nominal Tautology   150
7.4 Summary   154

Chapter 8 Conclusion   157

References   163
日本語の読者のための内容紹介   173
Index   185

Acknowledgments

This book is a revised version of my Ph. D. dissertation that I submitted to the Graduate School of Nara Women's University in January 2012. When I decided to go to graduate school, I never thought that I would see the day when my own thesis would be published. Many people have supported me and helped to bring this publication to completion. Here, I would like to offer my profound gratitude to them all.

First, I would like to express my deep appreciation to my supervisor, Professor Akiko Yoshimura. My encounter with her was a very wonderful thing. When I was a first-year undergraduate, I went to see her about choosing my major. This was the first time we met. I became discouraged many times during my graduate course, but she continued to encourage me, spare her time and offer valuable advice on my papers. Thanks to her, I have had many opportunities to deliver presentations and publish papers and thus sustain my career as a researcher. I owe what I am today to her friendly generous guidance. I am also extremely grateful to Professor Seiji Uchida, who was the sub-supervisor of my Ph. D. program. He always listened to me and provided deep insights regarding my work. Without his positive comments, I would not have decided to become a researcher. My heartfelt thanks go to Associate Professor Ayumi Suga. She offered different perspectives and very beneficial suggestions. I have been fortunate to receive instruction from these three teachers who taught me what a researcher and an educator should be, and thus allowed me to settle into studying linguistics, and especially pragmatics, as an undergraduate and graduate.

Furthermore, I greatly appreciate one of my Ph. D. examiners, Associate Professor Yoshio Nishide of the Faculty of Letters, Nara Women's University. He is an expert on Shakespeare and took the time to read my thesis and proffer suggestive advice. I would also like to express my gratitude to the teachers of the College of Liberal Arts, Nara University who have provided me with an outstanding work environment since I started working with them in Spring 2013. Special thanks go to Professor Kathleen Yamane, who gave me clear and pertinent advice. My sincere thanks go as well to Mr. David Meacock for correcting my English.

Let me also say thank you to those who have studied alongside me at Nara Women's University for their comments on my presentations and papers, encouragement and friendship. I thank Hituzi Syobo for agreeing to publish this thesis and the editor, Ms. Shiori Bando, for supporting me while I was preparing this work for publication. Every time I handed her a manuscript, she read it carefully and raised valuable points.

I could not have reached the publication stage without the support, encouragement and stimulation that I received from those mentioned above. Although I committed myself fully to this project, I am sure that certain inadequacies remain. I should certainly be obliged if readers would point out that any errors contained in this book.

I was supported by a Grant-in-Aid for Publication of Scientific Research Results (Scientific Literature, 255064) from the 2013 Japan Society for the Promotion of Science. I offer my deep appreciation to all the many people who were involved in awarding this grant.

Finally, I would like to thank my parents, Toshio and Shigeko Yamamoto, who have provided a warm and comfortable environment in which I can relax and devote myself entirely to studies. I also thank my sister, Takako Yamamoto, for her tender consideration.

January, 2014
Naoko Yamamoto

Chapter 1

Introduction

The word *tautology* has been used in several ways, for instance, in linguistics literature, to refer to expressions such as *War is war* and *Business is business*. In these expressions, the subject nouns have the same form as the predicate nouns. At first, these expressions appear redundant and uninformative, yet people can understand what is communicated by apparently nonsensical tautological statements, depending on the context. Such tautological expressions can be found even in children's literature.

(1-1)   'I'm sure I'm not Ada,' she said, 'for her hair goes in such long ringlets, and mine doesn't go in ringlets at all; and I'm sure I can't be Mabel, for I know all sorts of things, and she, oh! she knows such a very little! Besides, *she's she, and I'm I*, and — oh dear, how puzzling it all is! I'll try if I know all the things I used to know.
(Lewis Carroll, *Alice's Adventures in Wonderland*, p.14, my emphasis)

In this example, quoted from *Alice's Adventures in Wonderland*, Alice has fallen into a wonderland and because she experiences several strange occurrences, she begins to question who she is. To be sure, she tries to perform multiplication and to review lessons in geography but she cannot answer the questions. Then, she starts to think that she is so ignorant that she has become Mabel. She feels depressed that she has to live in a poor house without toys as Mabel does. In that situation, she suddenly utters the phrase *she's she, and I'm I*, based on her intuition that however stupid she may be, Alice is no one other than Alice. The phrase appears redundant but provides abundant information to readers.

Mysterious expressions such as (1-1) have fascinated many researchers. There have been many previous studies; however, most of them discuss data on English nominal tautologies. Certainly, they make instructive suggestions but overlook the fact that although nominal tautological expressions exist in most languages, the way of representing the expressional form is language dependent. It is generally said that an English nominal tautology is represented by the single form *A is A*. On the other hand, Japanese has three types of nominal tautological expressional forms: *A wa A da*, *A ga A da* and *A mo A da* because it has three different particles: *wa* (topic marker), *ga* (subject marker) and *mo* (Eng. 'also'/'too'). For example, consider the conversations between a woman and her husband as shown in (1-2)–(1-4):

(1-2) [A couple is talking about their son Taro's academic record. Taro scored poorly on an exam again.][1]
 Wife : *Watashi mo sonnani yoku dekinakattashi ne. Taro bakkari*
 I too very well did not do SFP Taro only
 semerarenai wa.
 (I will) not put a blame SFP
 'I didn't do very well, either. I won't put all the blame on him.'
 Husband : *Sonnakoto iuna yo.*
 that do not say SFP
 Oya wa oya da. *Boku ga hanashitemiru yo.*
 parent TM parent COP I SM try to talk (to him) SFP
 'Don't say anything like that. (lit.) Parents are parents. I try to talk to him.'

(1-3) [A couple is talking about their son Taro's academic record. Taro scored poorly on an exam again.][2]
 Husband : *Omae, seiseki dôdatta?*
 you how were (your) grades?
 'How were your grades?'
 Wife : *Un, mâ mâ. Dakara ne, Taro no seiseki ga*
 well so-so so SFP Taro of grade SM
 yokunainomo murimonai wa. Tokorode,
 not very smart understandable SFP by the way
 anata wa dôdatta?
 how were (your grades)?

'Well, they were so-so. So it is understandable that Taro is not very smart. By the way, how were your grades?'

Husband : *Mâ mâ.* **Oya ga oya da.**
so-so   parent SM parent COP
Dôshiyômonai   yo na.
there is nothing that can be done (about his grades) SFP SFP
'So-so. (lit.) <u>The parents are the parents</u>. There's nothing that can be done about his grades.'

(1-4) [A couple is talking about a boy named Taro and his father. The father is a notorious troublemaker.]

Wife : *Taro ga mata kurasumeito to kenkashitan datte.*
Taro SM again classmate with got into a fight HEAR
Hontoni yanchana ko yo ne.
really (he is) a naughty boy SFP SFP
'Taro got into a fight with a classmate again. He is really a naughty boy.'

Husband : *Mâ,* **oya mo oya da.** *Taro ga gakkô de*
well parent also parent COP Taro SM school P
mondai bakari okosu no mo murimonai yo.
(Taro) often gets into trouble P P no wonder SFP
'Well, (lit.) <u>the parent is also the parent</u>. No wonder Taro often gets into trouble at school.'

In (1-2), the husband's utterance *Oya wa oya da* is interpreted as an objection to his wife. On the other hand, the husband's utterance *Oya ga oya da* in (1-3) and the husband's utterance *oya mo oya da* in (1-4) are interpreted as agreeing with her. However, in the former, the people referred to by *oya* 'parent' (that is, the husband and wife) are criticized while in the latter, the person referred to by *oya* 'parent' (that is, Taro's father) is also subject to criticism in a context where his son, Taro, is criticized.

As briefly observed, these three expressions have the same subject and predicate noun but convey different meanings. On the other hand, it is hard in the English language to distinguish between these complicated meanings only through the nominal tautological form *A is A*, such as *Parents are parents*. This fact suggests that when discussing Japanese and English nominal tautologies, the formal variety should be kept in mind. Here the following two questions arise:

how does the expressional form of nominal tautology work?; and if there is a common feature in Japanese and English nominal tautologies, what is it?

To solve these questions, this study sets the following three goals: (i) to stipulate the meaning of *A wa A da*, *A ga A da* and *A mo A da*, (ii) to show that each of the three expressional forms encodes a specific meaning, and (iii) to generalize characteristics of Japanese and English nominal tautologies and to propose their common characteristics. This study is conducted based on the hypothesis that *A wa A da*, *A ga A da* and *A mo A da* are regarded as expressional forms, that is, constructions.[3] When this approach is adopted, the linguistic phenomenon of nominal tautology in Japanese can be successfully explained.

The following describes more specifically what each chapter covers. Chapter 2 provides an overview of the concepts of *tautology*. As mentioned at the beginning, the word *tautology* has been used in various senses. Roughly speaking, there are four possible uses of the word. To strengthen the foundation of this study, I should understand the differences between tautology in logic and in natural language. Therefore, I outline the meaning of tautology in propositional logic, clarify the differences between tautologies in logic and in natural language, and define the kind of tautology that is discussed in the study.

Chapter 3 outlines and discusses previous studies on nominal tautologies. Researchers have adopted the following five approaches: radical pragmatic approaches (traditional pragmatics), radical semantic approaches, non-radical approaches, cognitive linguistic approaches and relevance theoretic approaches (cognitive pragmatics). However, I provide counterexamples to previous studies and conclude that they cannot be accepted.

The subsequent three chapters examine three types of Japanese nominal tautologies. Chapter 4 focuses on the expressional form *A wa A da*. First, I critically discuss two previous studies: Tsujimoto (1996) and Nakamura (2000). Although they argue that the process of interpreting *A wa A da* can be explained from a viewpoint of negation, the use of *negation* varies from one author to another. I propose that *A wa A da* is used for objecting and rejecting requests from others, and therefore these functions lead us to a conclusion that *A wa A da*, which includes no explicit negative words such as *nai* 'not', can be regarded as negation. Furthermore, introducing the notion of the *Cognitive Structure of Negation* (CSN) proposed by Yoshimura (1992, 1994, 1999), I stipulate the meaning of the expressional form *A wa A da* and demonstrate that the meaning cannot be expected from the constituent parts of the sentence.

Chapter 5 focuses on the expressional form *A ga A da* and stipulates the meaning encoded in it. There have been a few previous studies on *A ga A da* such as Moriyama (1989) and Okamoto (1993). Presenting counterexamples, I first demonstrate that they cannot systematically explain how *A ga A da* is interpreted. Then I observe some cases of *A ga A da* in the given contexts and argue that the meaning of the expressional form cannot be entirely predicted by integrating the meanings of the lexical items of the sentence.

Chapter 6 focuses on the expressional form *A mo A da*, which has attracted little attention in linguistic literature. There have been only two previous studies on this topic by Moriyama (1989) and Okamoto (1993). I show that their conclusions have serious problems and do not apply to some data. Further, after observing some examples of *A mo A da* in context, I stipulate the meaning encoded in *A mo A da* and illustrate that the expressional form carries a meaning independent of the sentence's lexical items.

Chapter 7 first identifies differences between *A wa A da*, *A ga A da* and *A mo A da*, based on the research reported in the previous three chapters and further generalizes the characteristics of Japanese and English nominal tautologies, and pursue the possibility of providing nominal tautologies in natural languages including English with a unified characterization.

Finally, chapter 8 summarizes my main findings. The linguistic phenomenon of nominal tautology has been discussed mainly based on English data. However, the analyses cannot explain Japanese nominal tautologies with various forms and they cannot be regarded as a comprehensive theory. Further, this study adopts the approach that the three types of Japanese nominal tautologies are regarded as expressional forms, that is, constructions, and demonstrates that each expressional form encodes a specific meaning, in that it carries the meaning that is independent of the constituent parts of the sentence. The analysis conducted in this study provides a clear picture of the mechanism involved in interpreting nominal tautologies.

Notes

1 This book basically adopts the Hepburn system of romanization for writing Japanese words, whereby a long sound is represented with a circumflex ˆ. However, the representation of long sounds in the references follows the preferred notation. A Japanese nominal tautology

is emphasized in semibold and is translated directly into English. The subject and predicate nouns are identical in form, and it depends on the context whether the nouns are singular or plural and whether or not the nouns are translated with an article. The abbreviation (lit.) means a literal translation of a Japanese nominal tautology, which is underlined. The other abbreviations are also used for glossing Japanese. For more detail, see page 13.

2   An exchange similar to this is traced back to Okamoto (1993), but the husband and wife's words have been adapted.

3   In this book, I use the term *construction* loosely, not as a technical term for Construction Grammar.

Chapter 2

Concepts of Tautology

The word *tautology* has been extended to several fields and has been used in various senses. Before proceeding with a discussion of tautology, it is important to review the different concepts of tautology. This chapter begins with an explanation of the derivation of the word *tautology*, and clarifies the differences between tautology in logic and tautology in natural language.

2.1 What is *Tautology*?

The word *tautology* is derived from the ancient Greek word ταυτολογία, which was used to describe a rhetorical statement that involved saying the same thing twice. It has gained new meanings and its use has been extended to several fields. In propositional logic, *tautology* is used in a fairly technical way to describe a certain type of propositional formula. In daily conversation, *tautology* can have a number of meanings.

There are four possible uses for the word *tautology* as shown in (2-1):

(2-1)a. *Tautology* is an expression that "always receive[s] 'true' as [its] computed truth-value irrespective of the assignment of truth-values to the simple sentences of the expressions".　　　(Allwood et al. 1977: 50)
　　b. *Tautology* is an expression "in which you say the same thing twice using different words in a way which is not necessary".
　　　　　　　(*Longman Dictionary of Contemporary English*)
　　c. *Tautology* is an expression that is "used, metalinguistically, in order to explain the meaning of an unfamiliar word".　　(Lyons 1977b: 417)

d. *Tautology* is an utterance whose logical form is the same as a tautology in propositional logic. However, it conveys abundant information.[1]

Let us examine each in turn. First, *tautology* described in (2-1a) is a logical term and is strictly defined. For instance, the expression p ∨ ~ p is given as a simple tautology in propositional logic. The truth-value of such an expression is always true regardless of whether p is true or false.

Second, as regards (2-1b), according to the *Longman Dictionary of Contemporary English*, the sentence *He sat alone by himself*, for example, is regarded as a tautology. In this expression, either *alone* or *by himself* is redundant. In this sense, *tautology* can be replaced with the word *redundancy*.

Thirdly, when defining a word or phrase, *tautology* can be used in the sense of (2-1c) (cf. Lyons 1977b: 417). For example, when explaining the unfamiliar word *abiogenesis*, we might use the sentence *Abiogenesis is spontaneous generation*. The word *abiogenesis* is metalinguistically paraphrased by *spontaneous generation*. That is, metalinguistically speaking, the meaning of *abiogenesis* is the same as the meaning of *spontaneous generation*, so the sentence is only contingently true.

And finally, *tautology* type (2-1d) has been discussed within linguistic frameworks such as pragmatics, semantics and cognitive linguistics. Tautologies in natural language such as *Business is business* and *If it rains it rains* have the same truth-condition, whose logical form is always true, but unlike tautologies in propositional logic, they convey additional information. Most researchers have puzzled over the way in which tautological utterances are understood without reaching any concrete conclusions.

This study will focus on the fourth type (i.e. utterances whose logical form represents tautologies in logic). However, we first need to confirm what we mean by tautology in logic since without this knowledge confusion may occur when discussing tautologies in natural language. In what follows, I will outline tautology in propositional logic, clarify the differences between tautologies in logic and tautologies in natural language, and define the kind of tautology I discuss in this thesis.

2.2 Tautology in Logic

When people communicate their thoughts and feelings in natural language, they can non-demonstratively infer the communicated content. That is, natural language can deal with non-demonstrative inferences. Logical language, however, deals with demonstrative rather than non-demonstrative inferences. In other words, it deals with logically valid inferences.

Logic is usually divided into two types: propositional logic and predicate logic. The former focuses on the study of inter-sentential relations, while the latter focuses on the study of the intra-sentential relations.

Now, I shall outline tautologies in propositional logic.[2] According to Allwood et al. (1977: 50), the technical term *tautology* is defined as "complex expressions that always receive 'true' as their computed truth-value irrespective of the assignment of truth-values to the simple sentences of the expression". The truth-value of such expressions can be completely determined by using such techniques as the truth table method.[3] A typical tautological expression is descried with the logic symbol ∨, as shown in (2-2):

(2-2)   p ∨ ~ p [4]

For instance, suppose that p is *it's raining*. The disjunctive tautological expression (2-2) can be also described as (2-3):

(2-3)   It's raining or it's not raining.

The truth-value of (2-2) is always true whether p (e.g. *it's raining*) is true or false, as shown in the following truth table:

(2-4)   p   ~ p   p ∨ ~ p
         T   F   T
         F   T   T

This shows that *It's raining or it's not raining* in (2-3), which appears to be a tautological utterance, ignores empirical facts. The statement shows neither that it is true that it is raining nor that it is false that it is raining. We know nothing about the weather as an empirical fact. However, the sentence is not considered to be meaningless since whether or not it is logically true can be decided mechanically based on the truth table method — that is, it has a truth-value.

Tautologies can be produced infinitely. Typical tautologies are written as follows. All of them are always true in the light of the truth table.

(2-5)a. One proposition
    (i) Law of identity
$$p \equiv p^5$$
$$p \vee p \equiv p$$
$$p \wedge p \equiv p$$
    (ii) Law of double negation
$$p \equiv \sim \sim p$$
    (iii) Law of excluded middle
$$p \vee \sim p$$
    (iv) Law of contradiction
$$(\sim p \wedge \sim p)$$
b. Two or more propositions
    (i) Commutative law
$$p \vee q \equiv q \vee p$$
$$p \wedge q \equiv q \wedge p$$
    (ii) Associative law
$$\{p \vee (q \vee r)\} \equiv \{(p \vee q) \vee r\}$$
$$\{p \wedge (q \wedge r)\} \equiv \{(p \wedge q) r\}$$
    (iii) First distributive law
$$\{p \wedge (q \vee r)\} \equiv \{(p \wedge q) \vee (p \wedge r)\}$$
    (iv) Second distributive law
$$\{p \vee (q \wedge r)\} \equiv \{(p \vee q) \wedge (p \vee r)\}$$
    (v) Law of absorption
$$\{p \wedge (p \vee q)\} \equiv p$$
$$\{p \vee (p \wedge q)\} \equiv p$$
    (vi) De Morgan's law
$$\sim (p \wedge q) \equiv \sim p \vee \sim q$$
$$\sim (p \vee q) \equiv \sim p \wedge \sim q$$

(Araki and Arai 1992: 1470)

2.3 Tautology in Natural Language

Next, let us focus on tautology in natural language. As we have seen in the previous section, tautologies in propositional logic are complex statements that are necessarily true in every possible situation. Logical tautologies ignore empirical facts, so it is difficult to analyze how to interpret colloquial tautologies within a logical framework. Linguistic tautologies convey additional information.

Here, a question arises: what type of utterance should be treated as a tautology in natural language? As Ward and Hirschberg (1991: 508) state, when adopting the most straightforward definition based on propositional logic, only utterances such as *Either John will come or he won't* and *If he does it, he does it* are regarded as tautologies since their logical forms are represented in the same way as tautologies in propositional logic: p ∨ ~ p and p → p, respectively. However, many researchers have traditionally discussed tautological utterances such as *War is war* and *Boys will be boys*. These standard examples are not tautologies according to the definition of logical tautology since the nouns *war* and *boys*, and the future modality *will* cannot be represented propositional-logically.[6] Such an explanation excludes typical examples. Then, following both the definition in logic and what has traditionally been considered natural language tautology, Ward and Hirschberg (1991) regard the following forms as English tautologies:[7]

(2-6)a. Equatives: A is A
    e.g. Murder is murder.
  b. Disjunctions: (either) p or not p
    e.g. Either a ham has bone or it doesn't have a bone.
  c. Conditionals: if p (then) p
    e.g. If I miss, I miss.
  d. Subordinate conjunctions: when p, p
    e.g. When they're gone, they're gone.
  e. Headless relatives: p what p
    e.g. It means what it means.
            (adapted from Ward and Hirschberg 1991: 510)

Such tautological utterances occur in most natural languages. The Japanese language is no exception. Seto (1997: 64–65) states that the following forms could be regarded as Japanese tautologies:[8]

(2-7)a. A wa A da (Eng. 'A is A')
    e.g. *Kodomo wa kodomo da.* 'Kids are kids.'
  b. A ka A denai ka (no dochiraka) (Eng. '(either) A or not A')
    e.g. *Kare wa kuru-kamoshirenaishi ko-nai-kamoshirenai.* 'Either he may come or he may not come.'
  c. A naraba A (Eng. 'if A, A')

        e.g. *Maketa nonara maketa noda.* 'If (I) lost, (I) lost.'
- d. A no-toki wa A (Eng. 'when A, A')

  e.g. *Yaru toki wa yaru.* 'When (I) do (it), (I) do (it).'
- e. A dakara A (Eng. 'because A, A')

  e.g. *Suki dakara suki.* 'Because (I) like (it), (I) like (it).'
- f. A na-mono wa A (Eng. 'what is A is A')

  e.g. *Ii mono wa ii.* 'What (is) good is good.'

As mentioned above, there are many types of tautology in English and Japanese. However, almost all previous studies focus on nominal tautologies, especially English nominal tautologies. In general, an English nominal tautology is expressed in the single form *A is A* as shown in (2-6a). On the other hand, a Japanese nominal tautology is expressed in the form *A wa A da* in (2-7a). Here, we must take note of a particular fact. As is well known, Japanese has the topic marker *wa* and the subject marker *ga*. There are two different nominal tautologies: *A wa A da* and *A ga A da*. Furthermore, Japanese has another type of nominal tautology: *A mo A da*.

Tautological utterances are represented in relatively straightforward forms. However, despite their simplicity of form, they communicate further information. Discussions about tautologies cover a wide range of linguistic topics including context, syntactic forms, shared knowledge, and categorization. Many aspects influence the way in which people interpret tautological utterances, and many linguists have provided different proposals from different viewpoints. I will discuss this point in chapter 3.

2.4 Data in This Study

Faced with deciding what kind of tautology I should analyze in this study, I was troubled by the fact that there are many types as I have already shown in (2-6) and (2-7). I have been particularly interested in three types of Japanese nominal tautology: *A wa A da*, *A ga A da* and *A mo A da*. As we saw in chapter 1, Japanese nominal tautology conveys different meanings by using different forms, and it is difficult in the English language to distinguish between their meanings based on the form *A is A*. This could indicate that each of the three Japanese nominal tautological expressional forms encodes a specific meaning that is independent of the words in the sentence.

This study will focus on the nominal tautologies *A wa A da*, *A ga A da* and *A mo A da* in Japanese, and *A is A* in English, where *A* is a noun or a noun phrase. These nominal tautologies are defined as follows:

(2-8)   *Tautology* is an expression with a syntactic structure in which two nouns or noun phrases *A* are identical in form and are meaningfully linked with a certain word (i.e. the particles *wa*, *ga* and *mo* in Japanese; the linking verb *be* in English).

The following abbreviations are used for glossing Japanese vocabulary.

ACC	accusative
COP	copular predication
HEAR	quotative maker
P	particle
Q	question marker
SFP	sentence final particle
SM	subject marker
TM	topic marker

In this chapter, I observed the derivation of the word *tautology*, and clarified the differences between tautology in logic and in natural language. In the next chapter, I will discuss previous tautology studies, and show them to be incorrect.

Notes

1   I could not find a definition of *tautology* in the literature on linguistics. A tentative definition is given in (2-1d).
2   There is also a statement called *tautology* in predicate logic, which contains quantifiers. The statement occurs if there is an equivalence relation between a universal quantifier $\forall$ and an existential quantifier $\exists$. Concrete examples are as follows:

(i) $\sim (\forall x) f(x) \equiv (\exists x) \sim f(x)$
(ii) $\sim (\exists x) f(x) \equiv (\forall x) \sim f(x)$ (Araki and Yasui 1992: 1470)

3   Wittgenstein (1922) developed the most generally used method of determining whether a sentence is true or false by employing the truth table. He refers to *tautology* as follows:

"[a]mong the possible groups of truth-conditions there are two extreme cases. In the one case the proposition is true for all the truth-possibilities of the elementary propositions. We say that the truth-conditions are *tautological*" (4.46).

4   In propositional logic, logical relations between sentences come into focus. Sentential or propositional variables are used. Lower case letters from p onwards are usually chosen to represent variables.

5   Propositional logic deals with logical relations between sentences, so $p \equiv p$ in (2-5) represents the fact that sentence p is logically equivalent to sentence p. On the other hand, as I discuss later, equative (or nominal) tautological utterances such as *A is A* in English and *A wa A da* in Japanese have been regarded as tautologies in natural languages. Their logical form is represented as $A \equiv A$. In this case, since *A* identifies not a sentence but a noun or a noun phrase (that is, a non-sentence), equative tautologies in natural languages cannot be captured propositional-logically. Thus, $A \equiv A$ is different from $p \equiv p$.

6   The future modality *will* is studied in modal logic, which deals with possible worlds. See also note 5.

7   Ward and Hirschberg (1991) provide no definition of p and *A* (in their paper, the lower case letter *a* is used instead of *A*. The present study uses *A* to provide coherent notation). Based on their analysis, it is assumed that *A* represents a noun or a noun phrase and p represents a sentence or a clause. The latter case seems to be the same as p in propositional logic. See also notes 4 and 5.

8   Seto (1997) always uses *A* for the repeated part in a tautological sentence. His notation is extremely vague. It can be presumed that *A* represents a noun ((2-7a)), a sentence or a clause ((2-7b)), a verb ((2-7c)–(2-7e)) and an adjective ((2-7f)). The notation in (2-7) follows his rule.

Chapter 3

Previous Studies of Tautology

This chapter examines previous studies on tautology, in particular those on nominal tautology. The discussion covers five fields of earlier research: radical pragmatics (traditional pragmatics), radical semantics, a middle position between the two, cognitive linguistics, and relevance theory (cognitive pragmatics). A close examination reveals that none can be considered a comprehensive theory for interpreting nominal tautologies.

3.1 Introduction

Nominal tautological sentences are very simple and can be regarded as variants of copular sentences. It appears highly likely that a form of nominal tautology exists in every language. What is interesting, however, is that almost all previous tautology studies have been based on English data.[1] As we have already seen in (2-6), there are (at least) five types of English tautological utterance. In particular, tautologies such as *War is war* and *Boys will be boys* have been thoroughly discussed in the literature on tautological utterances. These examples are generally written with the formula *A is A*. The same two nouns *A* are repeated and the truth-value is always true. This formula appears to be nonsense when uttered in everyday conversation. However, contrary to this perception, people can readily obtain meaningful information from these apparently nonsense utterances. Why and how is this possible?

Many researchers have been fascinated by the linguistic phenomenon of tautology and have attempted to solve the mystery it presents with radical pragmatic approaches, radical semantic approaches, and non-radical approaches.

Furthermore, two new waves have emerged recently: cognitive linguistic approaches and relevance theoretic approaches. This chapter will introduce these five approaches and examine previous studies critically.

3.2 Radical Pragmatic Approach

A (traditional) pragmatic approach to tautological utterance interpretation is often called a radical pragmatic approach in contrast to Wierzbicka's radical semantic approach, which will be dealt with in 3.3. This approach minimizes semantic contributions to utterances and maximizes pragmatic contributions to utterances. It pushes "the burden of utterance interpretation almost entirely onto pragmatic inference" (Fraser 1988: 216).

Grice first mentioned tautological utterances within the framework of pragmatics. Most pragmatic analyses are more or less accounted for in terms of Grice's framework of conversational maxims (cf. Gazder 1979; Levinson 1983; Ward and Hirschberg 1991).[2] According to the Gricean pragmatists, tautological utterances are apparently uninformative but in fact contextually meaningful. It is concluded that their meanings can be universally calculated by employing the Cooperative Principle. The following subsections overview the analyses of the Gricean pragmatists.

3.2.1 Grice (1975, 1989)

Grice (1975, 1989) states that tautologies such as *Women are women* and *War is war* violate the first maxim of Quantity: make your contribution as informative as is required. These examples are uninformative at the level of what is said, thus flouting the first maxim of Quantity, while they are informative at the level of what is implicated. In this way, Grice deals superficially with understanding tautological utterances, but he provides no detailed account.

3.2.2 Levinson (1983)

Following Grice's analysis of the infringement of the maxim of Quantity, Levinson (1983: 111) argues that "if the assumption that the speaker is actually co-operating is to be preserved, some informative inference must be made", and that an implicature depends on the context in which a tautology is uttered. Consider (3-1a)–(3-1c):

(3-1) a. War is war. $[\forall x (W(x) \rightarrow W(x))]$
 b. Either John will come or he won't. $[p \vee \sim p]$
 c. If he does it, he does it. $[p \rightarrow p]$
(Levinson 1983: 111)

These examples share the same truth conditions since their logical forms ($\forall x (W(x) \rightarrow W(x))$, $p \vee \sim p$ and $p \rightarrow p$, respectively) are always true, but they would convey something like (3-2a)–(3-2c), respectively, based on pragmatic inference.

(3-2) a. [T]errible things always happen in war, that's its nature and it's no good lamenting that particular disaster.
 b. [C]alm down, there's no point in worrying about whether he's going to come because there's nothing we can do about it.
 c. [I]t's no concern of ours. (ibid.)

This analysis appears to describe how tautological utterances are interpreted, but as Levinson himself admits, it is unclear how the above implicatures are derived from the contexts. Besides, Levinson lists just one concrete implicature each for (3-1a)–(3-1c), as shown in (3-2a)–(3-2c), and does not extend this analysis to other examples. Consider the utterance *War is war* in the following context:

(3-3) [The president of the arms-manufacturing company is pleased when he hears the news that a war will start.]
Employee : But I'm afraid that this war will not last long.
President : *War is war*. (Nishikawa 2003: 48)

In (3-3), the company president, who is planning to increase arms sales, does not communicate that "terrible things always happen in war, that's its nature and it's no good lamenting that particular disaster" as shown in (3-2a). Rather he communicates that war makes profits and is a moneymaking event. The president's utterance *War is war* indicates a profitable war, not a terrible war. Levinson's claim provides no answer for why the same sentences *War is war* have different interpretations. It is not applicable to all tautological utterances.

As discussed above, Levinson appreciates the importance of inference and presents the implicatures derived from tautological utterances concretely. However, he fails to describe the way in which inference is involved with the interpretation process and how implicatures are derived from the contexts in which tautologies are uttered.

3.2.3 Ward and Hirschberg (1991)

Next, let us discuss Ward and Hirschberg's (1991) analysis, which is based on a large corpus of natural data.[3] Their claim is that tautological utterances are typical examples of generalized conversational implicatures, and that they convey that "specific alternative utterances have intentionally *not* been chosen" (ibid.: 510).[4]

Ward and Hirschberg illustrate the interpretation process of *A is A* as shown in (3-4):[5]

(3-4)   Assume that a speaker (S) has produced a tautological utterance to a hearer (H), say in the form of an equative such as *War is war* (or Sp. *El futbol es futbol* 'Soccer is soccer', or Turk. *Çocuk çocuktur* 'A child is a child'). Then H may reason as follows:
– S has affirmed a tautological utterance of the form *A is A* (or Sp. *A es A*, or Turk. *A A-dir*), which appears to add nothing to our mutual beliefs in general, and, in particular, nothing to our mutual beliefs about *A*;
– Assuming that S is observing the Cooperative Principle, then, by the maxims of Quantity and Relation, S has said as much as s/he truthfully can that is relevant about *A*;
– S might have produced utterances of a similar form, say *A is B* (where *A* and *B* are distinct, modulo referring expressions), which *could* have added something to our mutual beliefs about *A*,
– S chose *not* to utter such alternatives;
– thus S implicates that these alternatives are not relevant for the purposes of the exchange.
(adapted from Ward and Hirschberg 1991: 511)

To put it simply, the nominal tautological utterance *A is A* is used to convey that the alternative utterance *A is B* or *Some A is B* is not relevant. In the former case, *B* represents either some property of *A* or some distinct equivalence to *A*. In the latter case, *B* represents properties or equivalences of some subset of *A*. Consider (3-5) and (3-6):

(3-5) A State Department official said the administration was standing behind the statement made by Secretary of State George P. Shultz in a speech in New York last week: '*Terrorism is terrorism.* It deserves no sanctuary, and it must be stopped.' Messages went out to several U.S. embassies Monday night, saying the United States hoped governments would not yield to the hijackers. (ibid.: 514)

(3-6) Stolichnaya vodka has been a slow mover, though, said restaurant manager Bill Leung. But not because of politics. 'Hardly anybody orders it. In a small town, people don't know the difference between vodkas. ***Vodka is vodka****,*' he said. (ibid.)

Under Ward and Hirschberg's analysis, *Terrorism is terrorism* in (3-5) is analyzed as conveying the implicature that the alternative utterance *Terrorism is sometimes justifiable* is not relevant. George P. Shultz implicates that "the U.S. position is that terrorism is invariant, and that all terrorists must be treated in a uniform manner" (ibid.: 514). *Vodka is vodka* in (3-6) is analyzed as implicating that the alternative utterance *Some vodka is Russian* is not relevant. The speaker implicitly rejects the idea that "a property of vodka such as point-of-origin or brand-name makes any difference to the people of small town Minnesota" (ibid.).

Additionally, Ward and Hirschberg conceive a counterargument based on the notion of *prototype* and present irrefutable evidence for it. One possible criticism might be that the speaker of (3-5) utters *Terrorism is terrorism* to "convey that all terrorism is like some prototype of terrorism" (ibid.). However, they insist that this counterargument is not accepted since it does not hold true for the utterance *a million dollars is a million dollars* below:

(3-7) Treasure Hunt Organizer: You know, *a million dollars is a million dollars*. We couldn't just bury it anywhere. (ibid.: 515)

In their account, in (3-7), where the organizer explains why it has taken people a long time to hide the treasure, he implicates that "a million dollars represents a formidable amount of cash by implicating that alternatives such as 'a million dollars is easy to hide/not that much to hide/not such a huge amount' are in fact not relevant" (ibid.: 515).

As discussed above, Ward and Hirschberg's analysis is more systematic than Levinson's and thus seems promising. However, there are several problems with their proposal. First, their claim does not explain how and why the alternative utterances *A is B* and *Some A is B* are derived from the contexts in which the speaker produces the tautological utterance *A is A*. In their generalization shown in (3-4), (although it does not provide a clear definition of *A*,) *A* in *A is B* and *Some A is B* (probably) corresponds to *A* in the nominal tautological utterance *A is A* and thus would be identified. On the other hand, *B* is defined as either some property of *A* or some distinct equivalence to *A* for the case of *A is B*, and as either properties or equivalences of some subset of *A* for the case of *Some A is B*. This definition evokes *B* limitlessly and therefore cannot determine which *B* is more involved in the interpretation process in question. For example, as *B* in (3-7), Ward and Hirschberg simply list *easy to hide*, *not that much to hide*, and *not such a huge amount*. They do not explain how and why these three properties are derived as *B*.

Second, Ward and Hirschberg discuss the interpretation process of *A is A* at the level of generalized conversational implicatures, but provide no account of the process at the level of particularized conversational implicatures.[6] It seems to me that they consider the following implicatures to be particularized conversational implicatures: in (3-5), "the U.S. position is that terrorism is invariant, and that all terrorists must be treated in a uniform manner", and in (3-7), "a million dollars represents a formidable amount of cash" (ibid.: 514–515). Ward and Hirschberg's analysis does not explain what type of particularized conversational implicature is derived.

And finally, Ward and Hirschberg argue that *A is A* conveys the alternative utterance *A is B* or *Some A is B* is not relevant, that is, that *A is A* is interpreted as denying that any alternative of *A is A* "is relevant to the current exchange" (ibid.: 515). However, they do not explain why *A is A*, which includes no explicit negative words, is linked to negation. If (explicit or implicit) negative sentences are uttered, a felicitous context is established for them. According to Givón (1978: 109), "negatives are uttered in a context where corresponding affirmatives have already been discussed, or else where the speaker assumes the hearer's belief in – and thus familiarity with – the corresponding affirmative". So, if what is negated is unfamiliar to the hearer, she would think it odd. For instance, compare (3-8a) with (3-8b):

(3-8)   X (Woman) : What's happening?
            Y (Man)   : a. Oh, my wife's pregnant.

b. Oh, my wife's not pregnant.

(adapted from Givón 1978: 79–80)

Suppose that X meets her friend Y on the street and knows that he is married. When he answers her question as in (3-8a), she would feel that his answer sounds quite natural. In contrast, when he answers the question as in (3-8b), she would feel that it sounds quite odd. The oddness results from the assumption that she must previously have had additional information, for example, the information that his wife is pregnant. The above observation shows that contexts where negatives are used are something special. I shall postpone my discussion of negation in the process of interpreting nominal tautologies until chapter 4. The next subsection considers a radical semantic approach to tautological utterances.

3.3 Radical Semantic Approach

In contrast with the radical pragmatic approaches discussed in 3.2, a radical semantic approach maximizes semantic contributions to utterances and minimizes pragmatic contributions to utterances. Anna Wierzbicka, a prominent researcher adopting this approach, heavily criticizes radical pragmatic analyses based on Grice's universal principles.

Wierzbicka (1987: 103) insists that tautological syntactic structures of different languages encode language-specific meanings, which are defined in "a technical, language-independent, semantic metalanguage derived from natural language", and that the interpretation of tautological utterances depends on their forms. For example, the three patterns N_{abstr} is N_{abstr}, $N_{hum.\,pl}$ are $N_{hum.\,pl}$, and *(ART) N is (ART) N* encode the following respective meanings:

(3-9)a. N_{abstr} is N_{abstr}: "a sober attitude toward complex human activities"
 b. $N_{hum.\,pl}$ are $N_{hum.\,pl}$: "tolerance for human nature"
 c. (ART) N is (ART) N: "obligation"   (Wierzbicka 1987: 105–107)

Here, I shall illustrate each of them in further detail. First, N_{abstr} is N_{abstr} in (3-9a) expresses "a sober attitude toward complex human activities" (ibid.: 105) and N_{abstr} identifies a noun that conveys negative aspects of such activities. In Wierzbicka's judgment, *War is war*, *Politics is politics* and *Business is business* are acceptable, but *Wind is wind*, *Sneezing is sneezing* and *Wars are wars* are not.

Second, $N_{hum.\ pl}$ are $N_{hum.\ pl}$ in (3-9b) expresses "tolerance for human nature" (ibid.: 106). Typical examples are *Boys are boys*, *Kids are kids* and *Women are women*. The meaning of this pattern is close to that of the preceding one, but there are some differences between them. One difference is that N_{abstr} is N_{abstr} conveys bad aspects of N while $N_{hum.\ pl}$ are $N_{hum.\ pl}$ does not. For example, when the sentence *Kids are kids* is uttered, it would imply kids' noisiness, boisterousness or tiresomeness, but it does not imply anything bad about children. Another difference is that for N_{abstr} is N_{abstr}, the immutability is seen as "a matter of an inability to reach 'normal' standards of behavior", whereas for $N_{hum.\ pl}$ are $N_{hum.\ pl}$, it is seen as "a matter of (so to speak) grim necessity" (ibid.).

And finally, *(ART) N is (ART) N* in (3-9c) expresses "obligation", strictly speaking, "the obligation in question must be fulfilled, even if one prefers not to do so" (ibid.: 107), and *N* in this pattern is often a noun that refers to tasks agreed in contracts (e.g. *rule*, *bet*, *deal*, *test* and *agreement*), or human relational terms that refer to accepted obligations (e.g. *father*). The following examples are presented: *A rule is a rule*, *A bet is a bet* and *A father is a father*. For example, *A father is a father* means that "one has certain obligations toward one's father which should be fulfilled" (ibid.).

As we have seen above, Wierzbicka categorizes English nominal tautological patterns conforming to *(ART) N^i be (ART) N^i* based on what type of noun is used in the pattern, and explains the meaning encoded in the patterns. However, her claim has some problems. First, as some researchers have already pointed out, Wierzbicka seems to judge the acceptability of tautology on the basis of whether or not it holds true for her generalization. For example, she presents *Wind is wind* as one of the odd cases. However, Fraser (1988) demonstrates that if we assume that a kite flyer utters *Wind is wind* in response to a friend who complains that the wind is coming from the wrong direction, we would understand what the kite flyer meant. One possible interpretation of the utterance is that wind cannot be controlled by human beings. If a tautological utterance is uttered in an appropriate context, it is acceptable. This shows that pragmatic inference is involved in the process of interpreting tautological utterances.

Second, Wierzbicka insists that tautological utterances are language-specific and the Gricean maxim of Quantity cannot universally account for tautological utterances since some but not all tautologies can be translated into another language. There is doubt regarding whether or not her judgment about translatability is right. Compare (3-10) with (3-10'):

(3-10)　　War is war.
(3-10′)a. *La guerre est la guerre.　　　　Eng. 'War is war.'
　　　b. C'est la guerre.　　　　　　　　Eng. 'That's war.'
　　　　　　　　　　　　　　　　　　　　　　(Wierzbicka 1987: 97)

In Wierzbicka's analysis, the English tautology *War is war* in (3-10) is not translated into French. Its translation (3-10′a) is not acceptable. To express an idea similar to *War is war*, one would say something like (3-10′b), which is literally translated as *That's war*. However, according to Huang (2007), tautological expressions such as *War is war* appear in French in (3-11a) and (3-11b):

(3-11)a. La guerre, c'est la guerre.　　　Eng. 'War is war.'
　　　b. À la guerre comme à la guerre.　Eng. 'War is war.'
　　　　　　　　　　　　　　　　　　　　　　(Huang 2007: 30)

Wierzbicka assumes that literal translations should preserve their implicatures. However, perhaps not all languages are directly translatable into another language since different languages express a given logical form in different ways because of different grammars.

　Third, Wierzbicka's classification is too rigid to hold up in every case. Consider (3-12) and (3-13):

(3-12)　　… Now we have robots to help us — stronger, more useful, more capable than we are. Human beings are no longer alone. Have you ever thought of it that way?'
　　　　'I'm afraid I haven't.'
　　　　'To you, *a robot is a robot*. Made by humans and, if necessary, destroyed by humans. But you haven't worked with them, so you don't know them. They're cleaner, better creatures than we are. In the beginning, of course, robots couldn't talk.'　　　　　　　(Isaac Asimov, *I Robot*, pp.4–5)
(3-13)　　'Speedy!' shouted Powell into his radio. 'Come here!'
　　　　Speedy looked up and saw them. He stopped suddenly and remained standing for a moment. Then he turned and ran away, kicking up dust behind him. Over their radios, Donovan and Powell heard him singing a song. Donovan said weakly, 'Greg, he's crazy.'
　　　　'He's not crazy,' Powell said. '*A robot's only a robot*. There's something

wrong with him that's confusing his brain patterns. Once we find out what it is, then we can fix it.' (ibid., p.12)

(3-12) and (3-13) fall into the pattern *(ART) N is (ART) N* in (3-9c). Both utterances are expected to mean that "the obligation in question must be fulfilled, even if one prefers not to do so" (Wierzbicka 1987: 107). Contrary to this expectation, however, they are interpreted differently depending on the context. In (3-12), the robot psychologist Dr Susan Calvin and a male newspaper writer are talking about robots. The psychologist thinks robots are friendly towards human beings and are there to help them, while the newspaper writer disagrees. The italicized passage would be understood as communicating that (for the man) robots should be controlled by human beings and they are nothing more than machines. The interpretation of (3-12) is not true of *obligation*. In (3-13), mechanics Donovan and Powell are looking for the lost robot Speedy and finally find that Speedy is out of order. Donovan describes the faulty robot as *crazy* by analogy with a certain human situation. In this situation, the italicized passage would be understood as communicating that the robot is not crazy like a human being, but is out of order in the same way as other machines. The interpretation of (3-13) is not true of *obligation*, either. These two examples show that Wierzbicka's classification cannot properly predict the meaning of the tautology under discussion.

Fourth, Wierzbicka describes the meanings of tautological utterances without examining them in concrete contexts. A question arises: why does she consider a syntactic structure to have a specific meaning as shown in (3-9a)–(3-9c)? For example, she explains that *A rule is a rule* means *obligation*. It seems that the meaning derives not from the form itself, but from the noun *rule* in the form. Wierzbicka lists as *N* in the pattern *(ART) N is (ART) N*, *rule*, *bet*, *deal*, *test*, *agreement* and *father*. To some degree, these nouns appear to entail *obligation* in Wierzbicka's sense. However, some nouns do not entail the meaning but they are used in the pattern *(ART) N is (ART) N*. As we have observed above, the noun *robot* in (3-12) and (3-13) is not linked to the meaning of *obligation*, but is used in the pattern. This reveals that the interpretation of nominal tautologies depends not on what fills the subject or predicate in the sentence, but on the contexts. We need contextual information if we are to comprehend a tautological utterance.

And finally, Wierzbicka's claim is self-contradictory in relation to the fact that, as is words, some tautological sentences can have more than one meaning. According to Wierzbicka, *A husband is a husband* has four meanings: (i) "obligation (one must fulfill one's obligations toward one's husband)", (ii) "appreciation (everyone knows that there is something good about having a husband)", (iii) "indifference (one husband is neither better nor worse than another)", and (iv) "absolute penalization (all husbands are essentially the same – one knows what to expect from them)" (ibid.: 108). If, as Wierzbicka insists, a certain syntactic structure encodes plural meanings, there is a doubt as to how one can separate those meanings. Wierzbicka attempts to minimize pragmatic contributions to utterances. In fact, however, people make excellent use of contextual information when interpreting tautological utterances as discussed in (3-12) and (3-13).

As is obvious from the counterexamples above, Wierzbicka insists that the interpretation of tautological utterances depends on their forms, but her proposal is not satisfactory. She does not accept pragmatic contributions to the interpretation of tautological utterances. In fact, however, tautologies are understood differently in different contexts and they cannot be analyzed without their contexts. The next section will focus on a non-radical approach.

3.4 Non-Radical Approach

An approach that accepts both pragmatic and semantic contributions to tautological utterance interpretation is called a non-radical approach since it is located between the radical pragmatic approaches discussed in 3.2 and the radical semantic approach discussed in 3.3. This section provides an overview of Fraser (1988), which is generally considered to be research adopting this approach.

Fraser (1988) stipulates the conventional meaning of the English nominal tautology *NP$_i$-be-NP$_i$* as shown in (3-14):

(3-14) An English nominal tautology signals that the speaker intends that the hearer recognize:
    (i) that the speaker holds some view towards all objects referenced by the NP;
    (ii) that the speaker believes that the hearer can recognize this particular view;
    (iii) that this view is relevant to the conversation.
                                                                (Fraser 1988: 217–218)

In brief, "the very form of the sentence – a nominal tautology – signals that the speaker intends to convey the belief that the participants share a view towards some aspect of the objects referenced by the sentence noun phrase, and wishes to bring this belief to the hearer's awareness" (ibid: 218). On the other hand, he postpones dealing with the pragmatic aspect involved in understating nominal tautological utterances, and simply mentions that the pragmatic interpretation of nominal tautological utterances depends on the contexts in which they are uttered.

Fraser refutes Wierzbicka's radical semantic approach in which English nominal tautologies have several patterns based on the type of noun used in the pattern, and claims that "there is no linguistic constraint on the lexical of the subject NP in a nominal tautology" (ibid.: 219). If an appropriate context is established, some sentences are well-formed tautologies. For example, under Fraser's analysis, the sentence *Wind is wind*, which Wierzbicka considers to be inappropriate, is meaningfully interpreted in the context where a kite flyer responds to a friend who complains about the wind blowing from the wrong direction. The sentence *My son is my son* is construed in the context of a father being proud of his son for winning a scholarship.

Additionally, Fraser states that the reading of *be* in tautologies such as *Boys will be boys* and *Congress will be Congress* differs from that in tautologies such as *Business is business*. The reading of *be* is *to act like* or *to behave like*.[7] On this basis, the interpretation of *Boys will be boys* and *Congress will be Congress* is analyzed as follows: *Boys will act like boys* and *Congress will act like Congress*.

As we have observed above, Fraser attempts to explain how a nominal tautology is interpreted with a non-radical approach. However, this view has several shortcomings. First of all, as some researchers have already pointed out, the conventional meaning in (3-14) is too general to explain the unique feature of tautologies (cf. Tsujimoto 1996). For example, let us take a metaphorical utterance *Juliet is the sun*. This utterance suggests that Juliet is kind, warm, beautiful and so on in an adequate context. This is in line with Fraser's generalization. The English metaphor signals that the person uttering *Juliet is the sun* intends the hearer to recognize: (i) that the speaker holds some view towards a person referenced by *Juliet*; (ii) that the speaker believes that the hearer can recognize this particular view; and (iii) that this view is relevant to the conversation. The conventional meaning of NP_i-*be*-NP_i proposed by Fraser fits naturally into cases other than nominal tautology.

Second, Fraser understands the importance of pragmatic inference in the process of understanding nominal tautology, but he does not attempt to clarify the pragmatic aspect involved in the interpretation process. In accordance with his observation, *Wind is wind* implies advice to a friend complaining about the wind. *My son is my son* implies the father's pride in his son. Fraser does not explain how these implications are derived from the nominal tautological utterances.

And finally, Fraser does not determine when a nominal tautology should be read as meaning *to act like* or *to behave like* and when another nominal tautology indicates different readings for *be* from *to act like* or *to behave like*. In his analysis, the predicate *be* in *Boys will be boys* and *Congress will be Congress* is interpreted as *to act like* or *to behave like*. It is unclear how the predicate *be* in tautologies other than the two examples mentioned immediately above should be interpreted. If he insists that the interpretation of nominal tautologies depends on the reading of *be*, he must explain how we identify a nominal tautology as having a certain meaning of *be* and how many meanings are required.

This section outlined the non-radical approach provided by Fraser. He adopts a non-radical position but he does not attempt to clarify what sort of role pragmatic inference plays in the interpretation of nominal tautologies. The mechanism of the pragmatic contribution to our understanding tautological utterances remains unclear. In the next section, I will discuss previous studies that adopted cognitive linguistic approaches.

3.5 Cognitive Linguistic Approach

The cognitive linguistic approach is one of the new ways of dealing with tautological utterances.[8] Several cognitive linguists have attempted to clarify how tautological utterances are interpreted through cognitive concepts such as *frame model*, *categorization*, and *mental space* (cf. Mizuta 1995, 1996; Sakahara 1993, 2002; Koya 2002, 2003; Furumaki 2009a, 2009b; Sakai 2006b, 2008a).

3.5.1 Mizuta (1995, 1996)

First, let us focus on Mizuta's claim. Adopting the concept of *frame model*, Mizuta (1995, 1996) discusses the process of interpreting an apparently meaningless tautological sentence as meaningful, and argues that the comprehension depends on context and shared knowledge.[9] Consider the following exchange between John and Mike:

(3-15)   John : Oh, it's heavy! Would you bring anyone powerful?
　　　　Mike : Sure. Mary was around here. I'll bring her.
　　　　John : No. Not a woman. It's SO heavy.
　　　　Mike : Don't you know her power?
　　　　John : Not actually. But anyway, *a woman is a woman*.
　　　　Mike : Well …, it might be true.　　　(adapted from Mizuta 1996: 77)

Suppose that John wants someone to help carry a heavy pack and Mike advises him to ask Mary. One would interpret the above conversation as follows: Mike thinks that he should ask Mary to help since she is a physically strong woman, while John thinks that she should not be asked to help since "[i]n general, a woman is weak in muscular power. (So is Mary.)" (Mizuta 1996: 77).

Introducing the frame model, Mizuta accounts for how this interpretation arises as follows. John, who utters *a woman is a woman*, would have the knowledge about the category MAN and the category WOMAN modeled in Figure 3-1.

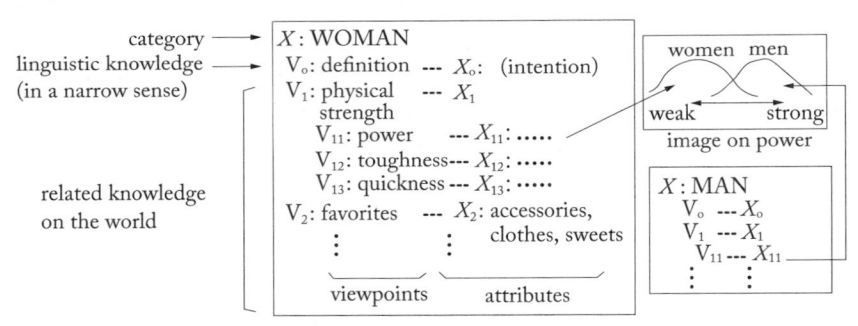

```
category        ──▶  X: WOMAN
linguistic knowledge ──▶  V₀: definition  ---  X₀: (intention)          women    men
(in a narrow sense)       V₁: physical    ---  X₁
                              strength                                weak        strong
                          V₁₁: power     ---  X₁₁: ……                image on power
                          V₁₂: toughness---  X₁₂: ……
                          V₁₃: quickness---  X₁₃: ……                 X: MAN
related knowledge         V₂: favorites  ---  X₂: accessories,        V₀ --- X₀
on the world                                       clothes, sweets    V₁ --- X₁
                           ⋮                 ⋮                        V₁₁--- X₁₁
                                                                       ⋮      ⋮
                          viewpoints     attributes
```

Figure 3-1. Knowledge representation of categories MAN and WOMAN
(Mizuta 1996: 79)

With regard to power, John's knowledge of the category WOMAN (= the upper category of MARY) is activated in his mind by Mike's utterance *Sure. Mary was around here. I'll bring her*. The relative weakness of women shown in Figure 3-1 occurs to him. He thinks that she should not be asked to help. Then, he refers to a general image of the physical strength of women (e.g. the relative weakness of women), applies the general idea to Mary, and indicates Mary's weakness.

On the other hand, the hearer Mike shares both the knowledge shown in Figure 3-1 and the context in which the utterances in (3-15) are exchanged, with the speaker John. Mike evokes an image of the physical strength of women from his own knowledge, based on the context. Then, he interprets John's utterance *a woman is a woman* as referring to the general idea of female weakness, and understands John's implication that Mary is weak in terms of physical strength, applying the general idea to Mary.

Consider another example:

(3-16) I promised my friend that I would say nothing of the matter, and *a promise is a promise*. (ibid.: 82)

Following Mizuta's (ibid.: 82) analysis, *a promise is a promise* in (3-16) would be readily interpreted to mean that "[a] promise should be kept, once it is made" without contextual information. The relative lack of dependence on the context is due to the limited attributions of the category PROMISE.

Based on the above observation, Mizuta concludes that the predicate *X* in the sentence *X is X* represents the stereotypical attribution of the category concerned in a given context and that hearers can understand the stereotypical attribution with the context and shared knowledge. As Mizuta argues, the hearer's interpretation evidently depends on the context. However, it does not always depend on shared knowledge since people necessarily memorize different information about an object due to differences in daily life experiences. For example, even when two people witness the same accident event, there may be a discrepancy between their representations of it (cf. Sperber and Wilson 1995[2]: 15–21).

Furthermore, Mizuta's proposal deals only with familiar tautologies such as *a woman is a woman* and *a promise is a promise*, and provides no explanation for unfamiliar tautologies. Familiar tautologies lead relatively easily to stereotypical attributions based on the category concerned in a given context while unfamiliar ones do not. Consider, for example, (3-17):

(3-17) Jake   : Nice! Good job, Nance. Good job, man.
        Senior : Nance. 5′04″. You're four seconds over.
        Jake   : Sir, give him another chance. He can make it.
        Senior : *5′04″ is 5′04″*.
        Jake   : It's four seconds. You know how far he's come?

(*Annapolis*)

Students in the naval school have to complete the final race within five minutes, but one of them could not. A student named Jake therefore asks his senior to pass the disqualified person on the test. The senior rejects his request by saying *5′04″ is 5′04″*. In this situation, it is difficult to select stereotypical attributions of the category of 5′04″. However, the utterance can be interpreted. Therefore, the predicate *X* does not always represent stereotypical properties of the category concerned in a given situation. Mizuta's claim must therefore be rejected.

Next, I will examine a series of studies initiated by Sakahara's analysis.

3.5.2 Series of Studies Initiated by Sakahara's Analysis

According to Sakahara (2002), the tautology *X wa X da* in Japanese is divided in four ways: *dôtei kyohi tôtoroji* 'identification-rejecting tautology', *kijutsu kyohi tôtoroji* 'description-rejecting tautology', *dôtei tôtoroji* 'identification tautology', and *kijutsu tôtoroji* 'description tautology'. The fourth tautology is further divided into *dôshitsuka tôtoroji* 'homogeneous tautology' and *ishitsuka tôtoroji* 'heterogeneous tautology'.[10] The classification is illustrated as shown in the diagram below:

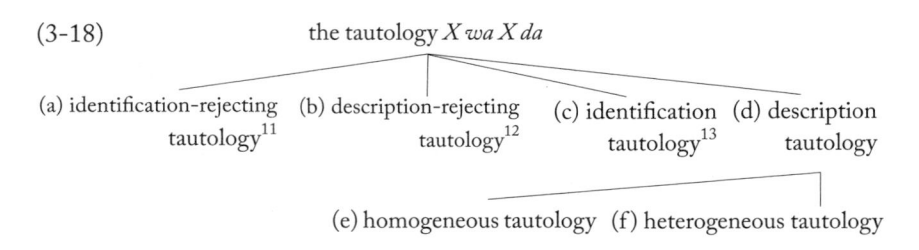

(3-18)   the tautology *X wa X da*

(a) identification-rejecting tautology[11] (b) description-rejecting tautology[12] (c) identification tautology[13] (d) description tautology

(e) homogeneous tautology (f) heterogeneous tautology

Description tautology in (3-18d) has proven particularly controversial. There have been various analyses. The details are presented below.

3.5.2.1 Sakahara (1993, 2002)

Sakahara (2002: 108) points out that the nature of the tautology *X wa X da* is double negation, strictly speaking, tautology is used to negate that "all of X is not always X" and that the tautology *X wa X da* is formally an affirmative sentence but indicates a double negation. To explain various interpretations of *X wa X da*, he proposes that description tautology be divided in two ways: *homogeneous tautology* in (3-18e) and *heterogeneous tautology* in (3-18f), whose respective interpretations are generalized as follows:

(3-19) a. Homogeneous interpretation: Every X is X.
  b. Heterogeneous interpretation: Distinguish X from its similar Y.[14]
                    (Sakahara 1993: 60–61, my translation)

These two interpretations are based on the category formations shown in Figure 3-2a and 3-2b, respectively:

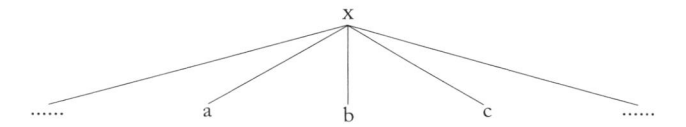

Figure 3-2a. Category formation of homogeneous tautology

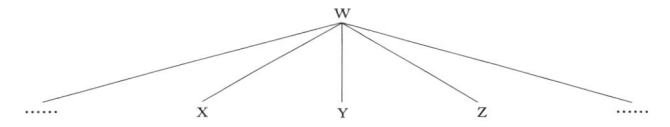

Figure 3-2b. Category formation of heterogeneous tautology
                    (Sakahara 2002: 110–111)

With homogeneous interpretation, *X wa X da* is used for focusing on the homogeneity among the members of category X. One thinks about category X and its members. On the other hand, with heterogeneous interpretation, *X wa X da* is used for focusing on the heterogeneity among the members of category W. X is considered a member of category W and is contrasted with Y, another member of category W (cf. Sakahara 2002: 109–110). To put it another way, the interpretations of tautology depend on whether X is regarded as a category or a member. The focus on categories emphasizes homogeneity among the members, while the focus on members emphasizes heterogeneity among the members.

To understand this analysis concretely, first, consider (3-20) and (3-21), which are examples of homogeneous tautology:[15]

(3-20) Speaking of numbers, it gets light and the sun rises. Then, it gets light and the sun rises. Then, it gets light and the sun rises. Three days have gone by. This is described with the number *three*. Three birds are flying. This is also described with the number *three*. It takes many years to begin to think that the *three* of *three days* is the same as the *three* of *three birds*.

However, the same sun rises when talking about the sun, while different birds fly when talking about the birds. Furthermore, the birds are definitely different from the sun. Despite that, human beings have a habit of thinking that they are not so different from one and another, I think.

Then, I imagine some people may think that *san wa san da* ((lit.) three is three) and the word *three* are unrelated to whether the object in question is a bird or the sun. Others may think that the number *three* comes from the *three* of *three birds*.

(Tsuyoshi Mori, *NHK Ningen Daigaku: Suugaku Bunka Jinsei*, cited by Sakahara 2002: 110–111, my translation)

(3-21) Nezumi wo toranaku temo, **neko wa neko da**.
mouse ACC (can) not catch even if cat TM cat COP
'Even if it cannot catch mice, (lit.) <u>a cat is a cat</u>.' (ibid.: 113)

In Sakahara's analysis, the writer of (3-20) (that is, the person referred to by the word *I*) discusses an abstraction process related to a numerical concept. The process is to eliminate differences between the states of affairs in question and extract their commonalities. The extracted commonality *X* (i.e. the category THREE) is homogeneous since it is not the case that the *three* in *three days* is more typical than the *three* in *three birds* or vice versa. The speaker of (3-21) rejects the categorization of the category CAT, which is divided into two parts based on whether or not the cat in question catches mice, and adopts the categorization of the category CAT, which is not divided based on the above criterion. That is, the speaker regards the category CAT as homogeneous. In these two examples, the writer and the speaker think about the category X and its members. *X wa X da* is used for focusing on homogeneity among the members of category X.

Next, consider (3-22) and (3-23), which are examples of heterogeneous tautologies:

(3-22) *Zasshu wa zasshu, hasuki wa hasuki*.
mutt TM mutt husky TM husky
'(lit.) <u>A mutt is a mutt, a husky is a husky</u>.' (ibid.: 123)

(3-23) *Asobi wa asobi, kekkon wa kekkon*.

game TM game   marriage TM   marriage
'(lit.) A game is a game, a marriage is a marriage.'   (ibid.: 124)

In (3-22), suppose that a woman criticizes a man for feeding leftover food to a mutt and steak to a husky, and in response to her criticism, the man says *Zasshu wa zasshu, hasuki wa hasuki*. In this case, he considers *mutt* and *husky* to be members of the category DOG (that is, the upper category of MUTT and HUSKY) and uses the tautological utterances to focus on the heterogeneity among the members of the category DOG. In (3-23), suppose that a man presents his idea about male–female relationships. In this case, he considers *game* and *marriage* as members of the (ad hoc) category MALE–FEMALE RELATIONSHIP (that is, the upper category of GAME and MARRIAGE) and he uses the tautological utterances to focus on the heterogeneity among the members of the category MALE–FEMALE RELATIONSHIP.

Thus far, I have overviewed Sakahara's classification of description tautology. Sakahara is devoted entirely to classifying nominal tautologies into certain types, and he provides no apparent explanation for the essence of the Japanese nominal tautology *X wa X da*. Certainly, he mentions that the nature of tautology is double negation, but does not describe the mechanism for interpreting *X wa X da* as double negation. As we have already observed in 3.2.3, in the contexts where (explicit or implicit) negative sentences are uttered, a certain condition is met. If you account for the interpretation process of tautology in terms of negation, you must make clear how and why a tautological utterance without explicit negative words is interpreted as negation.

In addition to this, his claim does not explain how the hearer derives what corresponds to member Y and category W from the contexts. Conceivably, the variables Y and W are determined based on contexts. If Sakahara insists that member Y and category W are involved in tautological utterance interpretation, we need an explanation of how an interpreter identifies member Y and category W.

And finally, a simple question arises: how do we understand when a tautology is homogeneously interpreted and when another tautology is heterogeneously interpreted? With heterogeneous interpretation, an antithesis *X wa X, Y wa Y* 'X is X, Y is Y' is often used as shown in (3-22) and (3-23). It is easy to identify Y as well as X. However, as Sakahara (1993) himself admits, the latter part of the antithesis (i.e. *Y wa Y* 'Y is Y') is not always uttered. If the latter part is not uttered (that is, only the former part of the antithesis (i.e. *X wa X* 'X is X') is uttered), we lose an important key for distinguishing heterogeneous interpretation from homogeneous interpretation whose form is *X wa X (da)*. Sakahara's claim does not succeed in explaining how a homogeneous tautology is interpreted.

As we observed, Sakahara attempts to classify description tautologies. Some researchers use his claim as a starting point for discussion.

3.5.2.2 Koya (2002, 2003)

Koya (2002) revises Sakahara's claim regarding description tautology interpretation shown in (3-19a) and (3-19b) (repeated as (3-24a) and (3-24b)) and argues that the interpretation of tautologies is almost always ambiguous: a tautology has *saihitei-no-imi* 'the meaning of difference-denying' in (3-25a) and *saikyôchô-no-imi* 'the meaning of difference-emphasizing' in (3-25b).

(3-24)a. Homogeneous interpretation: Every X is X.　　　　　(= (3-19a))
　　　b. Heterogeneous interpretation: Distinguish X from its similar Y.
　　　　　　　　　　　　　　　　　　　　　　　　　　　(= (3-19b))
(3-25)a. The meaning of difference-denying: Any type of X is not different from X.
　　　b. The meaning of difference-emphasizing: X is not Y.
　　　　　　　　　　　　　　　　　　(Koya 2002: 10, my translation)

(3-25a) and (3-25b) are a revised version of (3-24a) and (3-24b), respectively. Let us discuss Koya's analysis using the following example:

(3-26)　*Nihonjin　　wa　　nihonjin　　　da.*
　　　　Japanese people　TM　Japanese people　COP
　　　　'(lit.) Japanese people are Japanese people.'　　　　(ibid.: 11)

(3-26) is ambiguous in two ways. If we interpret (3-26) as meaning difference-denying, one possible interpretation would be that even if a Japanese person was born and brought up in a foreign country, that person is a Japanese person. Adopting the formula (3-25a) *Any type of X is not different from X*, we can represent the interpretation as follows: *Any type of Japanese people is not different from Japanese people*. Next, if we interpret (3-26) as meaning difference-emphasizing, one possible interpretation would be that Japanese people are not Chinese people.

The interpretation can be generalized as the formula (3-25b) *X is not Y*.

Koya adds that some tautologies are unambiguous. Consider (3-27):

(3-27)　*Anotoki　wa　anotoki　da.*
　　　　that time　TM　that time　COP
　　　　'(lit.) That time is that time.'　　　　　　　　　　(ibid.: 14)

Following his analysis, this example is used for contrasting *anotoki* 'that time' with *ima* 'now' and therefore it is interpreted not as difference-denying, but as difference-emphasizing. When a tautology has only one meaning, the meaning is difference-emphasizing, not difference-denying, since any category always has a contrastive category (even if they are not antonymous). Koya concludes that the primary meaning of tautologies is difference-emphasizing.

While Koya appears to explain how tautologies are interpreted, his account raises some questions. First, he uses the variables X and Y in stipulating the meanings of *X wa X da*, but he does not propose how an interpreter searches for those corresponding to X and Y. He states that X and Y in (3-25a) and (3-25b) represent a certain category, but postpones determining whether the two categories are similar in the sense that they are members of their upper category. That is, he does not define the two categories concretely. (Presumably) X corresponds to *X* in the sentence *X wa X da*. On the other hand, it is difficult to search for something that corresponds to category Y since Y is not uttered in (3-27). If Koya insists that category Y is involved in tautological utterance interpretation, we need an explanation of how an interpreter identifies category Y.

Second, Koya insists that tautology is ambiguous in two ways. However, the ambiguity dissolves since the interpretation is determined based on the context. He does not mention what role pragmatic inference plays in understanding nominal tautological utterances. The interpretation process is still unsolved until the role of pragmatic inference is clear.

And finally, in connection with the previous problem, even if, as Koya argues, tautology has two possible meanings, how do we determine when a tautology is interpreted as being difference-denying and when another tautology is interpreted as being difference-emphasizing? Koya's analysis cannot answer the question. As Koya himself points out, contrary to his claim, some tautologies can only have a difference-denying meaning. Here, reconsider (3-20). For convenience, it is repeated here as (3-28):

(3-28)   Speaking of numbers, it gets light and the sun rises. Then, it gets light and the sun rises. Then, it gets light and the sun rises. Three days have gone by. This is described with the number *three*. Three birds are flying. This is also described with the number *three*. It takes many years to begin to think that the *three* of *three days* is the same as the *three* of *three birds*.

However, the same sun rises when talking about the sun, while different birds fly when talking about the birds. Furthermore, the birds are definitely different from the sun. Despite that, human beings have a habit of thinking that they are not so different from one and another, I think.

Then, I imagine some people may think that ***san wa san da*** ((lit.) three is three) and the word *three* are unrelated to whether the object in question is a bird or the sun. Others may think that the number *three* comes from the *three* of *three birds*.   (= (3-20))

As we have already observed, the writer of (3-28) focuses on the abstraction process of the numerical concept and emphasizes the non-existence of differences among the states of affairs referred to by the number *three*. This example is interpreted as being difference-denying. Therefore (3-28) only has a difference-denying meaning. This is a clear-cut counterexample of Koya's analysis, which states that when a tautology has only one meaning, the meaning is difference-emphasizing. Koya's proposal is unsatisfactory.

3.5.2.3   Furumaki (2009a, 2009b)

Furumaki (2009a: 44) considers the Japanese tautology X *wa* X a construction, and argues that X *wa* X has "the constructional meaning of confirming its central category X, but not peripheral" and that the type of homogeneous tautology in Sakahara's (2002) sense is further divided into three usages: *ketteiteki-sokumen yôhô* 'critical-facet usage', *ta-sokumen yôhô* 'multiple-facet usage', and *hi-tokuteiteki yôhô* 'non-deterministic usage'.[16] According to his analysis, the interpretation mechanism of X *wa* X is illustrated as follows:

```
                    ╱──── Typical category X
         ┌ ─ ─ ─ ┐ ╱
        ╱   1    ╲╱
       │  ←─X─   │────── Category X
        ╲   2   ╱╲
         └ ─ ─ ─ ┘ ╲
                    ╲──── Peripheral category X
```

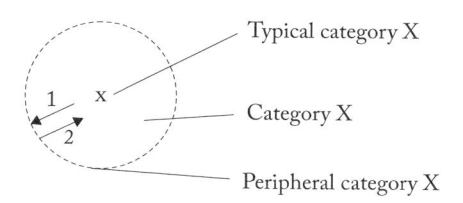

Figure 3-3. Interpretation mechanism of the *X wa X* construction   (Furumaki 2009a: 38)

The dotted line expresses a category X, whose center is more typical and whose edge is more peripheral. The arrowed lines 1 and 2 express a double negation, whose meaning is to emphasize the typical X but not the peripheral X. The function of the *X wa X* construction is characterized as emphasizing typicality but not peripherality.

The three usages are used to explain various homogeneous tautology interpretations. (3-29a)–(3-29c) are typical examples corresponding to each of the three usages:

(3-29) a. *Arukôru   ga   haittei   reba,   sake   wa   sake   da.*
        alcohol   SM   contain   if   liquor   TM   liquor   COP
        'If alcohol is contained in the beverage, (lit.) <u>liquor is liquor</u>.'

    b. *Shinkansen   ga   tomaranaku   temo,   daitoshi   wa   daitoshi   da.*
        bullet train   SM   (do) not stop   even if   large city   TM   large city   COP
        'Even if bullet trains do not stop at the city, (lit.) <u>a large city is a large city</u>.'

    c. ***Kinô   wa   kinô   da.***
        yesterday   TM   yesterday   COP
        '(lit.) <u>Yesterday is yesterday</u>.'   (ibid.: 34)

The three usages are illustrated as shown in Figure 3-4:

ketteiteki-sokumen yôhô	*ta-sokumen yôhô*	*hi-tokuteiteki yôhô*
'critical-facet usage'	'multiple-facet usage'	'non-deterministic usage'
(a)	(b)	(c)

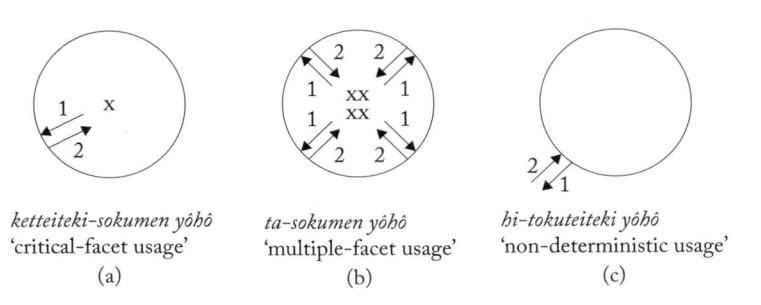

Figure 3-4. Three usages of homogeneous tautology   (ibid.: 39)

The first type called *critical-facet usage* in Figure 3-4a can be used for identifying category X as *X*, based on a critical facet. For instance, in (3-29a), the beverage in question is interpreted as *sake* 'liquor', based on the critical facet that it includes alcohol. The second type called *multiple-facet usage* in Figure 3-4b can be used for identifying an X as *X*, based on multiple facets. In (3-29b), the city in question is interpreted as *daitoshi* 'large city', based on the multiple facets relating to having a large population, being full of life and energy and so on. Finally, the third type called *non-deterministic usage* in Figure 3-4c can be used to identify an X as *X*, based on non-deterministic facets. In (3-29c), the day in question (that is, the day referred to by the word *kinô* 'yesterday') is interpreted as *kinô* 'yesterday', based on non-deterministic facets, that is, without specific proofs.

Furumaki might be able to explain how nominal tautologies are interpreted. However, he has the following two problems. First, he regards the tautological expression *X wa X* as a construction. If he adopts this approach, it should be said that (3-29a) and (3-29b) are different from (3-29c). The reason is that the expressional form *X wa X* does not always occur with a subordinate clause. The former two examples are embedded in another sentence while the latter example is not. Thus, these examples cannot be regarded as the same construction. Furumaki's claim is not about an analysis of tautologies, but about a classification of interpretations of expressions with tautologies.

Second, Furumaki categorizes homogeneous tautology in Sakahara's sense into three subtypes. He is devoted entirely to listing certain cases of nominal tautologies. I doubt whether the three subtypes are sufficient to describe the interpretation of tautologies and what determines which subtype is applied to the context in question. Although the above three types are expressed in the expressional form *X wa X*, Furumaki's claim cannot explain them from a unified point of view. He might reply to this counterargument as follows: the tautological construction *X wa X* has the function of emphasizing a typical case rather than a marginal case. However, such a response would be incorrect. Here, recall the numeral abstract example (3-28), which is a homogeneous tautology in Sakahara's sense. This example covers the abstract process of a numerical concept and ignores the point about which *three* is typical. That is, the category THREE is treated as homogeneous. This shows that the tautological construction *X wa X* does not always function as emphasizing a typical case rather than a marginal case. Thus, Furumaki's claim is unsatisfactory.

3.5.2.4 Sakai (2006b, 2008a)

Sakai (2006b) calls a certain case of homogeneous tautologies in Sakahara's (2002) sense, *saihitei gata tôtoroji* 'difference-negating tautology', and argues that it is used to deny the difference in question. The following examples are included in this type:

(3-30)a. *Nezumi wo toranaku temo,* **neko wa neko da.**
 mice ACC (can) not catch even if cat TM cat COP
 'Even if it cannot catch mice, (lit.) a cat is a cat.'
 b. *Kyô mo Ichiro wa Ichiro da.*
 today also Ichiro TM Ichiro COP
 'Today, (lit.) Ichiro is Ichiro.' (Sakai 2006b: 137)

He adopts the extended mental space theory, where two additional domains, namely the general knowledge domain (GKD) and utterance situation (US), are posited, in addition to discourse domain (DD), which contains mental spaces in Fauconnier's (1994, 1997) sense.[17] Following Sakai's proposal, the space configuration of the difference-negating tautology *X wa X da* is illustrated as follows:

(3-31)a. M1: C1 (X) = x
 b. M2: C2 (x′) = X
 c. C3 (x) = x′ (ibid.: 135)

The space configuration of (3-31) is illustrated as Figure 3-5:

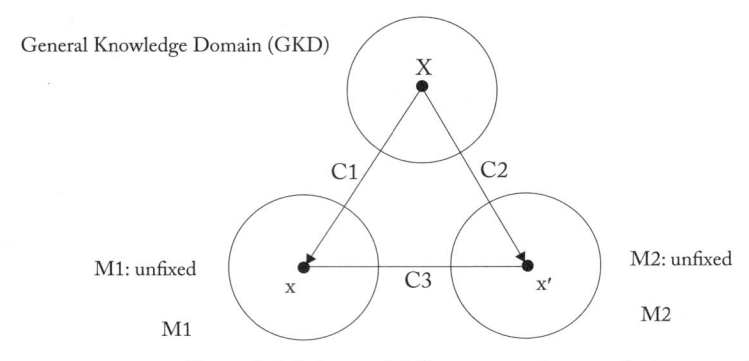

Figure 3-5. Schema of difference-negating tautologies   (ibid.: 136)

In this schema, the variable X in GKD corresponds to X in the sentence X *wa X da*. X's property is transferred to both x in M1 and x' in M2, and x and x' are regarded as the same individual since they are linked with the connector C3. M1 and M2 are unfixed, but they are fixed depending on context. For example, in (3-30b), X is *Ichiro*, M1 is the usual situation and M2 is *today* (that is, the day the utterance is produced). Ichiro's property (e.g. producing one hit after another) is transferred to both x in the usual situation (M1) and x' on the day the utterance is produced (M2), and Ichiro in the usual situation and Ichiro on the day the utterance is produced are regarded as the same individual since they are linked with the connector C3.

As we have just seen, Sakai proposes the space configuration and the schema of difference-negating tautologies. Here, a question arises: why does the hearer understand that the utterance (3-30b) conveys Ichiro's property of producing one hit after another? Sakai does not mention how the hearer chooses the property in question from some properties concerning Ichiro. Furthermore, within the framework of the extended mental space theory, Sakai (2008a) examines cases of *heiretsu gata tôtoroji* 'parallel tautology', which are categorized as *ishitsuka tôtoroji* 'heterogeneous tautology' in Sakahara's classification, and proposes the space configuration and the schema.[18] His proposal is simply a list of classifications of nominal tautologies and provides no apparent explanation for the essence of nominal tautologies.[19] Although difference-negating tautologies and parallel tautologies are represented in the expressional form *X wa X da*, his claim cannot explain them from a unified viewpoint. Thus, his claim is not promising.

In the course of the discussion in 3.5, we have found that several researchers adopting cognitive linguistic approaches have worked on classifying the usages of nominal tautology. The research style suggests that cognitive linguistic researchers do not discern the essence of nominal tautological utterances. Moreover, cognitive linguists often use the word *stereotypical* or *typical* when discussing nominal tautologies. However, tautological utterances are not always used to represent a stereotypical property or emphasize a typical one, as in the case of the numerical concept example (3-28).

3.6 Relevance Theoretic Approach

In this approach, Higashimori and Wilson (1996: 10) first mentioned that tautological utterances would be treated as "reminders, implicating that an obvious truth has been overlooked". Subsequently, studies adopting relevance theoretic approaches have progressed little. Mayumi Nishikawa, who is a relevance theorist, presents a challenging proposal.

Nishikawa (2003) argues that the tautological utterance *A is A* is interpreted via the pragmatic process of *ad hoc* concept construction.[20] The interpretation is summarized as follows:

(3-32) a. Utterance: *A is A*.
    b. Explicature: *A is A**.
    c. Higher-level explicature:
       The speaker intends the hearer to know that *A is A**.
    d. Implicatures: (They depend on the contexts.)   (Nishikawa 2003: 53)

The subject *A* is generically interpreted and the predicate *A* expresses contextually adjusted concepts but not encoded lexical concepts. For example, consider (3-33) and (3-34):

(3-33)   [Mary finds a penny on the street and picks it up.]
        Tom : Why did you pick it up? It's just a penny.
        Mary : *Money is money.*   (ibid.: 54)
(3-34)   [Mary won a lot of money in a public lottery. Her friend Jane is envious.]
        Jane : You are the happiest girl in the world, aren't you?
        Mary : *Money is money.*   (ibid.)

Following Nishikawa's analysis, in (3-33), Mary thinks that money is very important regardless of how much it is and expresses a scornful or critical attitude towards Tom, who considers a penny to be unimportant. In (3-34), Mary thinks that money is a tool for obtaining certain things and expresses a scornful or critical attitude towards Jane, who ignores the view that money is not the only thing in life. In both cases, the concept MONEY communicated by the predicate *money* is more specific than the concept that it originally encodes. These concepts are interpreted as MONEY* and MONEY** in (3-33′a) and in (3-34′a), respectively:

(3-33′)a. Explicature: Money is MONEY*.
    b. Higher-level explicature:
       Mary intends Tom to know that money is MONEY*.
    c. Implicated premise:
       We should not undervalue anything that has value.
    d. Implicated conclusions:
       Even a penny has value. We should not undervalue a penny. (ibid.)

(3-34′)a. Explicature: Money is MONEY**.
    b. Higher-level explicature:
       Mary intends Jane to know that money is MONEY**.
    c. Implicated premise:
       To be able to get a range of things does not necessarily mean happiness.
    d. Implicated conclusions:
       Mary is not necessarily that happy. (ibid.: 54–55)

In (3-33′), the concept MONEY* derived from the original encoded concept MONEY is connected to something important, and in (3-34′), the concept MONEY** is connected to something trivial.

Nishikawa's claim appears to be promising since it could provide a concrete process for understanding nominal tautological utterance. However, there are two problems with it. First, the word *they* in the generalized interpretation process of (3-32d) is defined metalinguistically. This shows that she thinks that the meaning of nominal tautologies appears only at the level of explicatures, and that she does not recognize the importance of stipulating what type of implicature is derived in the interpretation process.

Second, she insists that the subject *A* is interpreted generically. However, it is not always generic. Consider the following conversation between a woman and her mother in law:

(3-35) Daughter in law : So, I was talking to my dad about Jack potentially having an identity crisis, being half Japanese and half British, and not being either ... and my dad just said '*Jack is Jack*', which I thought was a very good way of thinking.
Mother in law : (Silence)
Daughter in law : Anyway, what time did you say we would have tea?
(Sasamoto 2012: 441)

Suppose that a woman is talking about her son with her mother in law in the lounge. The mother in law tends to have a stereotypical view about other cultures and the daughter wants to stop her saying inappropriate things about her mixed race baby son. The daughter cites her father's comment, *Jack is Jack*. In this example, the name *Jack* is a proper noun and therefore has no generic use.

Furthermore, I have a simple question: can her analysis apply to Japanese nominal tautology data? As mentioned in chapter 1, there are three types of nominal tautology in Japanese: *A wa A da*, *A ga A da* and *A mo A da*. The English nominal tautology *A is A* could be simply literally translated into the Japanese nominal tautology *A wa A da*. If so, Nishikawa's proposal for *A is A* could explain examples of *A wa A da*. However, it cannot apply to *A wa A da*. Here, let us discuss the following case of *A wa A da*:

(3-36) [A boy is asking his mother about an unfamiliar word *furin* 'adultery'.]
Son : *Nênê, furin   tte   nanno koto? Oshiete   yo.*
        well   adultery HEAR   what   tell (me) SFP
        'Well, what does "adultery" mean? Please tell me.'
Mother : *Sonnakoto   shiranakutemoî   no   yo.*
          it   (you do) not need to know   SFP   SFP
          'It's not something you need to know.'
Son : *Nê,   oshiete   yo.*
       please tell (me) SFP
       'Please tell me.'
Mother : *Dakara ne, furin   wa furin   nano. Sonnakoto*

so	SFP	adultery	TM	adultery	SFP	that

kikanaidechôdai.
do not ask (me)
'So, (lit.) <u>adultery is adultery</u>. Don't ask me any questions about that.'

In (3-36), suppose that a boy cannot understand the word *furin* 'adultery' and asks his mother for its meaning. In this situation, the son wants her to tell him the meaning of *furin*. On the other hand, by uttering *furin wa furin nano*, the mother communicates that she does not want to tell him the meaning of *furin*. The utterance *furin wa furin nano* is used to reject his request. That is, she simply rejects his request by producing a tautological utterance. If, following Nishikawa's analysis, the utterance *furin wa furin nano* might be interpreted as communicating that furin wa FURIN* da 'adultery is ADULTERY*'. The concept FURIN* 'ADULTERY*' indicates a narrowing or widening of the lexically encoded concept. However, by uttering *furin wa furin nano*, the speaker does not intend to communicate such an interpretation. Rather she intends to communicate that she does not want to tell him the meaning of the word *furin*. The communicated assumption is regarded not as an explicature, but as an implicature. Nishikawa's claim cannot explain the unfamiliar word example (3-36) and thus is rejected.

In this chapter, I have examined previous studies on nominal tautology that have adopted five different approaches: a radical pragmatic approach, a radical semantic approach, a non-radical approach, a cognitive linguistic approach and a relevance theoretic approach. They provide insightful suggestions, but cannot correctly predict the interpretation of nominal tautology. In the following three chapters, I will examine Japanese nominal tautology data and propose that each of the three types of Japanese nominal tautologies encodes a specific meaning.

Notes

1 Of course, there have been non-English tautology studies. An analysis of tautological expressions in colloquial Jordanian Arabic was undertaken by Fraghal (1992). Japanese nominal tautologies have been attracting scholarly attention. For detailed discussions of past studies of Japanese tautologies, see 3.5, 4.2, 5.2, and 6.2.
2 Gazder (1979) observes only disjunctive tautologies such as (i). I will not examine his claim here. For a more detailed argument, see Gazder (1979).

(i) Man : What are you doing this evening?
Woman : *I'll either go to Fran's or not.*
Man : You're not on call then. (adapted from Gazder 1979: 51–52)

3. Of their corpus, which includes 343 tokens collected from conversation and the media, Ward and Hirschberg (1991) use 169 tokens obtained from the Associated Press (AP) newswire (February–December 1988). The 169 tokens are presented in the following forms:

(i) a. Equatives: A is A
   e.g. Murder is murder.
   b. Disjunctions: (either) p or not p
   e.g. Either a ham has bone or it doesn't have a bone.
   c. Conditionals: if p (then) p
   e.g. If I miss, I miss.
   d. Subordinate conjunctions: when p, p
   e.g. When they're gone, they're gone.
   e. Headless relatives: p what p
   e.g. It means what it means. (= (2-6))

The following chart shows the distribution of each type.

Type	Numbers	Percent
Equatives	114	67.5%
Headless relatives	22	13.0%
Conditionals	14	8.3%
Disjunctions	13	7.7%
Subordinating conjunctions	6	3.6%
Total	169	100%

(Ward and Hirschberg 1991: 511)

This chart contains a slight error. The total percentage is said to amount to 100% but in fact, it is 100.1%.

4. Grice (1975, 1989) classifies conversational implicatures in two types: *generalized conversational implicature* and *particularized conversational implicature*. Generalized conversational implicatures are characterized as follows: "the use of a certain form of words in an utterance would normally (in the absence of special circumstances) carry such-and-such an implicature or type of implicature" (Grice 1989: 37). That is to say, a certain expression has the same implicature regardless of contexts. Particularized conversational implicatures are characterized as "cases in which an implicature is carried by saying that *p* on a particular occasion in virtue of special features in the context" (ibid.). Briefly, the same utterance has various implicatures in different specific contexts. See Grice (1975, 1989) for some relevant discussion.

5. In Ward and Hirschberg (1991), the formulas *a is a* and *a is b* is used instead of *A is A* and

A is B. However, the present study uses *A is A* and *A is B* to provide coherent notation.
6 See note 4.
7 Fraser (1988) mentions that there are many interpretations with the predicate *be* as the following sentences indicate:

    (i)a. John is a man   [meets the defining properties of]
       b. John is a fireman   [works as]
       c. John is in Boston   [is located in]
       d. John is happy   [has the mental attitude of]
       e. Be quiet   [act]
       f. There is a boy in here   [exists]   (Fraser 1988: 219)

8 A cognitive linguistic approach often uses the formulas *X is X* and *X wa X da*, not *A is A* and *A wa A da*, which are used in my analysis. Properly, I should adopt coherent notation. However, to avoid confusion, 3.5 follows the notation used by each of the cognitive linguists.
9 Mizuta (1996: 79) has previously admitted that "[t]he frame model is not perfect, as Lakoff (1987) points out, but it will do for our present discussion".
10 Sakahara (2002) asserts that description tautology has two contrastive interpretations: *dôshitsuka tôtoroji* 'homogeneous tautology' and *ishitsuka tôtoroji* 'heterogeneous tautology'. After that, he intentionally adds a third interpretation: *saika tôtoroji* 'difference tautology', since researchers are not aware of the existence of the interpretation. The following example is included as difference tautology.

    (i) Taro : *Nezumi wo tottekoso,*   **neko wa neko da.**
             mice ACC only if (it can) catch   cat TM cat COP
       'Only if it can catch mice, (lit.) <u>a cat is a cat</u>.'   (adapted from Sakahara 2002: 112)

In (i), the speaker Taro objects to the categorization of the category CAT that is not divided into two parts based on whether or not the cat in question catches mice, and adopts the one that is divided based on the above criterion.

    On this basis, one might argue that description tautology is divided into three subtypes. However, in the present book, it is assumed that there are two subtypes of description tautology in Sakahara's classification, since the meanings of homogeneous tautology and heterogeneous tautology are defined as (3-19a) and (3-19b) but that of difference tautology is not defined.
11 Identification-rejecting tautology is used to reject the identification of *X*, where *X* represents *X* in the sentence *X wa X da*. Consider the following example:

    (i) Shunsuke : *Ojisan, ojisan, hanashi ga arunda.*   *Chotto koi yo.*
                     uncle   uncle   (I) want to talk (with you)   bit   come SFP
                     'Uncle, uncle, I want to talk with you. Come here.'
        Soichiro : *Atode na, ima isogashi.*
                     later   SFP   now   (I am) busy
                   'I'll hear you later. I'm busy now.'

Shunsuke : *Daijina   hanashi   nanda.   Ato   tte   itsu   da?*
           important   talk   COP   later   HEAR   when   COP
           'I have something important to talk about with you. When will we talk?'
Soichiro : ***Ato   wa   ato   da.***   *Wakatteiru daro,   Shunsuke.*
           later   TM   later   COP   know   Q   Shunsuke
           '(lit.) <u>Later is later</u>. You know that, don't you? Shunsuke.'

(Sakahara 2002: 107)

Soichiro forgot his daughter's birthday and Shunsuke tries to remind him of it. In this situation, what Shunsuke wants to know is not the meaning of *ato* 'later' but its referent (i.e. when they will talk about the daughter's birthday). The tautological utterance *Ato wa ato da* is used to reject the identification of when they will talk about the daughter's birthday.

12 Description-rejecting tautology is used to reject the description of *X*, where *X* represents *X* in the sentence *X wa X da*. Consider (i):

(i) Child : *Kan-in   tte   nani?*
             adultery HEAR   what
             'What's "adultery"?'
   Mother : ***Kan-in   wa   kan-in.***   *Kodomo   wa   sonnakoto   wa*
            adultery   TM   adultery   child   TM   that kind of thing TM
            shira nakute   i   no.
            even if (you do) not know   (that is) no matter   SFP
            '(lit.) <u>Adultery is adultery</u>. Even if children don't know it, that's no matter.'

(Sakahara 2002: 107)

Suppose that a child cannot understand the word *kan-in* 'adultery' and asks his mother its meaning. She does not want to explain it to him. The tautological utterance *Kan-in wa kan-in* is used to reject the description of *kan-in*, or more specifically, its meaning.

13 Identification tautology is used to identify *X*, where *X* represents *X* in the sentence *X wa X da*. Consider (i):

(i) Taro : *Metonimi   tte   nani?*
           metonymy   HEAR   what
           'What's "metonymy"?'
   Jiro : ***Metonimi   wa   metonimi   da   yo.*** *Kinô,   jugyô de   yattajanai   ka.*
          metonymy   TM   metonymy   COP   SFP   yesterday   class   in   (we) learned (it)   Q
          '(lit.) <u>Metonymy is metonymy</u>. Yesterday, we learned it in the class, didn't we?'
   Taro : *Â,   are   ne.*
          ah   that   SFP
          'Ah, that's one.'

(Sakahara 2002: 128)

In (i), Jiro responds to Taro's question. At first, Taro does not understand the meaning of *metonimi* 'metonymy' but Taro identifies its meaning from Jiro's tautological utterance.

When comparing identification-rejecting tautology with identification tautology, whether or not identification tautology is used for rejection depends on the hearer's knowledge, namely, whether or not she has some knowledge about the object referred to by the noun in the sentence.

14 Sakahara (1993: 60–61) discusses the French tautology *X ÊTRE X* and argues that it has the following interpretations: (i) Every X is X and (ii) Distinguish X from its similar Y, but he does not call these two interpretations *homogeneous interpretation* and *heterogeneous interpretation*, respectively.

On the other hand, Sakahara (2002) discusses the Japanese tautology *X wa X da* and calls description tautologies with interpretations (i) and (ii) *homogeneous tautology* and *heterogeneous tautology*, respectively. Given that fact, I summarized Sakahara's two interpretations as shown (3-19a) and (3-19b).

15 In (3-20), the italicized part *san wa san da* 'three is three' is only written in Japanese. For reference, the original Japanese version is shown below. The italicized part in (3-20) corresponds to the underlined part in the following text.

数でいいますと、夜が明けてお日さまが出る、また夜が明けてお日さまが出る、また夜が明けてお日さまが出る、これで三日たった。これは3という数です。そこに鳥が三羽飛んでいる、これも3です。三日の3と鳥が三羽の3が同じ3と考えるようになるにはどれだけ長い年月がかかったか…［…］

しかし、お日さまのほうは同じお日さまは三回顔を出すのですが、鳥のほうは違う鳥が三羽飛んでいる。さらに鳥とお日さまとは違うに決まっています。違うものであるにもかかわらず、違うことを承知のうえで「同じだな」と思う癖が人間にはあると思います。

その場合に、鳥であろうがお日さまであろうが、<u>3は3だ</u>、3という世界が別個にあって処理できる対象だというウェートのほうが強い人と、なんとなく、これは鳥から出てきた3だというのを引きずるタイプとあると思います。

16 Furumaki uses the term *construction* as a technical term in Construction Grammar (Lakoff 1987; Goldberg 1995) and Cognitive Grammar (Taylor 2003).

17 Sakai (2005: 360) characterizes GKD, US and DD as follows:

(i)a. GKD contains elements already known and their properties.
   b. US contains elements which are in the utterance situation and the information concerning them.
   c. DD corresponds to traditional mental spaces and contains elements introduced by verbal expressions and the information concerning them.

18 Sakai (2008a) erroneously categorizes as difference tautology in Sakahara's (2002) classification, the following example dealt with in his paper:

(i) A : *Dôshite   Tama   bakkari   kawaigaru   no?*
        why   Tama   only   (you) love   Q
        'Why do you love only Tama?'
    B : *Shiro   wa   Shiro,   Tama   wa   Tama   da.*
        Shiro   TM   Shiro   Tama   TM   Tama   COP

'(lit.) <u>Shiro is Shiro, Tama is Tama</u>.' (adapted from Sakai 2008a: 106)

Correctly, this example, which Sakai names parallel tautology, is categorized as heterogeneous tautology. Thus, in the present book, I consider (i) to be an example of heterogeneous tautology in Sakahara's (2002) sense.
19 Sakai (2006b, 2008a, etc.) has energetically attempted to explain how tautological utterances are interpreted mainly with the extended mental space theory. Sakai (2012a) adopts a different approach based on Recanati's (2004) contextualism, and argues that the linguistic meaning of *X is X* does not correspond to any propositional content.
20 A process of *ad hoc* concept construction is one of replacing an encoded lexical concept appearing in the logical form with a contextually adjusted one. Adjusted concepts are represented with * (e.g. A*). For details, see 4.4.1.

Chapter 4

A wa A da

Some previous studies have suggested that the interpretation process of *A wa A da* could be accounted for in terms of negation, but the process has yet to be clearly characterized. This chapter discusses the meaning encoded in the Japanese nominal tautology *A wa A da* and proposes the following meaning: *A wa A da* must be processed in such a way as to communicate an assumption that contradicts and eliminates another assumption about the referent of the subject *A*, attributed to someone other than the speaker at the point of utterance.

4.1 Introduction

In this and the following two chapters, I will examine three types of Japanese nominal tautologies. As mentioned in chapter 1, Japanese has three types of nominal tautological expressional forms: *A wa A da*, *A ga A da* and *A mo A da*. These three expressional forms convey different meanings. Given the formal variety, it is important to keep these three forms in mind and discuss the overall picture. However, past studies of Japanese nominal tautologies have scarcely recognized their importance and are mainly devoted to investigating *A wa A da*. Analyses of *A ga A da* and *A mo A da* have made little progress. This imbalance has led to a lack of uniformity in terms of constructing a comprehensive theory of Japanese nominal tautologies. My suggestion is that we need to provide a unified analysis as regards the linguistic phenomenon of Japanese nominal tautologies by postulating an expressional form that encodes procedural information. As a starting point, this chapter aims to stipulate the encoded meaning of *A wa A da*.[1]

4.2 Previous Studies

As already discussed in chapter 3, there have been several previous studies on nominal tautology. They appear to have nothing in common. Some researchers point out that the interpretation process can be accounted for in terms of negation. However, they have different views about the way in which the notion of negation is associated with the process of understanding nominal tautologies. Before observing how a nominal tautological utterance is used and understood in a given context, it is instructive to confirm what aspect is regarded as negation in the nominal tautology interpretation process. Two researchers have analyzed nominal tautology from the perspective of negation: Tsujimoto (1996) and Nakamura (2000). First, I offer an overview of Tsujimoto's (1996) work.

4.2.1 Tsujimoto (1996)

Limiting her data to non-idiomatic nominal tautologies, Tsujimoto (1996) argues that *A is A* is used to strongly reargue what has been once negated in a situation where there is a disagreement between two or more people. More technically speaking, when a speaker has recognized that the hearer has a counter opinion to hers, which is formalized as *X is not A*, she utters the tautological statement *A is A* to strongly reargue that *X is A*.[2] Consider (4-1):

(4-1) '… You are always trying to find hidden meanings in things. Why? *A cigarette is a cigarette. A piece of silk is a piece of silk.* Why not leave it at that?' (Tsujimoto 1996: 133)

A man named Mr. Wilcox and a woman named Robyn are talking about a poster advertising the cigarette brand *Silk Cut*. The poster has a picture of a purple silk cloth with a deep slit in it. Robyn interprets the purple cloth as a symbol of the female body and states her opinion as follows:

(4-2) The shimmering silk, with its voluptuous curves and sensuous texture, obviously symbolized the female body, and the elliptical slit foregrounded by a lighter colour showing through, was still more obviously a vagina. The advert thus appealed to both sensual and sadistic impulses, the desire to mutilate as well as penetrate the female body. (ibid.)

In response to this opinion, Mr. Wilcox utters the statement in (4-1). First, let us look at Tsujimoto's analysis of *A piece of silk is a piece of silk*. In the situation described above, the woman sees the cloth not as a silk fabric, but as symbolizing the female body, while the man sees it simply as a silk fabric. There is a disagreement between the two people. If you apply the formulas *X is A* and *X is not A* to the utterance, *A* corresponds to *a piece of silk* and *X* corresponds to *the purple silk in the poster in question*. Mr. Wilcox has noticed that Robyn has a counter opinion to his, namely *the purple silk in the poster in question is not a piece of silk*. Then, he says *A piece of silk is a piece of silk* to strongly reargue that the purple silk in the poster in question is a piece of silk.

The same holds true for the other tautological utterance in (4-1) *A cigarette is a cigarette*. Here, the woman sees the *Silk Cut* cigarette as a symbol expressing more than cigarettes, namely, a symbolized female body, while the man sees it simply as a cigarette. They regard the *Silk Cut* cigarette differently. In Tsujimoto's analysis, *A* is *a cigarette* and *X* is *Silk Cut*. Mr. Wilcox has noticed that Robyn has a different view regarding *Silk Cut*, namely *Silk Cut is not a cigarette*. Then, he says *A cigarette is a cigarette* to strongly reargue that Silk Cut is a cigarette.

Tsujimoto targets English nominal tautologies. Her analysis seems to explain, mutatis mutandis, cases of Japanese nominal tautology *A wa A da*. The formulas *X is A* and *X is not A* would be translated *X wa A da* and *X wa A dewanai* in Japanese, respectively. Consider (4-3):

(4-3) [The defense claims that a defendant Taro has extenuating circumstances based on the fact that he was asked to kill Jiro.]

Defense : *Saibanchô! Taro wa, tanomarete Jiro wo koroshitan*
your honor Taro TM be asked Jiro ACC killed
desu. Dakara, Taro niwa jôjôshakuryô
COP therefore Taro P extenuating circumstances
no yochi ga aru to kangaemasu.
of room SM there are HEAR insist
'Your honor! Taro was asked to kill Jiro. Therefore, I insist that there are extenuating circumstances for his crime.'

Prosecutor : *Nani wo itteirun desu ka.* **Satsujin wa**
what ACC (you) are saying COP Q murder TM
satsujin desu.[3]
murder COP

'What are you saying? Murder is murder.'[4]

In (4-3), suppose that the defense insists that there are extenuating circumstances regarding the murder that Taro committed. The prosecutor disputes the claim, saying *Satsujin wa satsujin desu*. This utterance would be interpreted as follows: the murder that Taro committed should not be considered to have extenuating circumstances. There is a disagreement between the two people. In this situation, the defense sees the murder that Taro committed as a crime that has extenuating circumstances, while the prosecutor does not. If we apply the formulas *X wa A da* and *X wa A dewanai* to the utterance, *A* corresponds to *satsujin* 'murder' and *X* corresponds to *Taro ga yatta koto* 'what Taro did'. The prosecutor has recognized that the defense has a counter opinion to his, namely *Taro ga yatta koto wa satsujin dewanai* 'what Taro did is not murder'.[5] Then, he says *Satsujin wa satsujin desu* to strongly reargue that *Taro ga yatta koto wa satsujin da* 'what Taro did is murder'.

This, however, does not apply to all cases of *A wa A da*. First, *A wa A da* is not always used in a context where there is a disagreement between two or more people. Consider (4-4):

(4-4) [Haruko's friends keep on quitting the theater company. The fact initially made her consider giving up a professional acting career, but she finally decided to continue her study of acting.]
Haruko : (to herself) ***Watashi   wa   watashi.   Tanin   wa***
                   I   TM   I   other people   TM
kankeinai.
(I do) not care
'I am I. I don't care what other people think.'

Suppose that a woman named Haruko is talking to herself. We can imagine the following as an appropriate context in which (4-4) might be uttered: Haruko once decided to give up her professional acting career, but ultimately she decided not to give it up. There are no hearers in this situation, unlike (4-3). The speaker Haruko cannot inevitably notice that a hearer has a counter opinion to hers (that is, *X wa A dewanai*). Nevertheless, the tautological utterance *Watashi wa watashi* sounds natural. This shows that there is no need for disagreement between two or more people in the context where a tautological sentence is uttered.

A further question arises: what is the counter opinion expressed in the formula *X wa A dewanai*? In some cases, it is hard to identify anything corresponding to *X* in the formulas *X wa A da* and *X wa A dewanai*. Consider again the unfamiliar word example (3-36) discussed in the previous chapter. For convenience, it is given as (4-5):

(4-5)   [A boy is asking his mother about an unfamiliar word *furin* 'adultery'.]
    Son   : *Nênê,   furin   tte   nanno koto? Oshiete   yo.*
           well   adultery   HEAR   what   tell (me)   SFP
           'Well, what does "adultery" mean? Please tell me.'
    Mother : *Sonnakoto   shiranakutemoî   no   yo.*
           it   (you do) not need to know   SFP   SFP
           'It's not something you need to know.'
    Son   : *Nê,   oshiete   yo.*
           please   tell (me)   SFP
           'Please tell me.'
    Mother : *Dakara   ne,   furin   wa   furin   nano. Sonnakoto*
           so   SFP   adultery   TM   adultery   SFP   that
           kikanaidechôdai.
           do not ask (me)
           'So, (lit.) <u>adultery is adultery</u>. Don't ask me any questions about that.'   (= (3-36))

In (4-5), suppose that a boy wants to know the meaning of *furin* 'adultery', and his mother does not want to tell him about it. In this situation, there is a disagreement between the boy and the mother. However, he has no idea about what is being discussed, or in other words, about the meaning of *furin*, so the speaker, namely the mother, cannot inevitably notice the hearer's (that is, the boy's) counter opinion expressed in the formula *X wa A dewanai*. Besides, if she cannot identify such a formularized counter opinion, the tautological utterance *furin wa furin nano* cannot be analyzed as strongly rearguing that *X wa A da*. Therefore, Tsujimoto's proposal is rejected.

4.2.2   Nakamura (2000)

    Nakamura (2000: 72) argues that "*A wa A dearu* shows a non-continuum categorization of two categories A and B, against a continuum categorization of the two categories, and denies the continuum categorization".[6] To follow his analysis, let us consider (4-6):

(4-6) [Reporters are swarming around a sumo wrestler Takahanada. They are comforting him since he lost a close game.]
Takahanada : *Make wa make.*
defeat TM defeat
'Defeat is defeat.' (Nakamura 2000: 71)

The sumo wrestler Takahanada utters *Make wa make* to reject the reporters' comforting words. In this situation, the hearers (i.e. the reporters) consider the defeat to be nearly equal to victory, and think that there is no clear dividing line between *kachi* 'victory' and *make* 'defeat'. On the other hand, the speaker, Takahanada, considers defeat to be different from victory, and thinks that there is a clear dividing line between them. Under Nakamura's analysis, *Make wa make* shows the non-continuum categorization of two categories, namely category *kachi* 'victory' and category *make* 'defeat' (Figure 4-1a), against the continuum categorization of the two categories (Figure 4-1b), and denies the continuum categorization.

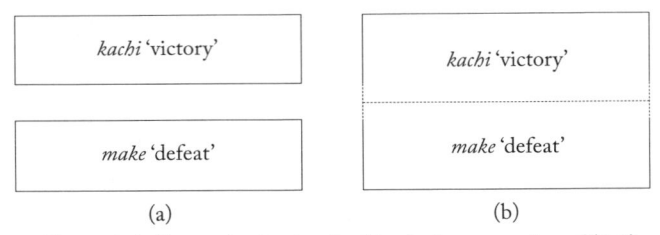

Figure 4-1. Categorization involved in the interpretation of (4-6)
(adapted from Nakamura 2000: 72)

In this way, Nakamura describes the way that an apparently meaningless tautological sentence gains a certain meaning with the notion of (non-)continuum categorization. However, his analysis does not always apply to examples of nominal tautologies. Here, recall the unfamiliar word example (4-5). In that situation, the son asks his mother the meaning of *furin* and has no idea what the word means. It is difficult to say that he attempts to show a (non-)continuum of category A (that is, category FURIN) and a certain category corresponding to B. The utterance *furin wa furin nano* cannot be explained only in term of (non-)continuum categorization. It follows from this that his analysis based on (non-)continuum categorization is crucially wrong.

Furthermore, Nakamura does not provide an accurate definition of category B, but his paper seems to suggest that the components of a pair of category A and category B are antonymous: e.g. *man* and *woman*, *boy* and *girl*. One typical example is the case of the antonyms *kachi* 'victory' and *make* 'defeat' as shown in (4-6). This suggests that Nakamura excludes cases of ad hoc categories. That is, he puts forward his analysis, focusing on existing categories expressed with antonymous words. However, after closely observing the data that Nakamura (2000) includes, it seems to me that he unconsciously includes a case of ad hoc categories. This leads to an incoherent analysis. See the following example:

(4-7)   Even if there are times when I don't have the price of a cup of coffee, *I'm still me*.
(English translation of *Momo* by J.M. Brownjohn, cited by Nakamura 2000: 73)

In his analysis (ibid.: 74), the sentence is interpreted as follows: "I, who do not have the price of a cup of coffee, am still me". Then an interpretation of the tautological sentence requires ad hoc categories: for example, the category *I who do not have the price of a cup of coffee* and the category *I who have the price of a cup of coffee*. Following Nakamura's claim, the tautology *I'm still me* can be analyzed as follows: it shows the continuum categorization of the category *I who do not have the price of a cup of coffee* and the category *I who have the price of a cup of coffee* (Figure 4-2a), against the non-continuum categorization (Figure 4-2b) and denies the non-continuum categorization.

I who do not have the price of a cup of coffee	*I who do not have the price of a cup of coffee*
I who have the price of a cup of coffee	*I who have the price of a cup of coffee*
(a)	(b)

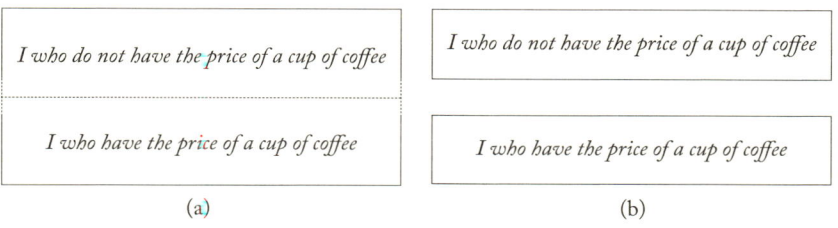

Figure 4-2. Categorization involved in the interpretation of (4-7)

This observation reveals that Nakamura's position is self-contradictory and that (if he allows his analysis to be expanded to ad hoc category cases,) there is a case where a nominal tautological utterance shows a continuum categorization of two categories, against a non-continuum categorization of the two categories, and denies the non-continuum categorization.

4.3   Tautology and Negation

So far, I have critically discussed Tsujimoto (1996) and Nakamura (2000). The discussion in the previous section shows their claims to be incorrect. Their claims are suggestive of the fact that it is generally accepted that the interpretation process of *A wa A da* (and *A is A*) can be analyzed from a viewpoint of negation. Of course, the use of *negation* in analyses depends on the researchers. In Tsujimoto's (1996) claim, *negation* appears in the formula *X is not A*. In Nakamura's (2000) claim, *negation* appears as negation of a continuum categorization of two categories.

Here, there is a slight confusion about the meaning of *negation*. According to van der Sandt (1991), *negation* is defined as follows:

(4-8)   [N]egation is a semantic notion. It is an operation on sentences, which assuming a bivalent logic simply reverses truth values. A negative sentence will thus always contain some sign of negation which contributes to the proposition expressed.   (van der Sandt 1991:331)

Following this definition, the nominal tautology *A wa A da* is not strictly regarded as negation since it does not contain such signs of negation as *nai* 'not'. In spite of this, why do we intuitively feel that *A wa A da* is negation? To answer the question, consider first the example cited in chapter 1:

(4-9)   [A couple is talking about their son Taro's academic record. Taro scored poorly on an exam again.]
Wife   : *Watashi mo   sonnani yoku   dekinakattashi   ne.   Taro*
          I   too very well   did not do   SFP   Taro
          bakkari semerarenai   wa.
          only   (I will) not put a blame SFP
          'I didn't do very well, either. I won't put all the blame on him.'
Husband : *Sonnakoto iuna   yo.*
          that   do not say   SFP

> *Oya wa oya da. Boku ga hanashitemiru yo.*
> parent TM parent COP I SM try to talk (to him) SFP
> 'Don't say anything like that. (lit.) <u>Parents are parents</u>. I try to talk to him.' (= (1-2))

In (4-9), where the wife implies that she blames herself for her son's poor score, the husband's utterance *Oya wa oya da* is interpreted as objecting to his wife's statement.

Consider another example:

(4-10) [A boy is asking his mother about an unfamiliar word *furin* 'adultery'.]
Son : *Nênê, furin tte nanno koto? Oshiete yo.*
well adultery HEAR what tell (me) SFP
'Well, what does "adultery" mean? Please tell me.'
Mother : *Sonnakoto shiranakutemoi no yo.*
it (you do) not need to know SFP SFP
'It's not something you need to know.'
Son : *Nê, oshiete yo.*
please tell (me) SFP
'Please tell me.'
Mother : *Dakara ne, furin wa furin nano. Sonnakoto kikanaidechôdai.*
so SFP adultery TM adultery SFP that
do not ask (me)
'So, (lit.) <u>adultery is adultery</u>. Don't ask me any questions about that.' (= (4-5))

This example, which was discussed above, is used to reject the son's request. It follows from these brief observations that the speakers who produce nominal tautological utterances intend to object to others and to reject offers from others.[7] These speakers' intentions lead us to conclude intuitively that *A wa A da*, which includes no explicit negative words such as *nai*, can be regarded as negation. This shows that the interpretation of *A wa A da* is associated with the notion of negation in a broad sense.

To be certain, here I confirm that negation is not associated with negative evaluations. Negation sometimes involves considering the bad sides of something or someone. However, when describing the phenomenon of nominal tautology, the word does not mean that the utterance *A wa A da* is always interpreted negatively. I show that *A wa A* can be interpreted as both a positive and a negative statement. One typical nominal tautology is given in (4-11):

(4-11) *Otokonoko wa Otokonoko da.*
boy TM boy COP
'Boys are boys.'[8]

This example is often thought of as an idiomatic expression and would therefore be assumed to have a fixed meaning. In fact, however, the expression has two possible interpretations, depending on the context: a positive interpretation and a negative interpretation. For instance, let us suppose the following two contexts. The first context is one where a couple is talking about their son's fight with his friend. The wife is worried about whether the son and his friend will be friends again and says, "They won't play together again". If in response to her comment, her husband replies with (4-11), it conveys that the boys are innocent. His statement can be easily understood as communicating a positive aspect of boys. The second context is one where a man has previously encountered a well-behaved boy in a public space and he then happens to see the boy running around in the same place. In this context, when he says (4-11) to himself, the utterance conveys that the boy is naughty. It can be naturally understood as communicating a negative aspect of boys. These observations reveal that what is communicated by *A wa A* is not limited to something negative.

This section proves that the interpretation of *A wa A da* is associated with negation in a broad sense and the content communicated by the utterance *A wa A da* is not limited to something negative. However, two points remain unclear: (i) why can *A wa A da*, which includes no explicit negative words, be accounted for in terms of negation?; and (ii) what does *A wa A da* mean? I will present a new proposal that answers these two questions by employing relevance theory. Before embarking on the discussion, I should outline the basis of the relevance theory that I adopt in this thesis.

4.4 Theoretical Background

4.4.1 Essence of Relevance Theory

Relevance theory is a cognitive pragmatic theory that was advocated by Sperber and Wilson (1986, 1995^2). The object of inquiry is ostensive-inferential communication, and the aim of the theory is to give a clear picture of the mechanism: how an addressee interprets what a communicator intends to convey. Within the relevance theoretic framework, relevance is a "property of the inputs to cognitive processes (whether perceptual or high-level conceptual); it is a positive function of cognitive effects and a negative function of the processing effort expended in deriving those effects" (Carston 2002: 44). As illustrated in the next part, there are three main kinds of cognitive effects (or contextual effects): the derivation of contextual implications, the strengthening of existing assumptions, and the contradiction and elimination of existing assumptions.

In the course of communication, a speaker intends to modify the hearer's cognitive environment. Human beings have a cognitive environment that consists of sets of manifest representations of the actual world. In more technical terms, the terms *manifest* and *cognitive environment* are defined as follows:

(4-12) A fact is *manifest* to an individual at a given time if and only if he is capable at that time of representing it mentally and accepting its representation as true or probably true.

(4-13) A *cognitive environment* of an individual is a set of facts that are manifest to him. (Sperber and Wilson 1995^2: 39)

Sperber and Wilson argue that there are three ways to modify a hearer's cognitive environment: derivation of contextual implications, strengthening existing assumptions, and contradicting and eliminating existing assumptions. Such modifications of the hearer's cognitive environment are called *cognitive effects*. I shall outline each of them in turn.

Derivation of Contextual Implications

The first way is to introduce contextual implications. Combinations of new and old information are interpreted as premises, and then consequents are added to the hearer's cognitive environment.

(4-14)a. If Bill came, the party was a success.
    b. Bill came.
    c. The party was a success.   (Higashimori and Yoshimura 2003: 16)

Suppose that a woman already has the assumption (4-14a) in mind and finds (4-14b). She will modify her cognitive environment by adding to it the consequent (4-14c) derived from the combination of old information (4-14a) and new information (4-14b). In this case, the assumption (4-14c) is called a *contextual implication*.

Strengthening Existing Assumptions

The second way involves strengthening existing assumptions. The strength of assumptions varies depending on context. In different cases, we may have more or less evidence for an existing assumption. New information may affect an existing assumption's strength.

(4-15)a. If Peter, Paul and Mary came to the party, it was a success.
    b. Peter came to the party.
    c. Paul came to the party.
    d. Mary came to the party.
(4-16)a. If the party broke up late, it was a success.
    b. The party broke up late.
(4-17)   The party was a success.   (ibid.: 16–17)

Suppose that a woman already has the assumption (4-15a) in mind and finds (4-15b)–(4-15d). She obtains the contextual implication (4-17). After that, the woman combines an existing assumption (4-16a) with new information (4-16b) and again obtains the contextual implication (4-17). The new information (4-16b) strengthens the confirmation of the existing assumption (4-17).

Contradicting and Eliminating Existing Assumptions

The third way involves contradicting and eliminating existing assumptions. When new and old information contradict each other, the old information is eliminated. This elimination involves a modification of the cognitive environment.

(4-18)a. Peter knows Russian.

b. Peter does not know Russian.
>
> (adapted from Higashimori and Yoshimura 2003: 17)

Suppose that a woman happens to see Peter carrying some Russian books. She would make the assumption (4-18a). After that, when he says, "I wish I knew Russian", at a party, she would make the assumption (4-18b). In this case, the new information (4-18b) contradicts and eliminates the old information (4-18a) and modifies her cognitive environment by eliminating the old one.

Using the above tenet as a basis, Sperber and Wilson (1995^2) propose two principles of relevance:

(4-19) Cognitive Principle of Relevance
Human cognition tends to be geared to the maximization of relevance.
(4-20) Communicative Principle of Relevance
Every act of ostensive communication communicates a presumption of its own optimal relevance. (Sperber and Wilson 1995^2: 260–270)

Here, one point I would like to emphasize is that these are not rules to be observed, but descriptions of an ostensive stimulus. A *presumption of optimal relevance* is defined as follows:

(4-21) Presumption of Optimal Relevance
a. The ostensive stimulus is relevant enough for it to be worth the addressee's effort to process it.
b. The ostensive stimulus is the most relevant one compatible with the communicator's abilities and preferences. (ibid.: 270)

The presumption of optimal relevance suggests a practical process for constructing hypotheses concerning the speaker's meaning. In brief, the addressee employs the following strategy:

(4-22) Relevance Theoretic Comprehension Strategy
a. Consider interpretations (disambiguations, reference assignments, enrichments, contextual assumptions, etc) in order of accessibility (i.e. follow a path of least effort in computing cognitive effects).
b. Stop when the expected level of relevance is reached.

(Carston 2002: 143)

Next, let us move on to four pragmatic processes involved in the derivation of explicatures.

4.4.2   Four Pragmatic Processes in Explicature Derivation

Relevance theory assumes that the assumptions communicated by a speaker are divided into two classes: *explicature* and *implicature*. They are defined as follows:

(4-23)   An assumption communicated by an utterance U is *explicit* [hence an 'explicature'] if and only if it is a development of a logical form encoded by U.
(4-24)   An assumption communicated by U which is not explicit is *implicit* [hence 'implicature'].
(Sperber and Wilson 1995^2: 182, cited by Carston 2002: 116)

This subsection will concentrate on explicature. Sperber and Wilson (1995^2) assumed that there are three sorts of pragmatic processes involved in explicature derivation, namely disambiguation, reference assignment and enrichment. Carston (2002, 2004a) has subsequently developed pragmatic processes and proposed that there are four processes involved in deriving explicatures, namely disambiguation, saturation, free enrichment and *ad hoc* concept construction. I review these four pragmatic processes below.

Disambiguation

When a linguistic expression used in an utterance has one or more meanings, one of the meanings must be pragmatically selected and determined in order to obtain an interpretation consistent with the principle of relevance. Let us consider the following situation. Suppose that a family has come to a riverside. The children talk about hiring a canoe and paddling down the river. The mother realizes that they have spent all their cash on lunch and says to her husband as in (4-25):

(4-25)   If the kids want to go on the river, I'll have to nip to the bank.
(Carston 2004a: 827)

In this example, there is a linguistic ambiguity to be solved. The lexical item *bank* has (at least) two meanings: (i) financial institution and (ii) the side of a river. In understanding the utterance, of the two meanings, the financial institution sense is selected and the meaning of *bank* is disambiguated, since accessible contextual assumptions include, for example, "they are standing on a river bank, so they do not need to nip to the riverbank".

Saturation

The word *saturation* is used among semanticists such as Recanati (1993). *Saturation* is a process of filling slots required by a linguistic expression used in an utterance. There are indexical expressions whose referents must be contextually filled in (4-26a) and (4-26b):

(4-26)a. She is lazy.
   b. That is green. (ibid.: 828)

Given an appropriate context, the referent of *she* in (4-26a) is contextually fixed. Similarly, the demonstrative *that* in (4-26b) requires a pragmatic inferential process to determine its value. These are given as examples of *reference assignment* in Sperber and Wilson's (1995^2) sense.

There are further examples, which are regarded as involving the pragmatic saturation of linguistically given slots.

(4-27)a. Paracetamol is better.   [than what?]
   b. It's the same.   [as what?]
   c. He is too young.   [for what?]
   d. It's hot enough.   [for what?]
   e. I like Sally's shoes.   [shoes in what relation to Sally?]
                                                    (ibid.: 830)

The above examples are semantically incomplete until answers for the bracketed questions are contextually supplied. Linguistics expressions, which require slots to be filled, are *better* (4-27a), *same* (4-27b), *too x* (4-27c), *x enough* (4-27d), and genitive markers (4-27e).

Free Enrichment

A process of *free enrichment* is one where further conceptual materials are added to the logical form without any linguistic mandate. Consider (4-28a)–(4-28e):

(4-28) a. It'll take time for your knee to heal.
   b. Ralph drinks.
   c. Emily has a temperature.
   d. He's a person with a brain.
   e. Something has happened. (ibid.)

Given the reference assignments in the above examples, each case is semantically complete (hence truth-evaluable), but it is trivially true. So it requires further pragmatic adjustments to recover the informative and relevant propositional forms. For instance, (4-28a) is a truism without further pragmatic adjustments, because we need time to recover from an injury. What the speaker intends to communicate as an explicature is that "it'll take quite a long time for your knee to heal". The utterance explicitly communicates that the recovery will take longer than expected. The constituent *quite a long* is added by a process of free pragmatic enrichment (i.e. without indication by any linguistic elements).

This sort of pragmatic process is widely applied to cases other than truisms. Consider (4-29a)–(4-29f):

(4-29) a. Jack and Jill went up the hill [together].
   b. Sue got a PhD and [then] became a lecturer.
   c. Mary left Paul and [as a result] he became clinically depressed.
   d. She took out her gun, went into the garden and killed her father [with the gun, in the garden].
   e. I'll give you £10 if [and only if] you mow the lawn.
   f. John has [exactly] four children. (ibid.: 830–831)

Without the bracketed elements, each case is semantically complete, but in the course of understanding the above utterances, the bracketed elements appear in the explicit content of those utterances to recover the proposition expressed by an utterance (i.e. explicature).

Ad hoc Concept Construction

In the process of deriving explicatures, it seems better to construe the concept communicated by an utterance as one replacing an encoded lexical concept appearing in a logical form. This process is called *ad hoc* concept construction. *Ad hoc* concepts are constructed pragmatically by a hearer via narrowing (or strengthening) or widening (or loosening) the encoded lexical concept. An asterisk * is used to distinguish lexicalized concepts (e.g. HAPPY) from ad hoc ones (e.g. HAPPY*), Consider (4-30):

(4-30) Kato (stating of O. J. Simpson, at his trial):
He was upset but he wasn't upset.
(= He was [upset*], but he wasn't [upset**].) (ibid.: 839)

This example seems to involve a contradiction, but we can understand what Kato wants to communicate. In the process of understanding the utterance, a hearer construes the encoded lexical concept UPSET as two different *ad hoc* concepts UPSET* and UPSET** via narrowing (or strengthening) the lexicalized concept. The second *upset* conveys certain implications, for instance, "he was in a murderous state of mind", but the first one does not convey the implication. What Kate explicitly communicates by the utterance in (4-30) is that O. J. Simpson had a property (that represented by UPSET*) at the time in question but lacked another (that represented by UPSET**).

The above example is a case of *ad hoc* concept constructions via narrowing (or strengthening). On the other hand, the following are examples involved in the process of widening (or loosening). Consider (4-31a)–(4-31e):

(4-31)a. Ugh, this custard is *raw*. [uttered by someone who has seen the custard being stirred over a flame]
b. You get *continuous* classics on Classic FM. [uttered by a radio announcer]
c. Jane is a *bulldozer*.
e. The *wilting violet* has finally left. [referring to a woman who has just left the room] (ibid.: 840)

For example, the word *raw* in (4-31a) communicates an *ad hoc* concept such as "much less cooked than the speaker wishes" by widening the lexicalized concept *raw*. The lexicalized concept *continuous* in (4-31b) is replaced by a widening concept such as "the classical music played on the radio station is interspersed with advertisements and the disk jockey's comments about the music, musicians, the recording and so on, but classics are played in all the music-playing slots". In these widening examples, the logical or defining property of the lexical concept is dropped. The property *uncooked* in the case of *raw* and the property *uninterrupted* in the case of *continuous* are dropped, and then loosening *ad hoc* concepts are regarded as constituents of the proposition expressed by an utterance.

Next, I move on to the distinction between conceptual and procedural encoding.

4.4.3 Conceptual Encoding and Procedural Encoding

In relevance theory, there are two types of information that can be encoded by linguistic elements: conceptual information and procedural information. The former is a constituent of conceptual representations, while the latter is a constraint on the way a conceptual representation is manipulated.

This dichotomy of linguistic semantics emerged from Blakemore's (1987) analysis of discourse connectives such as *so*, *after all*, and *but*. The essential function of procedural encodings is to constrain processes of pragmatic inference.[9] This idea is perhaps best conveyed through examples. Consider the utterance (4-32), which consists of two sequential clauses. For convenience, the first part is given as (a) and the second part is given as (b).

(4-32) a. Tom can open Ben's safe.
     b. He knows the combination.   (Blakemore 2002: 78)

The utterance (4-32) has two possible interpretations. The discourse connectives *so* in (4-33a) and *after all* in (4-33b) guide what computational path the hearer is expected to follow in order to arrive at the speaker's intended interpretation.

(4-33) a. Tom can open Ben's safe. *So* he knows the combination.
     b. Tom can open Ben's safe. *After all*, he knows the combination.
                                                                                                                     (ibid.: 79)

In (4-33a), (4-32a) provides evidence for (4-32b). Conversely, in (4-33b), (4-32b) provides evidence for (4-32a). These simple observations suggest that there are words and phrases that constrain inference procedures.

In what follows, let us observe the meaning encoded in *so* and *but*. See (4-34) and (4-35):

(4-34) There was $5 in his wallet. So I didn't spend all the money.
(4-35) Tom ate the condemned meat. So he fell ill. (Blakemore 1988: 184)

There seem to be various relationships between the two propositions connected with *so*. In (4-34), the proposition introduced by *so* (i.e. "I didn't spend all the money") is a conclusion derived from an inference in which the first proposition (i.e. "there was $5 in his wallet") is a premise. On the other hand, in (4-35), the proposition introduced by *so* (i.e. "he fell ill") is a causal consequence of the state of affairs described by the first proposition (i.e. "Tom ate the condemned meat").

Based on these observations, Blakemore (1988: 190) argues that "*so* constrains the relevance of the proposition it introduces by indicating that it must be interpreted as a contextual implication of some immediately accessible proposition". In (4-34), the proposition introduced by *so* "I didn't spend all the money" is a contextual implication derived from an inference in which "there was $5 in his wallet" (new information) and "if there is some money left in my wallet, I didn't spend all the money" (old information) are premises. In (4-35), the proposition introduced by *so* "he fell ill" is a contextual implication derived in an inference in which "Tom ate the condemned meat" (new information) and "if you eat condemned meat, you feel ill" (old information) are premises. The meaning encoded in *so* is the same in both cases.

Next, consider the encoded meaning of *but*. According to Blakemore (2000: 479), a hearer is "expected to access those contextual assumptions which allow him to interpret the second segment [the segment *but* introduces] as communicating a proposition that contradicts a proposition derived from the first segment [the preceding segment], and thus leads to its elimination". Consider (4-36):

(4-36) [X and Y are discussing the economic situation and decide that they should consult a specialist in economics.]
X : John is not an economist.
Y : But he is a businessman. (adapted from Blakemore 1987: 129)

In this example, the utterance (4-36X) communicates implicitly that "we should not consult him". The utterance (4-36Y) communicates implicitly that "we should consult him". The implication of Y's utterance contradicts that of X's utterance. The segment introduced by *but* (4-36Y) is interpreted as instructing the hearer to achieve relevance by contradicting and eliminating the preceding utterance's implicature "we should not consult him".

As discussed above, the concept of procedural encoding has played an important role in the analysis of what meaning words and phrases encode. Quite interestingly, Blakemore (2002: 9) deals with Prince's analysis of cleft sentences as shown in (4-37), and briefly mentions that "a particular linguistic form seems to encode information about the context in which the sentence that contains it should be used".[10]

(4-37)   It was Anna who found the money.   (Blakemore 2002: 9)

This suggests that Blakemore is aware of the possibility of applying a procedural analysis to expressional forms, or in other words, constructions. However, she has not provided detailed analyses. This subject still remains to be examined.

Here, I shall briefly overview Prince's analysis. Prince (1978) focuses on *wh*-cleft sentences such as (4-38a) and *it*-cleft sentences such as (4-38b), which have the same propositional content, and argues that they are not interchangeable since they are sensitive to different contextual information.

(4-38) a. What John lost was his keys.
       b. It was his keys that John lost.   (Prince 1978: 883)

According to Prince (1978: 883), in the *wh*-cleft case, "the presupposed part of a *wh*-cleft represents information that the speaker can assume the hearer is thinking about". In the *it*-cleft case, there are two types of information: the presupposed part represents (i) "information which the speaker assumes the hearer knows or can deduce, but is not presumably thinking about", and (ii) "information which the speaker takes to be a known fact, though definitely *not* known to the hearer".

First, consider the following *wh*-cleft example, which occurs discourse-initially:

(4-39)   What we have set as our goal is the grammatical capacity of children
         — a part of their linguistic competence.   (ibid.: 888)

This example is the outset of an article. Clearly, we have no information that is in fact given in the preceding linguistic context. However, we can construct an inferential bridge "from the situation or genre: the reader of a linguistics article *assumes* that its authors had a goal in writing the article" (ibid.: 888).

Furthermore, compare examples (4-40) and (4-40′), which are invented by Prince herself:

(4-40)a. *Hi! What my name is is Ellen.
    b. *Hi! What I've heard about is your work.
    c. *Hi! What you used to do was go to school with my brother.
(4-40′)a. Hi! My name is Ellen.
    b. Hi! I've heard about your work.
    c. Hi! You used to go to school with my brother.   (ibid.)

Suppose that each case occurs discourse-initially. *Wh*-cleft sentences in (4-40) are not acceptable but the corresponding 'non-clefted' sentences in (4-40′) are acceptable.[11] Following Prince's analysis, the different acceptability of (4-40) and (4-40′) is explained as follows. If the examples in (4-40) are accepted, the hearers have to infer the following information: the speaker has a name; the speaker has heard about something; and the speaker used to do something. However, such situations are odd or unnatural. On the other hand, the hearers in (4-40′) do not need to infer the above information. Based on these observations, Prince concludes that *wh*-cleft sentences constrain constructing an inferential bridge and the *wh*-clause of a *wh*-cleft sentence represents information that is assumed to be already present in the hearer's consciousness.

Next, I shall move on to a discussion of *it*-cleft sentences, which are divided into two types: the stressed-focus *it*-cleft sentence and the informative-presupposition *it*-cleft sentence. In the former case, the *that*-clause of an *it*-cleft sentence represents "known or old information, which is not assumed to be in the hearer's consciousness and which is not the theme" (ibid.: 898).[12] Consider the following example:

(4-41)   … So I learned to sew books. They're really good books. It's just the covers that are rotten.   (ibid.: 896)

In (4-41), from the fact that the speaker sews books, it is known that *something is rotten*. The theme of this discourse is not *what is rotten*, but *books*. Based on this observation, Prince concludes that the *that/wh*-clause of stressed-focus *it*-cleft sentences represents information that the speaker assumes the hearer knows or deduces, but is not presumably thinking about.

In the latter case, the informative-presupposition *it*-cleft sentence, a hearer is not expected to be thinking about the information in the *that*-clause. Nor is she expected to know it. Consider (4-42):

(4-42) It was just about 50 years ago that Henry Ford give us the weekend. On September 25, 1926, in a somewhat shocking move for that time, he decided to establish a 40-hour work week, giving his employees two days off instead of one.   (ibid.: 898)

This example is quoted from a newspaper. The *it*-cleft sentence is used to mark something as a fact known to the newspaper but unknown to the readers. It is concluded that the *that/wh*-clause of informative-presupposition *it*-cleft sentences represents information that is a known fact for the speaker and is an unknown fact for the hearer.

Prince has never used the concept of procedural encoding, but it seems to me that her claim can be restated using Blakemore's procedural encoding. The next section will move on to a discussion of the encoded meaning of *A wa A da*.

4.5   *A wa A da* Data

With the review of relevance theory in hand, let us pin down the encoded meaning of *A wa A da*. When we carefully observe some cases of *A wa A da*, it seems that two factors are related to their interpretation process. This section introduces concrete examples that show how *A wa A da* is used and understood, using the following notations: **Q** is a pre-existing assumption, and **R** is an assumption held by the speaker. First, Consider (4-43) and (4-44):

(4-43)   [The defense claims that a defendant Taro has extenuating circumstances based on the fact that he was asked to kill Jiro.]
    Defense   : *Saibanchô!   Taro   wa,   tanomarete   Jiro   wo   koroshitan*
                your honor   Taro   TM   be asked   Jiro   ACC   killed
                desu.   Dakara,   Taro   niwa   jôjôshakuryô

		COP		therefore	Taro	P	extenuating circumstances

      no yochi ga aru   to kangaemasu.
      of room SM there are HEAR insist
      'Your honor! Taro was asked to kill Jiro. Therefore, I insist
      that there are extenuating circumstances for his crime.'
   Prosecutor : *Nani wo itteirun   desu ka.* **Satsujin wa**
      what ACC (you) are saying COP Q murder TM
      satsujin desu.
      murder COP
      'What are you saying? Murder is murder.'   (= (4-3))

(4-44) [A couple is talking about their son Taro's academic record. Taro scored poorly on an exam again.]
   Wife : *Watashi mo sonnani yoku dekinakattashi ne. Taro*
      I too very well did not do SFP Taro
     bakkari semerarenai   wa.
     only (I will) not put a blame SFP
     'I didn't do very well, either. I won't put all the blame on him.'
   Husband : *Sonnakoto iuna   yo.*
      that do not say SFP
     Oya wa oya da. *Boku ga hanashitemiru   yo.*
     parent TM parent COP I SM try to talk (to him) SFP
     'Don't say anything like that. (lit.) <u>Parents are parents</u>. I try
     to talk to him.'   (= (4-9))

In (4-43), suppose that in court the defense and the prosecutor present arguments about the murder committed by Taro. In this situation, the defense thinks that **Q** [the murder that Taro committed should be considered to have extenuating circumstances]. On the other hand, by uttering *Satsujin wa satsujin desu*, the prosecutor communicates that **R** [the murder that Taro committed should not be considered to have extenuating circumstances]. In (4-44), suppose that a woman and her husband are talking about their son Taro's poor score. In this situation, the wife thinks that **Q** [she blames herself for Taro's poor score]. On the other hand, by uttering *Oya wa oya da*, the husband communicates that **R** [she is not blamed for Taro's poor score]. In (4-43) and (4-44), **Q** and **R** contradict each other, and the contradiction is resolved by eliminating **Q**. **Q** is communicated by the previous speaker's (i.e. the hearer's) utterance.

A tautological utterance does not always have a preceding utterance. Consider (4-45) and (4-46):

(4-45) [Haruko's friends keep on quitting the theater company. The fact initially made her consider giving up a professional acting career, but she finally decided to continue her study of acting.]
Haruko : (to herself) *Watashi   wa   watashi.   Tanin   wa*
　　　　　　　　　　　 I 　　　　TM 　I 　　　　other people　TM
kankeinai.
(I do) not care
'I am I. I don't care what other people think.' 　　(= (4-4))

(4-46) [A woman named Haruko is looking at a cutting board. It has become unserviceable soon after purchase.]
Haruko : (to herself) *398 en   wa   398 en   da   na.*
　　　　　　　　　　　398 yen　TM　398 yen　COP　SFP
'(lit.) 398 yen is 398 yen.'

In (4-45), suppose that a woman named Haruko is talking to herself. Her friends quit the acting company one after another. The fact initially made her consider abandoning a professional acting career, but she finally decided not to give up her acting studies. In this situation, the speaker previously thought that **Q** [she should give up her study of acting]. On the other hand, she currently thinks that **R** [she should not give up her study of acting]. In (4-46), suppose that the speaker bought a cutting board for 398 yen but now regrets it since the cutting board became unserviceable soon after purchase. In this situation, the speaker previously thought that **Q** [the cutting board was the best deal]. On the other hand, she currently thinks that **R** [the cutting board is not the best deal]. The above two examples have no preceding utterances but they sound quite natural. The contradiction between **Q** and **R** is resolved by eliminating **Q**. Here, **Q** is an assumption held by the speaker herself in the past.

Furthermore, consider another example:

(4-47) [A boy is asking his mother about an unfamiliar word *furin* 'adultery'.]
Son 　: *Nênê,   furin   tte   nanno koto?   Oshiete   yo.*
　　　　 well 　adultery　HEAR　what 　　　tell (me) 　SFP
'Well, what does "adultery" mean? Please tell me.'

Mother : *Sonnakoto   shiranakutemoî   no   yo.*
           it   (you do) not need to know SFP   SFP
           'It's not something you need to know.'
Son   : *Nê,   oshiete   yo.*
          please tell (me) SFP
          'Please tell me.'
Mother : *Dakara ne, **furin** **wa** **furin**   nano. Sonnakoto*
           so   SFP adultery TM   adultery   SFP   that
           kikanaidechôdai.
           do not ask (me)
           'So, (lit.) <u>adultery is adultery</u>. Don't ask me any questions about that.'   (= (4-10))

In (4-47), a boy is asking his mother about the unfamiliar word *furin* 'adultery'. In this situation, the son thinks that **Q** [he wants her to tell him the meaning of *furin*]. On the other hand, by *furin wa furin nano*, the mother communicates that **R** [she does not want to tell him the meaning of *furin*]. In this example, the contradiction between **Q** and **R** is resolved by eliminating **Q**. **Q** is communicated by the preceding utterance.

This section introduced apparently different cases of *A wa A da* and observed how they are used in a given context. The next section will attempt to provide the various examples dealt with in this section with a unified characterization from a relevance theoretic perspective.

4.6   Stipulating the Meaning of *A wa A da*

From the above observation, we first found that in (4-43)–(4-47), the contradiction between **Q** and **R** is resolved by eliminating **Q**. Moreover, it turned out that when stipulating the meaning of the expressional form, we need to take three points into account: **Q** (which is informally defined as a "pre-existing assumption"), **R** (which is informally defined as an "assumption held by the speaker"), and their relationship.

4.6.1   The Need for a Contrastive Assumption

First, I shall begin by looking at the third point: the relation between **Q** and **R**. Based on the observation described in the previous section, it can be said that in a context where *A wa A da* is uttered, it must be processed in such a way as to communicate **R** that contradicts and eliminates **Q**. For example, the husband's utterance *Oya wa oya da* in (4-44) is analyzed as follows: it must be processed in such a way as to communicate **R** "she is not blamed for Taro's poor score" that contradicts and eliminates **Q** "she blames herself for Taro's poor score". The same analysis holds true for the other examples. In a context where the expressional form *A wa A da* is uttered, a hearer is expected to interpret *A wa A da* in such a way as to raise a contradiction and abandon a pre-existing assumption. This shows that *A wa A da* must be processed in a context containing information that contradicts pre-existing assumptions, or in other words, in a context with a contrastive assumption. Then, what is a context with a contrastive assumption? To make this clear, the next subsection will introduce the notion of the *Cognitive Structure of Negation* (CSN). CSN helps us explain why *A wa A da*, which includes no explicit negative words, can be analyzed in terms of negation.

4.6.2 The Cognitive Structure of Negation

The explicit negative word *nai* 'not' does not appear in the expressional form *A wa A da*. However, the contrastive assumption required by *A wa A da* is parallel to that required by explicit negative sentences. Why does the contrastive assumption arise? To provide a theoretic explanation for this, I will first review the notion of the *Cognitive Structure of Negation* proposed by Yoshimura (1992, 1994, 1999). This notion synthesizes a series of studies by Givón (1978), Sperber and Wilson (1986, 1995[2]) and Blakemore (1987). It can explain the contrastive assumption required by both explicit and implicit negative sentences.[13]

First, let us look at Givón's (1978) claim. He discusses contexts where negative sentences are uttered. Consider (4-48):

(4-48) X (Woman) : What's happening?
        Y (Man)   : a. Oh, my wife's pregnant.
                    b. Oh, my wife's not pregnant.   (= (3-8))

Suppose that when X runs into Y, who is married, she asks him "What's happening?". If his answer is (4-48a), it would feel pragmatically natural to her. However, if his answer is (4-48b), it would feel pragmatically strange. The reason for this arises from the assumption that she must have previously had additional information such as "his wife is pregnant". On this basis, Givón (1978: 109) concludes as follows:

(4-49) [N]egatives are uttered in a context where corresponding affirmatives have already been discussed, or else where the speaker assumes the hearer's belief in – and thus familiarity with – the corresponding affirmative.

If we employ the terms *figure* and *ground*, following Givón's claim, the pre-existing affirmative assumption constitutes a *ground*, and the corresponding negative assumption constitutes a *figure*. Yoshimura (1992: 258) sets Givón's *figure* and *ground* within relevance theory, and proposes that "[t]he figure and ground discussed by Givón would then be a cognitive structure where the cognitive environment contains a logical form that leads to a contradiction when combined with that of a new assumption in the central system". The cognitive structure called the *Cognitive Structure of Negation* (CSN) is defined as follows:

(4-50) The Cognitive Structure of Negation (CSN)
$(\phi, \{\ldots, \psi, \ldots\})$ where ϕ and ψ lead to a contradiction.
(Yoshimura 1994: 603)

Formally, ϕ is the proposition most recently input into the central system, and ψ is the contrastive assumption in the context.

Furthermore, Yoshimura argues that Blakemore's analysis of *but* can be restated in terms of CSN. Recall Blakemore's example (4-36), which Yoshimura elaborates as follows:

(4-51) [X and Y are discussing the economic situation and decide that they should consult a specialist in economics.]
X : John is not an economist. (premise)
 If John isn't an economist, then we shouldn't
 consult him (John). (premise)
 We shouldn't consult John. (contextual implication)
Y : But he is a businessman. (premise)
 If John is a businessman, then we should
 consult him (John). (premise)
 We should consult John. (contextual implication)
(adapted from Yoshimura 1992: 259)

In this situation, the contextual implication drawn from X's utterance is that "we shouldn't consult John", while the one drawn from Y's utterance is that "we should consult John". The utterance which *but* introduces (that is, "he is a businessman") leads to a contradiction. It modifies the hearer X's cognitive environment. It follows from this that "restating Blakemore's generalization in our own terms, *but* is acceptable only if the proposition it introduces is processed in CSN" (Yoshimura 1992: 259).[14] In other words, the CSN approach converges with the analyses of negation and *but* and we may interpret the presence of *but* as an indicator of CSN.

Here, let us analyze the expressional form *A wa A da* by employing the notion of CSN. Recall the court example (4-43). In the CSN approach, the pre-existing affirmative assumption (**Q**) "the murder that Taro committed should be considered to have extenuating circumstances" constitutes a *ground*. The corresponding negative assumption (**R**) "the murder that Taro committed should not be considered to have extenuating circumstances" constitutes a *figure*. In the context described above, the two assumptions are contrastive. The CSN is established in the same way as explicit negative sentences. This observation provides a theoretical background for the following question: why can *A wa A da*, which includes no explicit negative words, be explained with the notion of negation?

4.6.3 The Definition of Q and R

So far, I have informally used the following notations: **Q** is a pre-existing assumption, and **R** is an assumption held by the speaker. Here, I shall precisely define **Q** and **R** involved in the interpretation process of *A wa A da*. First, I would like to define **Q**. There are clearly different types. For instance, **Q** in the court example (4-43) "the murder that Taro committed should be considered to have extenuating circumstances" is based on the previous speaker's (i.e. the defense's) utterance. Similarly, in the example of Taro's score (4-44) and the unfamiliar word example (4-47), **Q** ("she blames herself for Taro's poor score" and "he wants her to tell him the meaning of *furin*", respectively) is based on the previous speaker's utterance (i.e. the wife's utterance and the son's utterance, respectively). On the other hand, **Q** in the actress example (4-45) "she should give up her study of acting" is based on the previous thought of the speaker herself. The types of **Q** differ depending on the context. However, they can all be generalized as an "assumption about the referent of the subject *A*, attributed to someone other than the speaker at the point of utterance". For example, in the court example (4-43),

Q "the murder that Taro committed should be considered to have extenuating circumstances" is an assumption about the referent of the subject *satsujin* 'murder' (i.e. the murder that Taro committed), attributed to the defense. In the actress example (4-45), **Q** "she should give up her study of acting" is an assumption about the referent of the subject *watashi* 'I' (i.e. Haruko herself), attributed to the speaker herself in the past.

Next, **R** is defined as an "assumption communicated by the utterance *A wa A da*". For instance, **R** in the court example (4-43) is that "the murder that Taro committed should not be considered to have extenuating circumstances", which is an assumption communicated by the utterance *Satsujin wa satsujin desu*. The same characteristic is applicable to the other examples (4-44)–(4-47).

On the basis of the above observations, I propose (4-52) as the meaning of *A wa A da*:

(4-52) The Meaning of *A wa A da* :
A wa A da must be processed in such a way as to communicate an assumption (**R**) that contradicts and eliminates another assumption (**Q**) about the referent of the subject *A*, attributed to someone other than the speaker at the point of utterance.

My hypothesis about the meaning of *A wa A da* in (4-52) above can explain the difference in acceptability as shown in (4-44) (repeated below as (4-53)) and (4-53'):

(4-53) [A couple is talking about their son Taro's academic record. Taro scored poorly on an exam again.]
Wife : *Watashi mo sonnani yoku dekinakattashi ne. Taro*
I too very well did not do SFP Taro
bakkari semerarenai wa.
only (I will) not put a blame SFP
'I didn't do very well, either. I won't put all the blame on him.'
Husband : *Sonnakoto iuna yo.*
that do not say SFP
Oya wa oya da. Boku ga hanashitemiru yo.
parent TM parent COP I SM try to talk (to him) SFP
'Don't say anything like that. (lit.) Parents are parents. I try

to talk to him.' (= (4-44))

(4-53')a. Wife : *Taro nê, mata akaten totta no yo. Rainen*
Taro P   again failed a test SFP SFP next year
jukensei ni narutteiukoto
(he will be) sitting for entrance exams
wakatteiru no kashira.
(I am) wondering if (he) understands
Watashi, itsumo "Benkyôshinasai" tte itteru no yo.
I   always study hard   HEAR say SFP SFP
'Taro failed another test. I'm wondering if he understands he will be sitting for entrance exams. I'm always saying, "Study hard!"'

b. Husband : # *Sonnakoto iuna yo.*
that   do not say SFP
Oya wa oya da. Boku ga hanashitemiru yo.
parent TM parent COP I SM try to talk (to him) SFP
'# Don't say anything like that. (lit.) <u>Parents are parents</u>. I try to talk to him.'

(4-53b) is acceptable because the utterance *Oya wa oya da* is processed in such a way as to communicate an assumption (**R**) that contradicts and eliminates another assumption (**Q**) about the referent of the subject *A*, attributed to someone other than the speaker at the point of utterance, as shown above.

In contrast, (4-53'b), whose discourse context is slightly different from (4-53), becomes unacceptable since the utterance is a signal that it must be processed in the way described above but it is difficult to imagine any obvious contradictory assumption that could be residing in the cognitive environment. That is, the hearer is expected to recognize that the contradiction should be resolved by abandoning a certain pre-existing assumption, but she does not recognize it in the context (4-53') where the husband and wife think that Taro should study hard. That is exactly why the husband's utterance (4-53'b) is infelicitous. This strongly supports the stipulation of *A wa A da* in (4-52).

Here, someone might have a simple question. The discussion in 4.6.2 states that *A wa A da* is processed in CSN in the same way as negative sentences and a contrastive conjunction *but*, and that the presence of *but* is understood as an indicator of CSN, namely if an utterance is introduced by *but*, it is regarded as being processed in CSN. However, there is a case where an utterance *A wa A da*, which cannot be introduced by a contrastive conjunction *dakedo* 'but', is regarded as felicitous as shown in (4-54):

(4-54) [A boy is asking his mother about an unfamiliar word *furin* 'adultery'.]
Son : *Nêne, furin tte nanno koto? Oshiete yo.*
well adultery HEAR what tell (me) SFP
'Well, what does "adultery" mean? Please tell me.'
Mother : *Sonnakoto shiranakutemoi no yo.*
it (you do) not need to know SFP SFP
'It's not something you need to know.'
Son : *Nê, oshiete yo.*
please tell (me) SFP
'Please tell me.'
Mother : {a. *Dakara* /b.# *Dakedo*} *ne, furin wa furin nano.*
so but SFP adultery TM adultery SFP
Sonnakoto kikanaidechôdai.
that do not ask (me)
'{So / # But} (lit.) <u>adultery is adultery</u>. Don't ask me any questions about that.'

The mother's utterance *furin wa furin nano* is understood as a rejection of the son's request. However, in this context, the tautological utterance cannot be introduced by *dakedo* 'but' while there is no problem in it being introduced by *dakara* 'so'. This shows that CSN is not built in a 'simple' cognitive environment, namely representations of the actual world.

Where then does the contrastive assumption necessary for producing an utterance *A wa A da* come from? The answer to this is that the contrastive assumption arises in a structured cognitive environment, namely in representations of the desires of others. Sperber and Wilson (1995[2]: 2) define *assumptions* as "thoughts treated by the individual as representations of the actual worlds (as opposed to fictions, desires, or representations of representations)", and treat a cognitive environment as a simple set. In contrast to their claim, Yoshimura (1994, 1999) proposes that the cognitive environment is a structured database with sub-databases representing such things as possible worlds and the beliefs of others. If we adopt the structured cognitive environment approach, we can succeed in explaining the difference in acceptability as shown in (4-54a) and (4-54b), without need for further stipulation.

In the context in which *furin wa furin nano* is uttered, the son does not have any assumptions about the word *furin* in the actual world since he does not know anything about it. If we only consider actual world assumptions, it is problematic to assume that CSN arises. This is because there is no contrast relation in the actual world. However, as seen in 4.5, in a context such as (4-54), the son wants the mother to tell him the meaning of the word, while she does not want to tell him the meaning. That is, in a context like (4-54a), a contrastive assumption is built not in the representations of the actual world (i.e. a 'simple' cognitive environment), but in the beliefs of others (i.e. a structured cognitive environment; more strictly speaking, a sub-structured database representing the beliefs of others). Based on these observations, the use of *A wa A da* requires a contradiction leading to the abandonment of existing assumptions.

4.7 Validating the Hypothesis that *A wa A da* Has a Specific Meaning

Thus far, I have argued that *A wa A da* itself encodes a meaning as shown in (4-52). This means that the meaning of *A wa A da* is not revealed by integrating the meanings of the lexical items in the sentence, and that the meaning encoded by *A wa A da* is procedural rather than conceptual. If this is on the right track, other approaches should drop out of the picture. In this section, I will (i) hypothesize that the expressional form *A wa A da* has a certain meaning, (ii) conceive some counterarguments for the hypothesis, and (iii) reveal that the meaning of *A wa A da* cannot be explained in terms of the principle of compositionality.

Some may reject my hypothesis and argue that the meaning of *A wa A da* can be predicted from its constituent parts. The sentence *A wa A da* contains four components: the subject *A*, the particle *wa*, the predicate *A*, and the copular predication *da*. Rejections of the hypothesis fall broadly into three categories: counterarguments based on the uses of the particle *wa*, counterarguments based on formal similarities between *A wa A da* and *A wa B da*, and counterarguments from relevance theoretic perspectives.[15] As stated below, I shall tackle these counterarguments one by one and refute them.

Counterarguments Based on the Uses of the Particle Wa

The first type of counterargument is related to the uses of the particle *wa*. In Japanese linguistics, this particle is a rather controversial subject, as is the particle *ga*, which will be dealt with in the next chapter.[16] There have been many previous studies from different viewpoints. It seems to be generally argued that *wa* is used as a contrastive marker. Consider the following example:

(4-55)   *Taro   wa   gakusei   da.*
       Taro   TM   student   COP
       'Taro is a student.'

According to the general approach, this sentence is analyzed as implying that Taro is a student, but Haruko, for example, is not a student. This analysis might cover the interpretation of the noun preceding *wa*, but it does not describe how to comprehend the predicate. As we have observed in 4.5, the expressional form *A wa A da* has various interpretations. So, even if we focus attention on the uses or functions of the particle *wa*, we cannot find any clues as to the interpretation of *A wa A da*.

Counterarguments Based on Formal Similarities between A wa A da and A wa B da

Next, two possible counterarguments come to mind based on formal similarities between *A wa A da* and *A wa B da*. Someone might argue that *A wa A da* could be used to express identity relations or class inclusion relations since it has a similar form *A wa B da*. Quite clearly, the first possibility is nonsense. If *A wa A da* is interpreted as an identity assertion, it can be meaningless, since the first *A* and second *A* have the same referent.

How about the second possibility? When *A wa A da* is interpreted as a class inclusion, it is meaningful, since the first *A* and the second *A* have different referents. Then, is it appropriate that the class inclusion analysis is regarded as a comprehensive theory of the interpretation of the *A wa A da* utterance? If we follow this analysis, *Otokonoko wa otokonoko da* 'Boys are boys' would be analyzed as communicating that the boy named Taro is included in the class of people who behave like a stereotypical boy, since the first *otokonoko* 'boy' refers to tokens of a type (e.g. a boy named Taro) and the second *otokonoko* 'boy' refers to a type (e.g. the class of people who behave like a stereotypical boy). However, such an approach cannot explain all the examples of *A wa A da*. For example, without mentioning the unfamiliar word example (4-47), the mother's utterance *furin wa furin nano* is not entirely linked to a class inclusion interpretation since it is used to express rejection. Thus, the class inclusion analysis cannot provide a unified account for all of the examples and thus is unacceptable.

As discussed above, the expressional form *A wa A da* is not understood in the same way as the similar expressional form *A wa B da*. It is natural to attribute the contradiction-elimination meaning directly to the expressional from *A wa A da* itself. The conclusion can be regarded as supporting the validation of the hypothesis that the expressional form *A wa A da* encodes a certain meaning.

Counterarguments from Relevance Theoretic Perspectives

In the foregoing discussion, I presented a refutation of counterarguments based on the analogy between *A wa A da* and *A wa B da*. Furthermore, in terms of relevance theory, there are two further possible counterarguments for the hypothesis that *A wa A da* has a certain meaning and imposes the derivation of implicatures. If I am right, the assumption (**R**) communicated by *A wa A da* cannot be derived through the pragmatic processes involved in explicature derivation such as free enrichment and *ad hoc* concept construction.

First, I discuss the possibility of interpretation via free enrichment. For example, to support this possibility, reference may be made to scalar implicature cases such as cardinal number terms.[17] Cardinal number terms are cases of free enrichment that are considered a pragmatic contribution to the explicit content of the utterance. The critics apply this point to the numerical concept example (3-28) cited in 3.5.2.1 (*san wa san da* 'three is three'), and mention that the example would be understood as communicating that "three is exactly three". However, free enrichment analysis cannot explain other examples. For instance, in the case of refusing to answer the son's question such as (4-47), no matter how hard we try to interpret the tautological utterance *furin wa furin nano* via the process of free enrichment, we cannot. Its interpretation cannot be obtained by adding further conceptual materials to the logical form without a linguistic mandate. An analysis based on free enrichment is not regarded as a comprehensive theory of the *A wa A da* interpretation process.

Next, let us move on to the possibility of interpretation via *ad hoc* concept construction. *Ad hoc* concept construction is the process of replacing an encoded lexical concept appearing in a logical form with a contextually adjusted one. As discussed in 3.6, Nishikawa (2003) proposes an analysis of interpretation via *ad hoc* concept construction but her claim cannot explain all the examples with *A wa A da*. According to her analysis, with (4-43) *Satsujin wa satsujin desu*, suppose the context is one in which the speaker directly refutes the defense's allegation, then the relevant concept, SATSUJIN* 'MURDER*' might be broader than the encoded concept (e.g. the crime of deliberately killing someone). In the process of arriving at the intended interpretation, a defining feature of the lexically encoded concept such as *deliberately* is dropped. An *ad hoc* concept would be, for example, "the crime of killing someone (without regard to whether the crime is committed deliberately or at someone's request)".

If this analysis is right, it could explain other examples. However, in fact, it cannot. Following Nishikawa's analysis, for instance, the mother's utterance *furin wa furin nano* in (4-47) might be interpreted as communicating that furin wa FURIN* da 'adultery is ADULTERY*'. The *ad hoc* concept FURIN* 'ADULTERY*' would indicate a narrowing or widening of the lexically encoded concept. However, in the context in which *furin wa furin nano* is uttered, the speaker does not intend to communicate the interpretation via *ad hoc* concept construction. Rather she intends to communicate the assumption (**R**) that she does not want to tell him the meaning of the word *furin*. The assumption communicated by the utterance is regarded not as an explicature but as an implicature.

As mentioned above, Nishikawa's claim cannot explain these two examples from a unified viewpoint. However, the account presented in (4-52) can explain them in the same way. In the former case, the utterance *Satsujin wa satsujin desu* encourages the hearer to interpret it in such a way as to communicate (**R**) "the murder that Taro committed should not be considered to have extenuating circumstances" that contradicts and eliminates (**Q**) "the murder that Taro committed should be considered to have extenuating circumstances". In the latter case, the utterance *furin wa furin nano* instructs the hearer to process it in such a way as to communicate (**R**) "she does not want to tell him the meaning of *furin*" that contradicts and eliminates (**Q**) "he wants her to tell him the meaning of *furin*". Therefore, the analysis of the interpretation via *ad hoc* concept construction is not satisfactory.

It follows from the above observations that several possible counterarguments cannot provide a unified characterization of all the cases of *A wa A da*, and thus it is not reasonable that *A wa A da* is interpreted by combining lexical items in the sentence. This can be regarded as strong support for my hypothesis that *A wa A da* is an expressional form with the encoded procedural information involved in implicature derivation.

4.8 Summary

This chapter discussed the encoded meaning of *A wa A da*. Past studies have argued that *A wa A da* (and *A is A*) can be explained in terms of negation. However, they present problematic points and are rejected. In the course of observing the data in detail, I introduced the notion of the *Cognitive Structure of Negation* (CSN) proposed by Yoshimura (1992, 1994, 1999) and provided a theoretical background for the question: why can *A wa A da*, which includes no explicit negative words, be explained with the notion of negation? Also, I stipulated the meaning of *A wa A da* as follows: *A wa A da* must be processed in such a way as to communicate an assumption (**R**) that contradicts and eliminates another assumption (**Q**) about the referent of the subject *A*, attributed to someone other than the speaker at the point of utterance. An analysis of the combination of lexical items in the sentence cannot systematically predict the meanings of the constituent parts of the sentence.

In the next chapter, I will discuss the meaning encoded in *A ga A da*.

Notes

1. This chapter focuses on *A wa A da*, which is not embedded in other sentences. *A* in *A wa A da* represents a noun or a noun phrase. The copular predication *da* in *A wa A da* can sometimes be omitted, as exemplified in (4-4) *Watashi wa watashi*.
2. According to Tsujimoto (1996), in the formulas *X is A* and *X is not A*, *X* represents a thing or a situation that is under discussion at the point of utterance, and *A* represents a noun in the nominal tautological sentence *A is A*.
3. *desu* (polite form of *da*) and *da* are treated equally.
4. When *A wa A da* is translated literally, the translation *A is A* rarely makes sense. However, it seems that *Murder is murder*, which is an English version of *Satsujin wa satsujin desu*, is meaningful in a context such as (4-3). This also holds true for *Watashi wa watashi* in a context such as (4-4).
5. According to Tsujimoto's analysis, it follows that the defense believes that what Taro did was not murder. However, it is an overstatement to say that the defense presents such a strong view of what Taro did, since in this context the defense and the prosecutor are arguing about whether there are extenuating circumstances for Taro's crime, not about whether what Taro did is murder.
6. Nakamura (2000) observes cases of the Japanese nominal tautology *A wa A da* and the

English nominal tautology *A is A*, but he generalizes his observations with the formula *A wa A dearu*. The copular predication *dearu* in *A wa A dearu* is a variation of *da*. *A wa A dearu* is literally translated into English as *A is A*.

7 The function of objection is associated with denial. The term *denial* is defined as follows:

  (i) Denial is a concept of speech act theory. Its essential function is to object to a previous utterance. And the utterance objected to may have been made by means of a positive or negative sentence. So, depending on the polarity of the utterance objected to, a denial may be negative or a positive statement. (van der Sandt 1991: 331)

8 As with (4-3), the English version of *Otokonoko wa otokonoko da*, *Boys are boys* is meaningful. A native English speaker has said that *Boys will be boys* is more commonly used than *Boys are boys*, as the English version of *Otokonoko wa otokonoko da*.
9 Blakemore (1987) found that conceptual encoding contributes to the derivation of explicatures, while procedural encoding constrains the derivation of implicatures. Developing this idea, Wilson and Sperber (1993) argue that procedural encoding also contributes to the derivation of explicatures.
10 Blakemore does not agree with Prince's claim regarding the relation between the competence/performance and semantics/pragmatics distinctions. For some discussion, see Blakemore (2002).
11 Following Prince (1987), the term *non-clefted* is used as the opposition of *cleft*.
12 In Prince's terms, *known information* is that "information which the speaker represents as being factual and as already known to certain persons (often not including the hearer)" (Prince 1987: 903).
13 Yoshimura (1992, 1994, 1999) employs the notion of the *Cognitive Structure of Negation* to clarify the NPI-licensing condition.
14 Yoshimura (1999: 193) points out that "a context where *but* occurs is a subset of a context in which CSN arises. If CSN arises, *but* is not always acceptable. However, if *but* is acceptable, CSN always arises".
15 *A* and *B* in *A wa B da* represent a noun or a noun phrase.
16 The distinction between the Japanese particles *wa* and *ga* has been discussed from different points of view: topic–comment, old–new, theme–rheme, and so on. As Tanaka (1988: 3) points out, "[s]ome linguists regard these distinctions as grammatical, others as pragmatic; some argue that more than one such distinctions will be needed, while some see a need for only one". There is as yet no consensus about the specific details.
17 Scalar implicature cases remain controversial, but of the cases, cardinal number expressions appear to be nearing a resolution. In what follows, I provide a brief explanation of the relevance theoretic account of cardinal number expressions. Consider (i) and (ii):

  (i) X : Can you help me out?
      Y : I have 10p.
  (ii) X : Do you have 20p?
      Y : I have 10p. (adapted from Carston 1995: 228)

According to Carston (1995: 228), "a cardinal 'n' may be understood in at least the following three ways: 'exactly n', 'at most n', and 'at least n', and which of these is taken to have been communicated depends on context". In (i), suppose that X is trying to make a local call from a phone booth and X and Y both know that local calls cost 10p. (iX) asks whether Y has 10p or not. As a response to the question, (iY) is likely understood as communicating "I have at least 10p".

In (ii), (iiX)'s concern is about "whether Y has 20p", not about "whether Y has 10p". As a response to the question, (iiY) would be understood as communicating "I have at most (or only) 10p". It follows from these observations that scalar implicatures such as cardinal numbers are cases of free enrichment that should be considered a pragmatic contribution to the explicit content of the utterance.

Chapter 5

A ga A da

The expressional form *A ga A da* tends to be treated as an idiom. A few researchers have studied this expressional form, but their analyses are not clear-cut. Based on a detailed survey, this chapter stipulates the encoded meaning of *A ga A da* as follows: *A ga A da* must be processed in such a way as to evoke an assumption about the referent of the subject *A* that provides an explanation for the state of affairs that is under discussion at the point of utterance.

5.1 Introduction

The previous chapter discussed the Japanese nominal tautology *A wa A da*. This expressional form is similar to the expressional form *A ga A da* discussed in this chapter. Compare the husband's tautological utterance (5-1b) with (5-2c):

(5-1) [A couple is talking about their son Taro's academic record. Taro scored poorly on an exam again.]
  a. Wife : *Watashi mo sonnani yoku dekinakattashi ne. Taro bakkari*
      I too very well did not do SFP Taro only
      semerarenai wa.
      (I will) not put a blame SFP
      'I didn't do very well, either. I won't put all the blame on him.'
  b. Husband : *Sonnakoto iuna yo.*
      that do not say SFP
      ***Oya** wa **oya** da. Boku ga hanashitemiru yo.*
      parent TM parent COP I SM try to talk (to him) SFP

'Don't say anything like that. (lit.) <u>Parents are parents</u>. I try to talk to him.' (= (4-44))

(5-2) [A couple is talking about their son Taro's academic record. Taro scored poorly on an exam again.]

    a. Husband : *Omae,   seiseki   dôdatta?*
                  you   how were (your) grades?
                'How were your grades?'

    b. Wife : *Un, mâ mâ. Dakara ne, Taro no seiseki ga*
               well so-so so SFP Taro of grade SM
               yokunainomo   murimonai   wa. Tokorode,
               not very smart understandable SFP by the way
               anata wa dôdatta?
               how were (your grades)?
               'Well, they were so-so. So it is understandable that Taro is not very smart. By the way, how were your grades?'

    c. Husband : *Mâ mâ.* **Oya   ga   oya   da.**
                  so-so parent SM parent COP
                  Dôshiyômonai   yo   na.
                  there is nothing that can be done (about his grades) SFP SFP
                  'So-so. (lit.) <u>The parents are the parents</u>. There's nothing that can be done about his grades.' (= (1-3))

In the context of (5-1), the wife implies that she blames herself for Taro's score. The husband's utterance *Oya wa oya da* is interpreted as objecting to his wife. On the other hand, in the context of (5-2), the wife implies that it is understandable that Taro is not very smart. The husband's utterance *Oya ga oya da* is interpreted as agreeing with her. These two examples convey different meanings.

In contrast, in the above scenario, if the husband's utterance is produced using an English nominal tautology, it can be expressed in one way as in (5-3):

(5-3)   Parents are parents.

According to a native speaker, this English expression can be barely understood unless some more information is added to it.[1] It is highly unlikely that it communicates a meaning such as (5-2c). This suggests that the English nominal tautology *Parents are parents* has no way of expressing differences such as those embodied in (5-1b) and (5-2c).

This chapter discusses the encoded meaning of *A ga A da*.[2] In the following section, I start with examining past studies, and then prove their claims to be incorrect.

5.2 Previous Studies

As we observed in chapters 3 and 4, there have been relatively many previous studies on *A wa A da*. Strangely, there has been much less research on *A ga A da* than on *A wa A da*. This might be because the expression *A ga A da* tends to be listed as an idiom. Some researchers think that it is difficult to analyze *A ga A da* from a unified viewpoint. Is this view correct? As far as I know, there have been only two previous studies: Moriyama (1989) and Okamoto (1993).[3] They have discussed how *A ga A da* is used and understood, but their discussions are lacking in lucidity. In what follows, I will review the meaning of *A ga A da* mentioned in previous studies. According to a relevance theoretic account, if a word is regarded as encoding some sort of information, it should carry the information wherever it is used.

5.2.1 Moriyama (1989)

Moriyama (1989) argues that the subject *A* in the sentence *A ga A da* refers to a specific state of affairs, and the sentence means *futsû-dewanai* 'unusual' (or *sôteidôri-dewanai* 'not a good result'). He employs the following two examples to support his argument:

(5-4)a. *Jiken ga jiken da.* (*Dakara mina ga chûmokushita.*)
 affair SM affair COP so everyone SM paid attention to (it)
 '(lit.) The affair is the affair. (So everyone paid attention to it.)'
 b. *Jikan ga jikan da.* (*Dakara shokudô ga kondeiru.*)
 time SM time COP so restaurant SM is crowded
 '(lit.) The time is the time. (So the restaurant is crowded.)'

(adapted from Moriyama 1989: 6)

In each example, the second utterance is provided in parentheses, but the specific context is not mentioned. We cannot reexamine how these two examples would be interpreted and what aspect is considered *futsû-dewanai* (or *sôteidôri-dewanai*).

One point I would like to add is that Moriyama argues that *A mo A da*, which I will deal with in chapter 6, means *futsû-dewanai* 'unusual' (which is paraphrased as *ijôna* 'anomalous'). Moriyama paraphrases the term *futsû-dewanai* in two ways. It seems to me that the meaning of the term *futsû-dewanai* is vague, and that what Moriyama attempts to argue by employing the term *futsû-dewanai* in the interpretation process of *A ga A da* remains incomprehensible. It cannot be said that he offers a full explanation of the meaning of *A ga A da*. His analysis prompts the following questions:

(5-5)a. What is *futsû-dewanai* 'unusual' or *sôteidôri-dewanai* 'not a good result'?
    b. What is the meaning of *sôteidôri-dewanai* 'not a good result', which can be paraphrased as *futsû-dewanai* 'unusual'?

With respect to (5-5a), it would be safe to say that it is *A* that is unusual or is not a good result. Strictly speaking, it seems to me that it is the referent of the subject *A* that is unusual or is not a good result. For example, in (5-4b), *jikan* 'time' (= *A*) is not unusual, but *the time at the point of utterance* (= the referent of the subject *jikan*) is unusual. When discussing the meaning of *A ga A da*, we need to concretely describe what (the subject) *A* refers to. However, Moriyama provides no explicit explanation of this point.

Next, let us consider (5-5b). As mentioned above, Moriyama does not observe how *A ga A da* is comprehended in a given context. It is not clear what Moriyama intends with terms such as *futsû-dewanai* and *sôteidôri-dewanai*. Here, I attempt to find out what these terms mean. According to the Japanese dictionary, *Kojien*, *sôtei* means "to hypothetically imagine a certain state of affairs or a certain condition". If this is what *sôtei* means, *sôteidôri-dewanai* means "to be inconsistent with a certain hypothetically imagined state of affairs or condition". If we assume that this is used with the same meaning as *futsû-dewanai*, the term *sôtei* in Moriyama's sense would indicates "a certain state of affairs or a certain condition about an object (probably, *A*) that the speaker usually imagines". It therefore seems that the meaning of *A ga A da* is that "*A* is inconsistent with a certain state of affairs or a certain condition about an object (probably, *A*) that the speaker usually imagines". That is exactly the meaning of *A ga A da* proposed by Moriyama. For example, consider the following example:

(5-6)   [A couple is talking about their son Taro's academic record. Taro scored

Chapter 5 *A ga A da* 93

       poorly on an exam again.]
       Husband : *Omae,   seiseki dôdatta?*
                   you   how were (your) grades?
                   'How were your grades?'
       Wife   : *Un, mâ mâ. Dakara ne, Taro no seiseki ga*
                  well so-so   so   SFP Taro of grade SM
                yokunainomo   murimonai   wa. Tokorode,
                not very smart   understandable SFP by the way
                anata wa dôdatta?
                how were (your grades)?
                'Well, they were so-so. So it is understandable that Taro is not very smart. By the way, how were your grades?'
       Husband : *Mâ mâ.* **Oya   ga   oya   da***.*
                so-so   parent SM parent COP
              Dôshiyômonai   yo na.
              there is nothing that can be done (about his grades) SFP SFP
              'So-so. (lit.) <u>The parents are the parents</u>. There's nothing that can be done about his grades.'   (= (5-2))

The husband's utterance *Oya ga oya da* is understood as communicating that the husband and wife are not very smart. Following Moriyama's analysis, the meaning of the utterance might be analyzed as follows: *oya* 'parent' (strictly speaking, the referents of the subject *oya*, the husband and wife) is inconsistent of a certain state of affairs or a certain condition about *oya* (= *A*) that the speaker (i.e. the husband) usually imagines (e.g. "parents set a good example for children").

However, this does not apply to all cases of *A ga A da*. Consider (5-7):

(5-7)   [X and Y go to a restaurant close to their company in the lunch hour. Many people are lining up in front of the restaurant.]
        X : *Yappari,   kekkô   narandeiru   ne.*
          as expected   many (people) are lining up SFP
          'As expected, many people are lining up.'
        Y : *Mâ,* **jikan   ga   jikan   da***   kara   ne.*
          well   time   SM   time   COP because SFP
          'Well, because (lit.) <u>the time is the time</u>.'

In (5-7), Y's utterance *jikan ga jikan da* is understood as providing an explanation for the situation that many people are waiting in front of the restaurant. If explaining it in line with Moriyama's analysis, the utterance *jikan ga jikan da* is analyzed as follows: *jikan* 'time' (strictly speaking, the referent of the subject *jikan*, lunch time) is inconsistent with a certain state of affairs or a certain condition about *jikan* (= *A*) that the speaker usually imagines. However, it is difficult for us to find a state of affairs or a condition applicable to the above analysis. If we have to imagine a state of affairs or a condition in this context, "restaurants are crowded in the lunch hour" may come to mind. This is a widely accepted image, and is *consistent* with the situation described in (5-7). Thus, the utterance in question would be analyzed as follows: *jikan* (strictly speaking, the referent of the subject *jikan*, lunch time) is consistent with the condition that restaurants are crowded in the lunch hour. This is a clear counterexample to Moriyama's analysis.

Furthermore, Moriyama insists that the meaning of *A ga A da* is simply *unusual* (or *not a good result*). Here, a simple question arises: how does Moriyama explain why people receive more complicated content from the utterance *A ga A da*? As already observed above, the utterance *A ga A da* communicates various types of content. In spite of this fact, Moriyama assumes that all cases of *A ga A da* always have the meaning of *unusual* (or *not a good result*). He does not account for the fact that examples of *A ga A da* have different interpretations according to context. Thus, Moriyama's claim is unsatisfactory.

5.2.2 Okamoto (1993)

Okamoto (1993) argues that *A ga A da* indicates that the referent of *A* has undesirable qualities, and that when the referent in question is of high quality, *A ga A da* indicates that the referent of *A* has threatening qualities. First, let us observe examples that can be classified as having undesirable qualities:[4]

(5-8)   X : *Nê,   kyô   pikunikku   iku?*
             hey   today   shall (we) go on a picnic?
             'Hey, shall we go on a picnic today?'
         Y : *Sô nê,   otenki   ga   otenki   da   kara*
             well   weather   SM   weather   COP   because
             pikunikku   wa   yameyô   yo.
             let's cancel (the) picnic
             'Well, because the weather is (not good) weather, let's cancel the

picnic.'

(5-9) [The speaker is talking about a place that is considered dangerous.]
Basyo ga basyo da kara, ki o tuke-nasai.
place SM place COP because, be careful
'Because the place is (not a safe) place, be careful.'
(Okamoto 1993: 448–450)

According to Okamoto's (ibid.: 448–450) analysis, in (5-8), "[t]he undesirability of the weather is at issue". *Otenki ga otenki da* indicates that "the weather is not good". *Basyo ga basyo da* in (5-9) is used to "convey the undesirable nature of the item in question" and it "suggests that the place is dangerous". Okamoto considers these two examples to indicate that the referents of *otenki* 'weather' and *basyo* 'place' have undesirable qualities.

Next, consider (5-10) and (5-11), which are regarded as examples that can be classified as having threatening qualities:

(5-10) [The speaker is talking about the very formal wedding to which she is invited.]
Basyo ga basyo da kara, tyan to site ik-anakutya.
place SM place COP because, in a proper (dress) (I) must go
'Because the place is (not an ordinary) place, I must go in a proper dress.'

(5-11) [The speaker is talking about the tennis match in which he is facing a strong opponent.]
Nanisiro aite ga aite da kara,
at any rate opponent SM opponent COP because
katsu jishin wa nai yo.
self-confidence in winning (I) don't have
'At any rate, because the opponent is a (very strong) opponent, I'm not confident if I can beat him.'
(ibid.: 450–451)

With Okamoto's (ibid.: 450–451) claim, *Basyo ga basyo da* in (5-10) indicates that "the place of the wedding is not ordinary, but very fancy", and *aite ga aite da* in (5-11) is used to indicate the high quality of the referent of *aite* 'opponent'. "The contexts of [(5-10)] and [(5-11)] suggest that when *A ga A* [*da*] concerns high quality, the quality is considered almost too high or too threatening for those who are the person(s) involved". Based on these observations, Okamoto concludes that "whether the referent's quality is negative or positive in the abstract, by using *A ga A da* the speaker presents that quality as undesirable or threatening for those who are involved" (ibid.: 451). In brief, the meaning of *A ga A da* is *undesirable* or *threatening*. If we restate Okamoto's analysis within a relevance theoretic framework, we can say that these two meanings are encoded by *A ga A da*.

After observing her data, it is still unclear what a *high and threatening quality* is. As mentioned above, Okamoto claims when the referent in question is of high quality, *A ga A da* indicates that the referent of *A* has threatening qualities. However, *high* and *threatening* are subjective and the criterion for the judgment is vague. I still do not know what these qualities are. To answer this question, I shall identify what corresponds to a *high and threatening quality* in (5-10) and (5-11) above. It seems that Okamoto characterizes the following states of affairs as a *high and threatening quality*. In (5-10), the wedding ceremony hall referred to by the subject *basyo* 'place' has a high quality *formal*, which is positively evaluated, but because of that quality the speaker has to take care to wear the right clothes; and in (5-11), the speaker's opponent referred to by the subject *aite* 'opponent' has a high quality *strong*, which is positively evaluated, but because of that quality the speaker is not confident of winning the game. It follows from this that in Okamoto's analysis, a *high and threatening quality* means "the referent of the subject *A* has a high quality, which is positively evaluated, but that quality leads to a negative consequence". This is exactly the meaning of *A ga A da* in Okamoto's sense.

If so, when the referent of the subject *A* is of high quality, which is positively evaluated, the quality always leads to a negative consequence. However, this does not hold true for the following example:

(5-12) [X and Y are talking about an actress Haruko. She is a big-name actor's daughter.]

X : *Saikin, Haruko wo terebi de yoku mikakeru yo ne.*
these days Haruko ACC television on often see SFP SFP
Rukkusu mo i shi, engi mo umaishi.
(she) looks so good and (she) performs well
'These days, we often see Haruko on television. She looks so good and performs well.'

Y : *Dakedo, oya ga oya da kara ne.*
but parent SM parent COP because SFP

'But, because (lit.) <u>the parent is the parent</u>.'

In (5-12), X and Y are talking about an actress named Haruko. X thinks that Haruko frequently appears on television because she looks so good and is a fine actress. On the other hand, Y thinks that Haruko frequently appears on television because her father is a famous actor. Y's utterance *oya ga oya da* is understood as providing an explanation for the fact that Haruko appears often on television. If we analyze this with Okamoto's analysis, we find that it is used to indicate the high quality of the referent of *oya* 'parent' (i.e. being a famous actor), and that the quality does not lead to a negative consequence, but to a positive one. The reason for this is that it is commonly known to be good for those involved in show business to perform often on television. Thus, Okamoto's analysis does not apply to (5-12). It cannot be said that when the referent of the subject *A* is of high quality, which is positively evaluated, that quality always leads to a negative consequence.

Furthermore, consider the following example:

(5-13) [In early autumn, X and Y are talking about new confectionery products at a convenience store. In Japan, autumn is a perfect season to have a good appetite. Many new confectionery products arrive in stores.]
X : *Sôsô.   Kinô,   konbini ni ittara,*
     oh yeah   yesterday   when (I) went to a convenience store
     shinshôhin   no   okashi   ga   ippai   atta   wa.
     new products of   confectionery   SM   many   (I) saw   SFP
     'Oh, yeah. When I went to a convenience store yesterday, I saw many new confectionery products.'
Y : *Mâ,   jiki   ga   jiki   da   kara   ne.*
     well season SM season COP   because   SFP
     'Well, because (lit.) <u>the season is the season</u>.'

In (5-13), Y thinks that new confectionery products are displayed because it is early autumn. By uttering *jiki ga jiki da*, Y provides an explanation for the fact that many new confectionery products were on sale at the convenience store. The sentence *jiki ga jiki da* does not mean that the referent of *jiki* 'season' (i.e. the present season) has undesirable or threatening qualities. As I have already discussed above, Okamoto insists that *A ga A da* has two meanings: *undesirable* or *threatening*. However, the observation of (5-13) reveals that *A ga A da* cannot be characterized as encoding these two meanings. Thus, Okamoto's claim is rejected.

In this section, I have proved Moriyama's (1989) and Okamoto's (1993) claims to be incorrect. Then, what kind of alternative proposal can I offer? In the next section, I will introduce some examples of *A ga A da* to illustrate how they are interpreted in concrete contexts.

5.3 *A ga A da* Data

The discussion in the previous section showed that studies of *A ga A da* have not been fully explored. The *A ga A da* data should be scrutinized. Then, how we start our discussion? As a starting point, in this section, I shall introduce and look at the *A ga A da* data to see how they are interpreted in a given context.

When some examples of *A ga A da* are examined closely in concrete contexts, it seems that two factors are involved in their interpretation process. To illustrate the interpretation process, I shall informally use the following notations: **P** is what is discussed at the point of utterance, and **S** is an assumption that the utterance *A ga A da* evokes. First, consider (5-12) and (5-13) discussed above. For convenience, they are given in (5-14) and (5-15), respectively:

(5-14) [X and Y are talking about an actress Haruko. She is a big-name actor's daughter.]

X : *Saikin,   Haruko wo   terebi   de   yoku mikakeru yo   ne.*
these days Haruko ACC television on often see   SFP SFP
Rukkusu mo i   shi,   engi mo umaishi.
(she) looks so good and   (she) performs well
'These days, we often see Haruko on television. She looks so good and performs well.'

Y : *Dakedo,   oya   ga   oya   da   kara   ne.*
but   parent   SM   parent COP   because SFP
But, because (lit.) the parent is the parent.'   (= (5-12))

(5-15) [In early autumn, X and Y are talking about new confectionery products at a convenience store. In Japan, autumn is a perfect season to have a good appetite. Many new confectionery products arrive in stores.]

X : *Sôsô.   Kinô,   konbini ni ittara,*
oh yeah   yesterday   when (I) went to a convenience store

        shinshôhin   no okashi   ga ippai atta   wa.
        new products of confectionery SM many (I) saw SFP
        'Oh, yeah. When I went to a convenience store yesterday, I saw many new confectionery products.'
    Y : *Mâ, jiki   ga jiki   da   kara   ne.*
        well season SM season COP because SFP
        'Well, because (lit.) <u>the season is the season</u>.'   (= (5-13))

In (5-14), the hearer (that is, X) would construct the following interpretation: **P** [Haruko frequently appears on television] because **S** [her father is a famous actor]. In (5-15), the hearer (that is, X) would construct the following interpretation: **P** [many new confectionery products are displayed] because **S** [the season at the point of utterance is a perfect season to have a good appetite]. In these two examples, **S** is understood as providing a reason for **P**. Such a cause-consequence relation is established even if the utterance in question is not followed by *kara* 'because', whose function is to express a cause or a reason. Consider the following examples:

(5-16)   [A couple is talking about their son Taro's academic record. Taro scored poorly on an exam again.]
    Husband : *Omae, seiseki dôdatta?*
                you   how were (your) grades?
                'How were your grades?'
    Wife   : *Un, mâ mâ. Dakara ne, Taro no seiseki ga*
                well so-so so   SFP Taro of grade   SM
              yokunainomo   murimonai   wa. Tokorode,
              not very smart understandable SFP by the way
              anata wa dôdatta?
              how were (your) grades?
              'Well, they were so-so. So it is understandable that Taro is not very smart. By the way, how were your grades?'
    Husband : *Mâ mâ. **Oya   ga   oya   da.***
              so-so   parent SM parent COP
            Dôshiyômonai   yo   na.
            there is nothing that can be done (about his grades) SFP SFP
            'So-so. (lit.) <u>The parents are the parents</u>. There's nothing that

can be done about his grades.' (= (5-6))

(5-17) [A couple is talking about a boy named Taro and his father. The father is a notorious troublemaker.]

Wife : *Taro ga mata kurasumeito to kenkashitan datte.*
Taro SM again classmate with got into a fight HEAR
Hontoni yanchana ko yo ne.
really (he is) a naughty boy SFP SFP
'Taro got into a fight with a classmate again. He is really a naughty boy.'

Husband : *Mâ, oya ga oya da. Taro ga gakkô de*
well parent SM parent COP Taro SM school P
mondai bakari okosu no mo murimonai yo.
(Taro) often gets into trouble P P no wonder SFP
'Well, (lit.) <u>the parent is the parent</u>. No wonder Taro often gets into trouble at school.'

(5-18) [X and Y are talking about Mr. Yamada. He is a businessperson working at a competitor and he does anything to get a contract.]

X (Man) : *Honto, shinjiraremasen yo. Annafûni*
really (I) cannot believe SFP in that way
rokotsuni jamasuru nante.
undisguisedly hamper P
'I can't really believe that Mr. Yamada hampered me undisguisedly.'

Y (Woman) : *Mâ, aite ga aite yo ne.*
well competitor SM competitor SFP SFP
Saisho kara wakatteta koto yo. Yamada-san
the beginning from know thing SFP Mr. Yamada
wa, neratta keiyaku wa
TM once he sets his mind on getting something
zettai toru noyo.
(Mr. Yamada) never lets up SFP
'Well, (lit.) <u>the competitor is the competitor</u>. I knew that from the beginning. Mr. Yamada never lets up once he sets his mind on getting something.'

In (5-16), the hearer (that is, the wife) would construct the following interpretation:

P [Taro got a poor score on an exam again] because **S** [she and her husband are not smart]. In (5-17), the hearer (that is, the wife) would construct the following interpretation: **P** [Taro got into a fight with a classmate] because **S** [his father is a notorious troublemaker]. In (5-18), the hearer (that is, X) would construct the following interpretation: **P** [his business is hampered] because **S** [Mr. Yamada does anything to get contracts]. In (5-16)–(5-18), **S** is readily taken as a reason for **P** in the same way as (5-14) and (5-15). The cause-consequence interpretation has no connection with whether the utterance *A ga A da* is followed by *kara* or not.

Furthermore, consider another type of example typified by (5-19):

(5-19) "*Gomennasai.* — *Â,   onaka ga suita.*
 sorry ah (I am) hungry.
 Fuseijitsuna   ayamarikata   da   ga, honne   dearu.
 insincere the way of apologizing COP but real feeling COP
 Pan   mo   tabeteinai.   Inokori   no nakama to
 bread even (I) have not eaten staying after school of group with
 Fantaorenji   wo   nonda   dake da. Hontôni, pekopeko.
 Fanta orange ACC (I) drank just COP really (I am) starving
 "*Jikan ga   jikan da   kara   ne,*
 time SM time COP because SFP
 oyatsu nanka   tabenai   de   gohan ni shinasai."[5]
 snack such like do not eat P have dinner
 "'Sorry, but I'm hungry.' That's an insincere apology but my real feeling. I haven't even eaten any bread. I only drank Fanta orange with friends. I'm starving. "Because (lit.) <u>the time is the time</u>. Have dinner instead of eating snacks."'   (Kaoru Kitamura, *Sukippu*, p.8, my translation)

In (5-19) quoted from the novel by Kaoru Kitamura, a girl, who is the heroine of the novel, comes home late because she has been involved in school festival preparation. Her mother greets her at the door, saying "You're late!". The girl says "I'm hungry" shortly after apologizing for arriving home late. In this situation, the hearer (that is, the girl) would construct the following interpretation: **P** [she should have dinner instead of snacks] because **S** [the time at the point of utterance is just before dinnertime]. In this example, **S** is regarded as presenting a ground for **P**, which is why the suggestion **P** is made. The ground-conclusion relation is also established in a context where *A ga A da* is uttered.

5.4 Stipulating the Meaning of *A ga A da*

Through the above observations, it should be noticed that in all these cases, a natural interpretation is that S provides an explanation for P. To put it differently, by producing an utterance *A ga A da*, the speaker gives a certain reason for why P happened, or a certain ground for how the speaker reached the conclusion P. It is worth emphasizing that S precedes P temporally. So in the process of interpreting an utterance *A ga A da*, a hearer evokes an assumption corresponding to S from her memory. It seems to follow that the utterance *A ga A da* is an expressional form that indicates an inferential procedure.

Thus far, I have used the following notations informally: P is what is discussed at the point of utterance and S is an assumption that the utterance *A ga A da* evokes. Here, I shall define P and S precisely.

First, let us concentrate on P. There are various types of P. For example, P in (5-14) "Haruko frequently appears on television" is based on the preceding utterance (i.e. X's utterance). Similarly, P in (5-15) "many new confectionery products are displayed" is based on the preceding utterance (i.e. X's utterance). The same explanation is applicable to P in (5-17) and (5-18). On the other hand, P in (5-16) "Taro got a poor score on an exam again" is not based on a previous utterance, but on the previous situation where Taro scored poorly at school. Furthermore, P in (5-19) "she should have dinner instead of snacks" is based on the speaker's own utterance (i.e. the mother's utterance). However, they can all be generalized as "the state of affairs that is under discussion at the point of utterance". For example, P in (5-17) "Taro got into a fight with a classmate" is the state of affairs that is under discussion at the point of utterance. The same characterization can be applied to the other examples.

Next, S should always be generalized as an "assumption about the referent of the subject *A*, which the utterance *A ga A da* evokes". For instance, S in (5-14) "Haruko's father is a famous actor" is an assumption about the referent of the subject *oya* 'parent', which the utterance *oya ga oya da* evokes. Similarly, S in (5-19) "the time at the point of utterance is just before dinnertime" is an assumption about the referent of the subject *jikan* 'time', which the utterance *Jikan ga jikan da* evokes.

From the above discussion, it follows that *A ga A da* encodes the information as in (5-20):

(5-20)　**The Meaning of *A ga A da* :**
　　　A ga A da must be processed in such a way as to evoke an assumption (S) about the referent of the subject *A* that provides an explanation for the state of affairs (P) that is under discussion at the point of utterance.

According to this stipulation, the expressional form *A ga A da* encodes the information that the hearer must access her encyclopedic information about the referent of the subject *A*, and derive an assumption that is understood as providing an explanation for the state of affairs that is under discussion at the point of utterance.

If we assume that the expressional form *A ga A da* encodes something like (5-20), we can explain a difference between the acceptabilities of (5-21a) and (5-21b):

(5-21)　[In a front of a movie theater at 13:00, Taro and Jiro are meeting their friend Saburo. The movie starts at 13:15. It gets to 13:30. Saburo is late.]
　　　Taro : [looking at his watch and saying to Jiro]
　　　　a.　*Jikan　ga　jikan　da.　　Hayaku eigakan ni hairô.*
　　　　　　time　SM　time　COP　let us hurry inside theater
　　　　　　'(lit.) The time is the time. Let's hurry inside the theater.'
　　　　b. # *Jikan　ga　jikan　da.　　Môsukoshi matô.*
　　　　　　time　SM　time　COP　(we will) wait for (him) a little longer
　　　　　　'(lit.) The time is the time. We will wait for him a little longer.'

Suppose the following context: Taro and Jiro are waiting for their friend Saburo who is late. In the case (5-21a), *Jikan ga jikan da* is acceptable, while in the case (5-21b), it would be unacceptable or odd.

As we have seen, the inferential route signaled by *A ga A da* is to instruct the hearer to process it in such a way as to evoke an assumption (S) about the referent of the subject *A* that provides an explanation for the state of affairs (P) that is under discussion at the point of utterance. (5-21a) is felicitous, since the hearer is given immediate access to an assumption (S) (e.g. the time at the point of utterance has past the start time of the showing) providing an explanation for the state of affairs (P) that is under discussion at the point of utterance (i.e. 'we' should hurry inside the theater). In contrast, (5-21b) is not felicitous, since the hearer cannot be given access to an assumption (**S**) providing an explanation for the state of affairs (**P**) that is under discussion at the point of utterance (i.e. 'we' will wait for him a little longer). More simply speaking, the interpreters retrieve no appropriate assumption providing an adequate explanation for Taro's proposal that they wait for Saburo, from his encyclopedic information about the time at the point of utterance since the time at the point of utterance has already past the start time of the showing and cannot therefore access any obvious assumption that might be relevantly interpreted as providing any explanation for '"we' should wait for Saburo". This strengthens the accuracy of the above stipulation of the meaning of *A ga A da* as shown in (5-20).

Thus far, I have discussed the meaning of the Japanese nominal tautology *A ga A da*. It can be said that the interpretation process of *A ga A da* is different from that of *A wa A da*, and it is not connected with negation. As discussed in the previous chapter, some previous studies have suggested that nominal tautologies such as *A wa A da* (and *A is A*) can be illustrated in terms of negation. They actually exclude the other types of nominal tautology from their argument. This shows that they do not comprehensively explain the mechanism involved in interpreting nominal tautologies, and it is important to keep the formal variety in mind.

Here, let us discuss the question of why (5-1) and (5-2) (=(5-16)), which are cited at the beginning of this chapter, are interpreted as objection and agreement, respectively. For convenience, these two examples are repeated below:

(5-1) [A couple is talking about their son Taro's academic record. Taro scored poorly on an exam again.]
Wife : *Watashi mo   sonnani yoku   dekinakattashi   ne.*
　　　　I   too   very well   did not do   SFP
　　　　Taro   bakkari semerarenai   wa.
　　　　Taro   only   (I will) not put a blame SFP
　　　　'I didn't do very well, either. I won't put all the blame on him.'
Husband : *Sonnakoto   iuna   yo.*
　　　　　that   do not say   SFP
　　　　　Oya   wa   oya   *da. Boku ga hanashitemiru   yo.*
　　　　　parent TM   parent COP   I   SM try to talk (to him) SFP
　　　　　'Don't say anything like that. (lit.) <u>Parents are parents</u>. I try

to talk to him.'

(5-2) [A couple is talking about their son Taro's academic record. Taro scored poorly on an exam again.]

Husband : *Omae, seiseki dôdatta?*
you   how were (your) grades?
'How were your grades?'

Wife : *Un, mâ mâ. Dakara ne, Taro no seiseki ga*
well so-so so SFP Taro of grade SM
yokunainomo   murimonai   wa. Tokorode,
not very smart understandable SFP by the way
anata wa dôdatta?
how were (your grades)?
'Well, they were so-so. So it is understandable that Taro is not very smart. By the way, how were your grades?'

Husband : *Mâ mâ. **Oya ga oya da.***
so-so parent SM parent COP
Dôshiyômonai   yo na.
there is nothing that can be done (about his grades) SFP SFP
'So-so. (lit.) <u>The parents are the parents.</u> There's nothing that can be done about his grades.'   (= (5-16))

In (5-1), where the wife implies that she blames herself for her son's poor score, the husband's utterance *Oya wa oya da* is interpreted as an objection to his wife. As we examined in chapter 4, the utterance *A wa A da* is a signal that the utterance must be processed in a context that has a contrastive assumption. This contrastive assumption links easily to a disagreement between the husband and wife. It follows that the husband's utterance *Oya wa oya da* in (5-1) is connected to the interpretation of objection.

On the other hand, in (5-2) (= (5-16)), where the wife implies that it is understandable that Taro is not very smart, the husband's utterance *Oya ga oya da* is interpreted as agreeing with her. As discussed in 5.3, in a context such as (5-2), the utterance *Oya ga oya da* evokes the assumption (**S**) "she and her husband are not very smart". Understanding the utterance requires subsidiary premises such as "it is generally said that parents' academic ability tends to be passed on to their child". Given the evoked assumption and the generally accepted tendency as premises, the interpreters readily derive the conclusion "it is understandable that Taro (that is, the husband and wife's child) is not very smart". The conclusion coincides with the wife's implication. It follows from this that the husband's utterance *Oya ga oya da* in (5-2) is connected with the interpretation of agreement.

5.5 Validating the Hypothesis that *A ga A da* Has a Specific Meaning

So far, I have proposed that *A ga A da* itself encodes a meaning as shown in (5-20). If this proposal is right, the meaning of *A ga A da* cannot be predicted by combining the meanings of the lexical items in the sentence. However, it inevitably leads to a simple question: is it an appropriate claim that the expressional form *A wa A da* itself has a certain meaning? In what follows, I shall refute the doubtful point to support my proposal. In this section, I will (i) hypothesize that the expressional form *A ga A da* has a certain meaning, (ii) conceive some counterarguments for the hypothesis, and (iii) reveal that the meaning of *A ga A da* cannot be explained in terms of the compositionality principle. Ultimately, it will lead to the conclusion that the meaning encoded by *A ga A da* is procedural rather than conceptual.

A criticism of my hypothesis is that the meaning of *A ga A da* is determined by integrating the meanings of its component parts. First of all, let us check the constituents of *A ga A da*. The sentence consists of the subject *A*, the particle *ga*, the predicate *A* and the copular predication *da*. Given this point, counterarguments to the hypothesis fall into three types: counterarguments based on the uses of the particle *ga*, counterarguments based on formal similarities between *A ga A da* and *A ga B da*, and counterarguments from relevance theoretic perspectives.[6] In what follows, I shall investigate these three kinds of counterarguments individually.

Counterarguments Based on the Uses of the Particle Ga

The first sort of counterargument is related to the uses of the particle *ga*. As already mentioned in 4.7, the Japanese language has a topic marker *wa* and a subject marker *ga*. The distinction between these particles is a rather controversial issue in Japanese linguistics. A vast number of studies have been written (c.f. Kuno 1973a; Kuroda 1979; Mikami 1960, 1963).

Here, I shall outline the main points briefly. Some researchers have proposed that there are two uses of the particle *ga* (c.f. Kuno 1973a; Kuroda 1979). One is *neutral description*. The other is *exhaustive listing*. Consider (5-22) and (5-23):

(5-22) *Sora ga aoi ne.*
sky SM blue SFP
'The sky is blue.' (Kuno 1973a: 33)

(5-23) *Taro ga gakusei desu.*
Taro SM student COP
'Taro is a student.' (ibid.: 32)

In (5-22), *ga* is understood as a neutral description. Sentence (5-22) represents a thetic judgment. On the other hand, in (5-23), *ga* is understood as an exhaustive listing. Sentence (5-23) implies that for example, "only Taro is a student and nobody else is a student". Such an interpretation requires a particular context. For example, we can imagine the following context: two women X and Y are talking about Taro, Haruko and Natsuko, and of the three persons, Taro is a student. In the context, X says (5-23) above, in reply to Y's question (5-24).

(5-24) *Dare ga gakusei desu ka.*
who SM student COP Q
'Who is a student?' (ibid.)

The utterance (5-23) is interpreted as communicating that only Taro is a student and the others are not students.

As we have seen above, the particle *ga* has two uses: *neutral description* and *exhaustive listing*. These two uses alone cannot predict the meaning of *A ga A da*. The reason is that these uses explain the interpretation of the noun preceding *ga*. Through the discussion in 5.3, we have understood that the expressional form *A ga A da*, which is a simple form, conveys complicated content that depends on the context. The variety of what is communicated by *A ga A da* extends easily beyond the rage covered by the particle *ga*.

Counterarguments Based on Formal Similarities between A ga A da *and* A ga B da

What next comes to mind when we consider arguments against the proposal that *A ga A da* has a specific meaning? The next counterargument is based on formal similarities between *A ga A da* and *A ga B da*. Some might apply the analyses of the particle *ga*, which was dealt with in the previous part, and think that *A ga A da* is understood in the same way as the similar expression *A ga B da*. We can respond to this objection as follows. For example, as we have already observed, a possible reading of *A ga B da* involves interpreting *A ga* as representing an exhaustive listing.[7] The expression *A ga B da* is interpreted to mean that "only A is B and nobody else is B". In other words, it means "to list completely all of the objects that apply to B, within a certain limit". I have already confirmed the use, but to facilitate future discussion, I confirm the use of an exhaustive listing, using the following example:

(5-25)   *Haruko   ga   pianisuto   da.*
         Haruko   SM   pianist   COP
         'Haruko is a pianist.'

Suppose that when an orchestra conductor walks into a room with her manager, she finds three people there: Haruko, Natsuko and Akiko. She wants to know which of them is a pianist, and asks the manager the question. If the reply is something like (5-25), it is understood to communicate that "of the people concerned (i.e. Haruko, Natsuko and Akiko), only Haruko is a pianist". Then, by analogy with the similarity of the form, it would follow that *A ga A da* would be interpreted as communicating that with a certain limit, only *A* is *A*. This, however, is nonsense. As we observed in 5.3, the hearer of *A ga A da* does not assume a certain limit. Furthermore, after broadening the interpretation of *A ga B da*, critics might again argue that *A ga A da* would be interpreted as communicating that within a certain limit, only the referent of the subject *A* has the property of *A*. Nevertheless, this is also problematic since the interpretation of *A ga A da* is different from that of *A ga B da*. For instance, if the utterance in (5-14) is interpreted as a case of *A ga B da*, it would be interpreted as communicating that "within a certain limit, only Haruko's father (the referent of the subject *oya*) has a property of *oya* (e.g. a person who brings up children). In fact, as we have seen above, the utterance communicates (**S**) "Haruko's father is a famous actor" in the context described above. The communicated content does not include interpretations such as "within a certain limit," "only Haruko's father," and a certain property of parents. (What is noticeable here is that the property of being a famous actor is regarded not as a property of parents, but as a property of Haruko's father. I will discuss this point in the part that immediately follows.) The same argument can be applied to the other examples. Thus, it can be said that *A ga A da* cannot be interpreted in the same as *A ga B da*.

Counterarguments from Relevance Theoretic Perspectives

As we have seen, the expressional form *A ga A da* is not interpreted in the same way as the similar expressional form *A ga B da*. It is natural to attribute the fact-explanation interpretation directly to the expressional form *A ga A da* itself. This conclusion supports the hypothesis that the expressional form *A ga A da* has a certain meaning. However, from a relevance theoretic viewpoint, there would be two further possible counterarguments. Some relevance theorists might argue that the interpretation of *A ga A da* can be determined through the pragmatic processes involved in explicature derivation such as free enrichment and *ad hoc* concept construction. In what follows, I demonstrate that the counterargument is false.

First, let us discuss the possibility of interpretation via free enrichment. As noted in chapter 4.4.2, free enrichment is the process of recovering what is explicitly communicated without any linguistic mandate. For someone arguing the interpretation process of free enrichment, for example, the utterance *Oya ga oya da* in (5-16) might be understood as follows:

(5-16′)   Oya ga oya [who are not very smart] da.[8]
'The husband and wife are parents [who are not very smart].'

In (5-16′), a particular outcome of the enrichment process might be suggested in the brackets. Critics might argue that if the utterance in question is interpreted by the process of free enrichment, the concept [who are not very smart] would be provided contextually for purely pragmatic reasons, without being linguistically mandated. However, the utterance (5-16) does not encourage the hearer to draw such an interpretation as (5-16′). Thus, (5-16′) is not regarded as the speaker's intended interpretation. As we already observed in 5.3, what is communicated by the utterance in (5-16) is (**S**) "she and her husband are not very smart". Similarly, it is highly unlikely that the speaker's intended interpretations in the other examples will be obtained by adding further conceptual materials to the logical form without a linguistic mandate. The interpretation via free enrichment is not supportable.

Next, let us discuss the possibility of interpretation via *ad hoc* concept construction. Here, let us recall *ad hoc* concept construction. As outlined in 4.4.2, it is the process of replacing an encoded lexical concept appearing in a logical form with a contextually adjusted one. For someone arguing explicature derivation via the process of *ad hoc* concept construction, the predicate *A* in the sentence *A ga A da* is understood as expressing not the concept it encodes but a contextually adjusted concept. For example, (5-14) and (5-19) might be understood as follows:

(5-14′)   Oya ga OYA* da.⁹
           'The parent is PARENT*.'
(5-19′)   Jikan ga JIKAN* da.
           'The time is TIME*.'

In a context such as (5-14), when the utterance *oya ga oya da* is produced, the hearer, namely X, attempts to interpret the utterance in accordance with the presumption of optimal relevance. Then, those who approve the *ad hoc* concept construction analysis might argue that what the speaker explicitly communicates by the predicate *oya* is not the lexically encoded concept, but rather something much more specific, for instance, "famous actors", which is indicated by OYA* 'PARENT*' in (5-14′). Similarly, it might be argued that in a context like (5-19), the speaker, Y uses the word *jikan* to communicate a concept that is not a lexically encoded concept, but rather something much more specific, for instance, JIKAN* 'TIME*' in (5-19′), which would be something like "time to have dinner instead of snacks". However, these utterances do not yield an adequate interpretation with a measure of pragmatic adjustments, because the above apparently contextually adjusted concepts should not regarded as *ad hoc* concepts of the concept that the predicate *A* encodes lexically. Quite clearly, in (5-14) and (5-19), the predicate *A* does not communicate a lexical meaning. Nor does it communicate encyclopedic knowledge concerning the original encoded concept *A*. For example, the following information is included in the encyclopedic entry for the predicate OYA 'PARENT':

(5-26)   Encyclopedic Entry for OYA 'PARENT'
         a. bring up children
         b. being sober
         c. complaining about children

However, concepts such as "famous actors" are far from the above encyclopedic information. The reason is that the concept "famous actors" does not concern the original encoded concept OYA, but rather concern the referent of the subject *oya* (that is, Haruko's father). For example, in (5-14), assumption **S** "Haruko's father is a famous actor", evoked by the utterance *oya ga oya da*, is not derived until the utterance itself guides the hearer to access her encyclopedic information about the referent of the subject *oya*, which is regarded as providing an explanation for the state of affairs under discussion at the point of utterance. The same explanations can apply to the other examples. In the dinner-or-snacks example (5-19), assumption **S** "the time at the point of utterance is just before dinnertime" is not derived until the utterance *Jikan ga jikan da* instructs the hearer to access her encyclopedic information about the referent of the subject *jikan*, which is understood as providing an explanation for the state of affairs under discussion at the point of utterance. In the *A ga A da* interpretation process, the expressional form the speaker uses is just a hint or a clue that helps the hearer to pick out the assumption about the referent of the subject *A* that can be interpreted as an explanation in the fact-explanation relationship. Thus, the possibility of interpretation via *ad hoc* concept construction is not accepted.

The above observations revel that *A ga A da* cannot be understood through the pragmatic process of free enrichment and *ad hoc* concept construction involved in explicature derivation. This strongly supports my hypothesis that *A ga A da* is an expressional form with encoded procedural information that constrains derivation implicature.

In this section, I examined several possible counterarguments to my hypothesis. These counterarguments should not be regarded as a comprehensive theory. This shows that the expressional form *A ga A da* encodes procedural information as in (5-20), that is, the *A ga A da* construction exists.

5.6 Summary

In this chapter, I have shown that we can analyze *A ga A da* as an expressional form encoding procedural information. Moriyama (1989) and Okamoto (1993) argued the meaning of the expressional form. Some of the explanations were ambiguous. The earlier studies are not accepted as a comprehensive analysis of the interpretation of *A ga A da*. After closely examining several concrete examples to discover its essential meaning, I reached the following conclusion: *A ga A da* must be processed in such a way as to evoke an assumption (**S**) about the referent of the subject *A* that provides an explanation for the state of affairs (**P**) that is under discussion at the point of utterance. When we think this way, we can explain the interpretation process of all the examples of *A ga A da* comprehensively and appropriately.

To this point, I have discussed two types of Japanese nominal tautology: *A wa A da* and *A ga A da*. There is another nominal tautology in Japanese. In the next chapter, I will discuss the meaning of *A mo A da*.

Notes

1 The informant is an American female in her thirties. I would like to thank her for her useful suggestions.
2 This chapter focuses on *A ga A da*, which is not embedded in other sentences, and *A ga A da*, which is followed by *kara* 'because' and whose consequent part is not verbalized. *A* in *A ga A da* represents a noun or a noun phrase.
3 Kubo (1992) discusses *A ga A da* with the concept of role-value relationship advocated by Fauconnier and attempts to clarify the semantic structure of tautology. For a detailed discussion, see Kubo (1992).
4 (5-8)–(5-11) are quoted from Okamoto (1993), so the transcription methods and conventions used for the example follows her rules.
5 The *A ga A da* in question is followed by *kara* and the consequent part is verbalized. However, I regard it as a target for discussion in this chapter, since the utterance appears with *ne*, whose function is to indicate the end of a sentence.
6 *A* and *B* in *A ga B da* represent a noun or a noun phrase.
7 It might be said that another possible interpretation of *A ga A da* is a neutral description. The use of a neutral description is limited to cases where the predicate of a sentence represents an action, the existence of someone or something, and a temporary state of affairs (cf. Kuno 1973a) and therefore does not explain the interpretation process of *A ga A da*.
8 It is assumed that the subject in (5-16′) has already been identified via reference assignment.
9 It is assumed that each referent of the subjects in (5-14′) and (5-19′) has already been identified via reference assignment.

Chapter 6

A mo A da

The Japanese nominal tautology *A mo A da* is unique and intriguing but related studies have made little progress. The interpretation process remains unclear. On the basis of a detailed observation, this chapter stipulates the encoded meaning of *A mo A da* as follows: *A mo A da* must be processed in such a way as to evoke an assumption about the referent of the subject *A* that provides one of several explanations for the state of affairs that is under discussion at the point of utterance.

6.1 Introduction

This chapter will focus on the Japanese nominal tautology *A mo A da*. The expressional form cannot be translated into an English nominal tautological form. If it has to be replaced by an English nominal tautological form, its English version might be *A is also A* or *A is A, too* and these translated expressions include the additional word *also* or *too*. *A mo A da* and its English versions are quite different from each other. In fact we can safely say that there are no English expressions corresponding to *A mo A da*. An analysis of *A mo A da* plays an important role in giving a clear picture of Japanese nominal tautologies.

Here, recall the following example cited in chapter 1:

(6-1)　[A couple is talking about a boy named Taro and his father. The father is a notorious troublemaker.]
　　　　Wife　　: *Taro　ga　mata　kurasumeito　to　kenkashitan　datte.*
　　　　　　　　　Taro　SM　again　classmate　　with　got into a fight　HEAR

>   *Hontoni yanchana ko   yo   ne.*
>   really   (he is) a naughty boy SFP   SFP
>   'Taro got into a fight with a classmate again. He is really a naughty boy.'
>
> Husband : *Mâ,   oya   mo   oya   da.   Taro ga   gakkô de*
>   well parent also parent COP   Taro SM   school P
>   *mondai bakari okosu   no   mo   murimonai   yo.*
>   (Taro) often gets into trouble P   P   no wonder   SFP
>   'Well, (lit.) <u>the parent is also the parent</u>. No wonder Taro often gets into trouble at school.'   (= (1-4))

In (6-1), where the wife implies that Taro is responsible for the fight, the husband thinks that Taro's father is also responsible for the fight. Why and how do we intuitively derive such an interpretation from the apparently meaningless tautological sentence *oya mo oya da*?

As mentioned above, to gain new insights into the linguistic phenomenon of Japanese nominal tautologies, *A mo A da* is a highly stable object of research, but little attention has been directed towards the expressional form. It is even unclear what remains unresolved. The aim of this chapter is to pin down the information encoded in *A mo A da*, and to show that it is an expressional form that has procedural information.[1] In what follows, let us start with a review of the literature as regards *A mo A da* and clarify some of the principal issues mentioned in previous studies.

6.2   Previous Studies

There have been few previous studies dealing with *A mo A da*. What is more, even analyses of *A mo A da* that have been undertaken are poor in terms of detail and some aspects have not been explicitly mentioned. My first task is to appreciate precisely what previous research on *A mo A da* has attempted to argue. This section presents a critical examination of Moriyama (1989) and Okamoto (1993).

6.2.1   Moriyama (1989)

Moriyama (1989) states that *A mo A da* means a juxtaposition of *unusual* (or *anomalous*) states of affairs.[2] In his paper, the following examples are presented as examples of *A mo A da*:

(6-2) a. *Kyôshi ga kyôshi nara,* **gakusei mo gakusei da**.
   teacher SM teacher if student also student COP
   '(lit.) <u>If the teacher is the teacher, the student is also the student.</u>'
 b. *Kyôshi ga kyôshi da shi,* **gakusei mo gakusei da**.
   teacher SM teacher COP because student also student COP
   '(lit.) <u>Because the teacher is the teacher, the student is also the student.</u>'
   (adapted from Moriyama 1989: 7)

(6-2a) and (6-2b) are examples of *A mo A da* with a subordinate clause. In Moriyama's view, *A mo A da* is *basically* regarded as an expression similar to *A ga A da* and is an independent form of the latter part of *X ga X nara, Y mo Y da* 'If X is X, Y is also Y' in (6-2a), and of *X ga X da shi, Y mo Y da* 'Because X is X, Y is also Y' in (6-2b). And, *A mo A da*, like *A ga A da*, "expresses a unusual state of affairs in a specific situation" (ibid.: 8). On the basis of this short discussion, Moriyama jumps to the conclusion that the meaning of *A mo A da* is a juxtaposition of *unusual* (or *anomalous*) states of affairs.

In the same way as Moriyama (1989), Okamoto (1993) also mentions similarities between *A mo A da* and *A ga A da*, but her view about the meaning of *A mo A da* differs from Moriyama's slightly.

6.2.2 Okamoto (1993)

Okamoto (1993) claims that *A mo A da* indicates that the item in question is undesirable, presupposing the existence of another item that is equally undesirable, which is to say that *A mo A da* means a juxtaposition of *undesirable* persons or things.[3] Let us consider some examples:

(6-3) [An elderly man criticizes the casual way young married men and single women have affairs.][4]
   Otoko mo otoko nara, **onna mo onna da**.
   men also men if women also women COP
   ittai   kanozyo-tati wa yome ni itte kara wa,
   how in the world   after they get married,
   donna katee   o tukuru   no daroo.
   what kind of family   (they) will make (I) wonder

'(lit.) If men are also men, then women are also women. (I find both the men and the women undesirable.) I wonder what kind of families they will make when they get married.' (Okamoto 1993: 451)

(6-4) *Oya ga oya da kara* **kodomo mo kodomo da**.
parent SM parent COP because child also child COP
'Because the parents are (bad) parents, the child is also (a bad) child.'
(ibid.: 452)

(6-5) *Anata mo anata yo.*
you also you SFP
'(lit.) You are also you. (You, too, are bad/ undesirable.)' (ibid.)

Following Okamoto's (1993: 452) analysis, in (6-3), "both the men and the women are considered undesirable", and the latter part in (6-4), *kodomo mo kodomo da* "indicates the child, like the parents, is not commendable". (6-5) presupposes that besides *anata* 'you' (that is, the hearer), there is someone else to be criticized, and it is used for criticizing *anata*.[5]

6.2.3 *A mo A da* on which Moriyama (1989) and Okamoto (1993) Focus
6.2.3.1 What is *A mo A da*?

So far, we have looked at previous studies on *A mo A da*. There is a significant overlap between Moriyama's and Okamoto's analyses. The overlapping points are summarized below:

(6-6) a. The subject for research consists of examples of *A mo A da* with a subordinate clause.
b. *A mo A da* communicates that the referent of the subject *A* has negative (i.e. *unusual* (or *anomalous*) and *undesirable*) features.
c. *A mo A da* presupposes that in addition to the referent of the subject *A*, there is another person or thing with negative features.

There is no great difference between the two analyses. It might be said that they immediately take a step towards resolution. However, a careful examination proves that they deal with only part of the *A mo A da* data. To clarify their problems, I shall first show the kinds of examples found in their papers.

As we confirmed in (6-6a), Moriyama and Okamoto deal only with examples of *A mo A da* with a subordinate clause. Their examples are given in (6-7)–(6-9):

(6-7)a. *Kyôshi ga kyôshi nara,* **gakusei mo gakusei da**.
　　　　 teacher SM teacher if　　 student also student COP
　　　　 '(lit.) If the teacher is the teacher, the student is also the student.'
　　　　　　　　　　　　　　　　　　　　　　　　　　　　　(= (6-2a))

b. *Kyôshi ga kyôshi da shi,* **gakusei mo gakusei da**.
　　 teacher SM teacher COP because student also student COP
　　 '(lit) Because the teacher is the teacher, the student is also the student.'
　　　　　　　　　　　　　　　　　　　　　　　　　　　　(= (6-2b))

(6-8) *Otoko mo otoko nara,* **onna mo onna da**.
　　　 men also men if　　 women also women COP
　　　 '(lit.) If men are men, then women are also women.'　　(= (6-3))

(6-9) *Oya ga oya da kara* **kodomo mo kodomo da**.
　　　 parent SM parent COP because child also child COP
　　　 'Because the parents are (bad) parents, the child is also (a bad) child.'
　　　　　　　　　　　　　　　　　　　　　　　　　　　　(= (6-4))

On the other hand, their data lack examples of *A mo A da* that are not embedded in other sentences, namely those that occurs in isolation (hereafter referred to as isolated *A mo A da*), such as (6-10) and (6-11):

(6-10)　[A couple is talking about a boy named Taro and his father. The father is a notorious troublemaker.]
　　　　Wife　　: *Taro ga mata kurasumeito to kenkashitan datte.*
　　　　　　　　　 Taro SM again classmate with got into a fight HEAR
　　　　　　　　　 Hontoni yanchana ko yo ne.
　　　　　　　　　 really (he is) a naughty boy SFP SFP
　　　　　　　　　 'Taro got into a fight with a classmate again. He is really a naughty boy.'
　　　　Husband : *Mâ,* **oya mo oya da**. *Taro ga gakkô de*
　　　　　　　　　 well parent also parent COP Taro SM school P
　　　　　　　　　 mondai bakari okosu no mo murimonai yo.
　　　　　　　　　 (Taro) often gets into trouble P P no wonder SFP
　　　　　　　　　 'Well, (lit.) the parent is also the parent. No wonder Taro often gets into trouble at school.'　　(= (6-1))

(6-11)　[A man writes about famous sumo-lovers in his blog.]
　　　　Sugiyama Kunihiro ya Uchidate Makiko wa

Sugiyama Kunihiro and Uchidate Makiko TM
dono basho de   kao wo mitemo odoroka nai   ga,
at any sumo tournament if (I) see (them) (I would) not be surprised but
maikai   areru   3 gatsu no   osakabasho   wa
every   close bouts March   the Osaka tournament TM
Omura Kon,   Hayashiya Pee,   Kyo Utako   nado   wa
Omura Kon   Hayashiya Pee   Kyo Utako   and so on   TM
jôren   nanode   tanoshimida. Shiranakattano   dakedo,
regular attendees because (I) enjoy   (I) did not know   although
ryôrinin no Kandagawa Toshiro wa shômen-shôbu-shinpan-seki no
chef   of Kandagawa Toshiro TM the main referees' seats   of
*aidani   suwatteiru toiu. **Basho   mo   basho   da.***
between   seated   HEAR ringside seat also ringside seat COP
Kôshitsu   desae anzen wo   kangaete tamariseki   niwa
imperial family even   safety ACC think   ringside seat at
suwarenai.   Hitogara   ga   shinobareru tokoro   da.
can not have a seat personality SM (one can) guess   COP

'I wouldn't be surprised to meet Kunihiro Sugiyama and Makiko Uchidate at any sumo tournament. I enjoy nothing better than meeting Kon Omura, Pee Hayashi, and Utako Kyo at the Osaka tournament every March because they are regular attendees. That tournament is well known for its close bouts. Although I didn't know it before, I heard that the chef, Toshiro Kandagawa, always watches the bouts, seated between the main referees' seats. (lit.) <u>The ringside seat is also the ringside seat</u>. Even the imperial family can't have ringside seats for safety reasons. One can guess the chef's personality from that.'

(adapted from http://punkhermit.jugem.cc/?eid=2055, my translation)

The above observation shows that Moriyama's and Okamoto's data are part of the data on the form *A mo A da*. If, as Moriyama argues, *A mo A da* is an independent case of the latter part of *X ga X nara, Y mo Y da*, and of *X ga X da shi, Y mo Y da*, the independent part can be formally considered the same as the isolated *A mo A da*. This raises a question regarding the extent to which the previous analyses (discussed in 6.2.1 and 6.2.2) can account for cases of isolated *A mo A da*.

Before answering this question, let us consider the nature of *A mo A da* with a subordinate clause. Neither Moriyama nor Okamoto mentions the object of their research. In the course of rethinking designed to identify their research target, the characteristics came to light. Here, recall the following examples:

(6-12) Kyôshi   ga   kyôshi   da   shi,   **gakusei   mo   gakusei   da.**
       teacher SM   teacher   COP because student also student COP
       '(lit.) Because the teacher is the teacher, the student is also the student.' (= (6-7b))

(6-13) Oya   ga   oya   da   kara   kodomo   mo   kodomo da.
       parent SM parent COP because child   also   child   COP
       'Because the parents are (bad) parents, the child is also (a bad) child.' (= (6-9))

It is immediately noticeable that (6-12) and (6-13) are regarded as expressions that are arranged pairwise since the tautological expressional forms *A ga A da* and *A mo A da*, which include different particles *ga* and *mo*, are used in a subordinate clause and a main clause, respectively, and correlative words (e.g. *kyôshi* 'teacher' and *gakusei* 'student' in (6-12), *oya* 'parent' and *kodomo* 'child' in (6-13)) are used for the repeated part of the sentence.

Another notable aspect is that both *A ga A da* and *A mo A da* can be used in a subordinate clause. As we have already seen in 6.2.1, after first modifying his pronouncement with the word *basically*, Moriyama states that *A mo A da* is an independent form of the latter part of *X ga X nara, Y mo Y da* and of *X ga X da shi, Y mo Y da*. On the other hand, Moriyama cites examples of *A mo A da* used in a subordinate clause such as *Kyôshi mo kyôshi nara, gakusei mo gakusei da* 'If the teacher is also the teacher, the student is also the student', and *Kyôshi mo kyôshi da shi, gakusei mo gakusei da* 'Because the teacher is also the teacher, the student is also the student'. In fact, these examples are undoubtedly produced in a particular context so *A mo A da* is likely to be considered an independent form of the former part or the latter part of *X mo X nara, Y mo Y da* and of *X mo X da shi, Y mo Y da*. Thus, contrary to Moriyama's analysis, it cannot be said in a strict sense that *A mo A da* is an independent form of the latter part of *X ga X nara, Y mo Y da* and of *X ga X da shi, Y mo Y da*. Okamoto also gives *Otoko mo otoko nara, onna mo onna da* 'If men are men, women are also women' in (6-7), as a example of *A mo A da* used in a subordinate clause, and does not distinguish examples of *A mo A da* used in a subordinate clause from that of *A ga A da* used in a subordinate clause.

The above observation shows that a discussion of *A mo A da* with a subordinate clause requires answers to the following two questions: what is the difference between *A ga A da* used in a subordinate clause and *A mo A da* used in a subordinate clause?; and why can these two expressions be used in a subordinate clause? However, Moriyama's and Okamoto's views regarding these two questions are unclear.

6.2.3.2 What is the Meaning of *A mo A da*?

The previous subsection showed that examples on which Moriyama and Okamoto concentrate constitute part of the data related to the form *A mo A da*. This reveals that the two linguists' analyses are not comprehensive accounts of the interpretation process. According to a relevance theoretic account, if a word is regarded as encoding some sort of information, it should carry the information wherever it is used. Adopting this claim, I shall next describe the meaning of *A mo A da* that Moriyama and Okamoto propose as clearly as possible, and disconfirm their claims.

As confirmed in (6-6b) and (6-6c), Moriyama and Okamoto share two common views: (i) *A mo A da* communicates that the referent of the subject *A* has negative features such as *unusual* (or *anomalous*) and *undesirable*, and (ii) *A mo A da* presupposes that in addition to the referent of the subject *A*, there is another person or thing with negative features. In brief, they conclude that the meaning of *A mo A da* is a juxtaposition of persons or things with negative features. This conclusion seems to be drawn from examining examples in concrete contexts, but in fact, the two researchers arrive at their conclusions based on a discussion of examples largely isolated from concrete contexts. How is this possible? The reason might be that some examples of *A mo A da* with subordinate clauses are used as idioms that indicate a juxtaposition of persons or things with negative features. For example, according to the Japanese language dictionary, *Daijisen*, *Oya mo oya nara, ko mo ko da* 'If the parent is also the parent, the child is also the child' is "an expression for criticizing parents and children in a situation where the parent does evil and so does their child". Native Japanese speakers intuitively understand that this expression indicates a criticism of the people concerned. However, contrary to Moriyama's and Okamoto's claims, it is not true to say that all cases of *A mo A da* with a subordinate clause always indicate something *unusual* (or *anomalous*) and *undesirable*. Following Okamoto's (1993: 452, my italics) analysis, *Otoko mo otoko nara, onna mo onna da* in (6-8) indicates that "the men and the women are considered *undesirable*", while the latter part of *Oya ga oya da kara, kodomo mo kodomo da*, that is, *kodomo mo kodomo da* in (6-13) indicates that "the child, like the parents, is *not commendable*". Certainly, *undesirable* and *not commendable* might be the same in that they have a negative meaning. However, Okamoto's analysis cannot explain why the meaning is *not undesirable* in (6-13). When people hear an utterance *A mo A da*, they receive more complicated and diverse messages than *undesirable* and *not commendable* from the utterance. In spite of this fact, Moriyama and Okamoto assume that all cases of *A mo A da* with subordinate clauses always have the meaning of *undesirable* and *not commendable*, but they cannot explain why examples of *A mo A da* with subordinate clauses, such as (6-8) and (6-13) discussed above, are interpreted differently depending on context. Therefore, Moriyama's and Okamoto's claims must be rejected.

Here, let us consider what Moriyama and Okamoto intend to argue by using the words *unusual* (or *anomalous*) and *undesirable*. As stated above, the two researchers do not examine the expressional form in question in a specific context. So we cannot reanalyze what aspect they interpret as *unusual* (or *anomalous*) and *undesirable* in the above examples. However, the two meanings express the speaker's subjective negative evaluation of the referent of the subject *A* and another person or thing. Accordingly, it is concluded that Moriyama and Okamoto regard *A mo A da* as meaning the speaker's subjective negative evaluation of the referent of the subject *A* and another person or thing.

6.2.3.3 Applicability to Data not Included in Moriyama (1989) and Okamoto (1993)

Moriyama and Okamoto did not observe examples of the isolated *A mo A da*. However, as seen above, the data of the expressional form *A mo A da* includes the isolated *A mo A da* as well as the *A mo A da* with a subordinate clause. Here, I shall respond to the question posed above regarding the extent to which the previous analyses discussed in 6.2.1 and 6.2.2 can account for cases of the isolated *A mo A da*.

First, previous studies argue that *A mo A da* with a subordinate clause communicates that the referent of the subject *A* has a negative feature. However, as illustrated immediately below, it cannot be said that the isolated *A mo A da* encodes the meaning that the referent of the subject *A* has a negative feature.

(6-14)   [A man writes a blog about the coincidence that his friends, Taro and
         Jiro, wrote about the same topic on the same day.]
         Sôsô.   Taro to   Jiro   ga,   onajihi ni

oh yes Taro and Jiro SM on the same day
onaji naiyô no burogu *wo* *kaitete* *uketa.* **Kisetsu**
a blog article about the same topic ACC wrote so funny season
mo *kisetsu* *da* *kara* *ne.*
also season COP because SFP

'Oh, yes. Taro and Jiro wrote a blog article about the same topic on the same day. The coincidence is so funny. Because (lit.) <u>the season is also the season</u>.' (adapted from http://blog.livedoor.jp/tek_nishi/tag/%E7%82%8A%E9%A3%AF%E5%99%A8, my translation)

(6-15) [A man writes a blog about cicadas.]
Jiki *mo* ***jiki*** *da. Sasugani* *minmin-zemi*
season also season COP as would be expected minminzemi cicada
to *abura-zemi* *no daisôon* *wa* *sukunakunari,*
and large brown cicada of loud buzz TM grow fainter and fainter
izentoshite Yoshida Shigeru-zô-hiroba
still the Square of the Bronze Statue of Shigeru Yoshida
no *okuno* *sakura no taiboku* *niwa* *takusan*
of back the large cherry tree on many
haritsuiteiru monono, tsukutsukubôshi *ga*
cling to while (the number of) meimuna opalifera cicadas SM
hijôni *ôkunatta.*
greatly is increasing

'(lit.) <u>The season is also the season.</u> As would be expected, the loud buzz of the minminzemi cicadas and large brown cicadas grows fainter and fainter. While many minminzemi cicadas and large brown cicadas still cling to the large cherry tree at the back of the Square of the Bronze Statue of Shigeru Yoshida, the number of meimuna opalifera cicadas is greatly increasing.' (http://homepage2.nifty.com/poppobora/mushitori.html, my translation)

For example, in (6-14), the man mentions that his friends, Taro and Jiro, coincidently wrote a blog about Christmas lights on the same day. The sentence *Kisetsu mo kisetsu da* does not mean that the referent of the subject *kisetsu* 'season', that is, *fuyu* 'winter' has some sort of negative connotation. Similarly, the sentence *Jiki mo jiki da* in (6-15) does not mean that the referent of the subject *jiki* 'time', that is, *hachigatsu gejun* 'late August' has some sort of negative feature. Thus, the isolated

A mo A da cannot be characterized as encoding the meaning that the referent of the subject *A* has a negative feature.

Next, I discuss the idea that *A mo A da* means a juxtaposition of persons or things with negative features. For example, (6-16) could be understood as meaning a juxtaposition of a person and a thing with negative features.

(6-16) [Taro could not deal with company X's complaint properly. The company complained about the cancellation of a contract.]
Boss : *Hontoni,   anata   mo   anata   yo.   Naze   hitori de*
really   you   also   you   SFP   why   by yourself
shorishiyô to shita   no. itte kurenake   reba
(you) tried to deal with   Q   do not tell (me)   if
wakaranai   desho. Konna ôkina koto ninatte shima tara,
(I do) not know   SFP   serious   have become   so
dônimodekinai   no   yo.
(it does) not seem to be getting anywhere   SFP SFP
'Really, (lit.) <u>you are also you</u>. Why did you try to deal with the complaints by yourself? I can't know about it if you don't tell me, right? The complaint has become serious. So it doesn't seem to be getting anywhere.'
Taro : *Hontôni   môshiwake arimasen deshita.*
really   (I am) very sorry
'I am very sorry.'

In this example, both Taro and company X are to be criticized. It might be concluded that (6-16) presupposes that in addition to the referent of the subject *anata* 'you' (that is, Taro), company X is also to be criticized. Thus, the utterance *anata mo anata yo* is regarded as an example of a juxtaposition of a person and a thing with negative features.

If the expressional form *A mo A da* encodes a juxtaposition of persons or things with negative features, it should always carry the meaning wherever it appears. In fact, however, this expectation contradicts the actual situation. Here, let us recall the concrete words used to represent negative features in the previous studies, and consider the following example:

(6-17) [There are two men in a meeting room.]

Boss : [looking at the clock] *Jikan mo jikan da. Sorosoro*
time also time COP soon
hajimeyôka.
let us start (the meeting)
'(lit.) <u>The time is also the time</u>. Let's start the meeting soon.'

Subordinate : *Sô desu ne.*
oh right COP SFP
'Oh, right. Boss.'

The boss's utterance *Jikan mo jikanda* is understood as providing grounds for starting the meeting. Possible grounds include the fact that "many people have gathered in the room", and "there are many topics to be discussed", as well as the fact that "the referent of the subject *jikan* 'time' (namely, the time at the point of utterance) is past the time scheduled for the meeting to start". Certainly, the boss's utterance can be analyzed as meaning that the referent of the subject *jikan*, that is, the time at the point of utterance, has a negative feature such as *unusual* (or *anomalous*) because the time scheduled for the meeting to start has passed. However, it is hard to say that someone or something other than the referent of the subject *A*, for example, the attendees and the topics to be discussed, can be understood as meaning a negative feature.

Similarly, Okamoto's analysis of a juxtaposition of *undesirable* persons or things cannot explain the following example:

(6-18) [A woman posts a question about wedding gifts for guests on an electronic bulletin board.]
Saikin tomodachi no kekkonshiki ni hisashiburini
recently my friend's wedding to for the first time in a long time
detandesuga, hikidemono ga kojinmarishiteite,
attend gift given to the gests SM small
un un itsumono eraberu purezento da nâ
all right always a gift could be freely chosen by the gests COP SFP
to omotteimashita. Soshite ouchini kaeritsui te
HEAR (I) knew then (I) went back (my) house and
fukuro no naka wo mitemi tara, bâmukûhen to
(I) looked into the bag if (a packet of) baumkuchen and

yubiwa	*no*	*hako*	*wo*	*sukoshi nagakushita*		*yôna*	*hako*
ring	of	box	ACC	small long		like	box
ga	*hitotsu.*	*Kono kobako*		*ni*	*eraberu gifuto*		
SM	one	this small box in		a gift could be freely chosen by the gests			
ga	*haitteiruwakedemonashi,*			*yubiwa*	*dat*	*tara*	*sugoi*
SM	not include			ring	COP	if	very
iyadanâ		*to*		*osoruosoru*		*akeruto*	
(I do) not feel good		HEAR		feel slightly worried		(I) open (the box)	
Kumano no keshôfude				*wo*	*hakken!*	*Ô*	*jiki*
a make-up brush produced in Kumano				ACC	(I) found	oh	season
mo	*jiki*	*da*	*mon*	*ne!*	*to*	*chotto*	*tenshon ga agarimashita!*
also	season	COP	because	SFP	HEAR	a little	(I) felt tense

'Recently I attended my friend's wedding ceremony and it was my first wedding in a long time. I knew that the gift given to the guests could be freely chosen by the guests since the bag containing the gift was small. Then, I went back to my house and looked into the bag. In it, I found a packet of baumkuchen and a small long gift box. When I saw the box, I guessed there was no catalog from which to make my choice. I thought I hope the gift isn't a ring. With that in mind, I opened the box feeling slightly worried and then I found that the gift was a make-up brush produced in Kumano! Oh, because (lit.) <u>the time is also the time.</u> I felt a little tense!'

(adapted from http://wa.chobirich.com/qa/show/2893, my translation)

(6-18) is part of a question about gifts given to guests at a wedding reception. At the time the question was contributed, the women's national soccer team had just received the People's Honor Award for its historic victory in the Women's World Cup final. There was a lot of talk about make-up brushes produced in Kumano, which were given to the team as a supplementary prize. In this context, it cannot be said that *jiki mo jiki da* means that the referent of the subject *jiki* 'time', namely, the point of utterance, has a negative feature. Thus, (6-18) cannot be analyzed as meaning a juxtaposition of persons or things that have a negative feature such as *undesirable*.

The above observation reveals that contrary to Moriyama's and Okamoto's claim, the isolated *A mo A da* cannot be characterized as meaning a juxtaposition of persons or things with negative features.

6.3 *A mo A da* Data

From the above discussion, it should be noted that the two previous studies deal with only part of the *A mo A da* data. Their proposals are not considered to be comprehensive analyses. Then, what is a convincing analysis of *A mo A da*? When examining several examples of *A mo A da* in concrete contexts, it seems that their interpretation involves three factors. To provide a clear explanation, the following notations are provisionally used: **P** is what is discussed at the point of utterance, **Q** is a pre-existing assumption, and **T** is an assumption that the utterance *A mo A da* evokes. Let us first consider examples (6-19) and (6-20).

(6-19) [A couple is talking about a boy named Taro and his father. The father is a notorious troublemaker.]

Wife : *Taro ga mata kurasumeito to kenkashitan datte.*
Taro SM again classmate with got into a fight HEAR
Hontoni yanchana ko yo ne.
really (he is) a naughty boy SFP SFP
'Taro got into a fight with a classmate again. He is really a naughty boy.'

Husband : *Mâ,* **oya mo oya da.** *Taro ga gakkô de*
well parent also parent COP Taro SM school P
mondai bakari okosu no mo murimonai yo.
(Taro) often gets into trouble P P no wonder SFP
'Well, (lit.) <u>the parent is also the parent</u>. No wonder Taro often gets into trouble at school.' (= (6-10))

(6-20) [Fred is talking to his elder sister Linda's husband (whose name is Douglas). Douglas is very jealous, so he has refused to let his wife meet his younger brother-in-law, Fred.]

Boku wa otôto nandesu yo. Shikamo jitsuno.
I TM younger brother COP SFP besides (we are) real family
Boku nimade yakimochiyaite, ane wo tôzaketeokukoto wa
(you are) jealous of me elder sister ACC keep away from TM
nai desho. Dôse, ie no nakani irutte koto wa wakatteirun desu yo.
don't you anyway my sister is there TM (I) know COP SFP
Yoshi, boku ga hipparidashitekuruto-shiyô. **Ane mo**

all right	I	SM	will find (my sisiter)	elder sister also

ane   desu yo. Itsumadetattemo, anatano inarininatteirun
elder sister COP SFP always   whatever (you) want (her) to do
da   kara.
COP   because

'I'm her younger brother. Besides, we are real family. You are jealous of me and you want to keep her from me, don't you? I know my sister is there. All right! I'll find her. (lit) <u>The elder sister is also the elder sister</u>. She's always doing whatever you want her to do.'

(Mariko Koike, *Daisan Suiyoobi no Jooji*, p.101, my translation)

In (6-19), the hearer (that is, the wife) would construct the following interpretation: **P** [Taro got into a fight with a classmate], because **Q** [Taro is naughty] and **T** [his father is a notorious troublemaker]. In (6-20), the hearer (Douglas) would construct the following interpretation: **P** [the speaker (Fred) cannot see his elder sister], because **Q** [he (Douglas) is extraordinarily jealous] and **T** [the elder sister (Linda) is always eager to avoid displeasing him]. In these two examples, **Q** and **T** are interpreted as providing a reason for **P**.

However, in the following example, **Q** and **T** are not considered as providing a reason for **P**.

(6-21)   [There are two men in a meeting room.]

Boss   : [looking at the wall clock] *Jikan mo   jikan   da.*
                                          time   also time   COP
             Sorosoro hajimeyôka.
             soon   let us start (the meeting)
             '(lit.) <u>The time is also the time</u>. Let's start the meeting soon.'
Subordinate : *Sô   desu   ne.*
              oh right COP   SFP
              'Oh, right. Boss.'   (=(6-17))

In (6-21), the hearer (that is, the subordinate) would construct the following interpretation: **P** ['we' shall start the meeting], not only because **Q** [many people have gathered in the room] and **Q′** [there are many topics to be discussed] but also because **T** [the time at the point of utterance is past the time scheduled for the meeting to start]. In this case, **Q**, **Q′** and **T** are regarded as providing grounds for **P**, which is why the judgment **P** is reached. Additionally, it seems to me that unlike (6-19) and (6-20) above, some assumptions corresponding to **Q** in (6-21) can be widely derived.

Furthermore, consider another example, where it is hard to identify specific assumptions corresponding to **Q**:

(6-22) [A man writes about famous sumo-lovers in his blog.]

Sugiyama Kunihiro ya Uchidate Makiko wa
Sugiyama Kunihiro and Uchidate Makiko TM
dono basho de kao wo mitemo odoroka nai ga,
at any sumo tournament if (I) see (them) (I would) not be surprised but
maikai areru 3 gatsu no osakabasho wa
every close bouts March the Osaka tournament TM
Omura Kon, Hayashiya Pee, Kyo Utako nado wa
Omura Kon Hayashiya Pee Kyo Utako and so on TM
jōren nanode tanoshimida. Shiranakattano dakedo,
regular attendees because (I) enjoy (I) did not know although
ryōrinin no Kandagawa Toshiro wa shōmen-shōbu-shinpan-seki no
chef of Kandagawa Toshiro TM the main referees' seats of
aidani suwatteiru toiu. **Basho mo basho da.**
between seated HEAR ringside seat also ringside seat COP
Kōshitsu desae anzen wo kangaete tamariseki niwa
imperial family even safety ACC think ringside seat at
suwarenai. Hitogara ga shinobareru tokoro da.
can not have a seat personality SM (one can) guess COP

'I wouldn't be surprised to meet Kunihiro Sugiyama and Makiko Uchidate at any sumo tournament. I enjoy nothing better than meeting Kon Omura, Pee Hayashi, and Utako Kyo at the Osaka tournament every March because they are regular attendees. That tournament is well known for its close bouts. Although I didn't know it before, I heard that the chef, Toshiro Kandagawa, always watches the bouts, seated between the main referees' seats. (lit.) <u>The ringside seat is also the ringside seat</u>. Even the imperial family can't have ringside seats for safety reasons. One can guess the chef's personality from that.' (= (6-11))

In (6-22), the readers would construct the following interpretation: **P** [Toshiro Kandagawa loves sumo more than any other famous sumo fans], because **Q** [?] and **T** [a ringside seat makes you feel close to bouts but involves risk]. In this case, like examples (6-19) and (6-20) above, **T** is understood as giving a reason for **P**, but it is hard to identify clearly specific assumptions corresponding to **Q**. Some readers do not seem to have much confidence in finding a concrete assumption corresponding to **Q**.

6.4   Stipulating the Meaning of *A mo A da*

Based on the observation in the previous section, the first point we notice is that the factor common to all the examples of *A mo A da* in (6-19)–(6-22) is that both **Q** and **T** are understood as providing some sort of explanation for **P**. More concretely, both **Q** and **T** explain why **P** happened, or how the speaker reached the conclusion **P**. One point I would like to add is that **Q** and **T** are understood to be temporally prior to **P**. That is exactly why a hearer needs to evoke **Q** and **T** from memory when she interprets the utterance *A mo A da*. As regards the interpretation process of *A mo A da*, the expressional form instructs a hearer to interpret it in the way described above. In other words, it constrains the hearer's inferential computation.

Second, it should be noted that in terms of constraints on inferential computation, **T** is certainly strongly derived as providing some sort of explanation for **P**, while **Q** comes with varying degrees of strength. For example, in (6-19), where Taro got into a fight with a classmate, the hearer entertains **Q** "Taro is naughty" relatively readily. The same applies to the jealous husband example (6-20). However, the other two examples appear somewhat different. In (6-21), where the boss encourages the subordinate to start the meeting, there is no single strong assumption **Q** that automatically comes to mind. The hearer entertains a less clear range of **Q**s (e.g. "many people have gathered in the room", "there are many topics to be discussed"). Thus the hearer has to take slightly greater responsibility for the resulting interpretation than she does with (6-19) and (6-20). Moreover, with the sumo wrestling example (6-22), there is no obvious strong assumption **Q**. The readers try to find an appropriate assumption **Q** from a wide range of very weak assumptions. Someone who is familiar with sumo would access entire range of available information about the chef, Toshiro Kandagawa, extend the context, and evoke an assumption such as "Toshiro Kandagawa talked about sumo with enthusiasm on a TV program". In contrast, someone who is not familiar with sumo would have great difficulty in evoking an assumption corresponding to **Q**.

The above observation reveals that **Q** comes to mind with varying degrees of strength, and when producing the utterance *A mo A da*, not all the cases evoke **Q** as strongly as **T**. Given the fact that the utterance *A mo A da* indicates **Q** ranging from a particularly strong assumption to a wide range of very weak assumptions, it can be said that the expressional form *A mo A da* instructs a hearer to "evoke **T** that is interpreted as providing one of several explanations for **P**". Following this hypothesis, the four examples discussed above can be analyzed in the same way. For instance, the utterance *oya mo oya da* in (6-19) is analyzed as evoking **T** "his father is a notorious troublemaker", which gives one of several explanations for **P** "Taro got into a fight with a classmate". Similarly, the utterance *Basho mo basho da* in (6-22) is analyzed as evoking **T** "a ringside seat makes you feel close to bouts but involves risk", which gives one of several explanations for **P** "Toshiro Kandagawa loves sumo more than any other famous sumo fans". Following this hypothesis, the four examples discussed above can be analyzed in the same way, verifying that the fact-explanation analysis of *A mo A da* is valid.

So far, I have provisionally used the following notations: **P** is what is discussed at the point of utterance and **T** is an assumption that the utterance *A mo A da* evokes. Here, I shall precisely define **P** and **T**.

First, let us concentrate on **P**. **P** in (6-19) "Taro got into a fight with a classmate" is based on the wife's previous utterance. On the other hand, **P** in (6-20) "the speaker (Fred) cannot see his elder sister" is not based on the preceding utterance, but on the preceding situation where the speaker cannot readily see his elder sister. **P** in (6-21) "'we' shall start the meeting" is based on the speaker's own utterance. **P** in (6-22) "Toshiro Kandagawa loves sumo more than any other famous sumo fans" is based on the preceding context where the writer is writing about famous sumo fans. As we have just seen, the types of **P** vary depending on the context. However, they can all be generalized as "the state of affairs that is under discussion at the point of utterance". For example, **P** in (6-19) "Taro got into a fight with a classmate" is the state of affairs that is under discussion at the point of utterance. The same characterization can be applied to (6-20)–(6-22).

Next, **T** can be generalized as an "assumption about the referent of the subject *A*, which the utterance *A mo A da* evokes". For instance, **T** in (6-19) "his father is a notorious troublemaker" is an assumption about the referent of the subject *oya* 'parent', which the utterance *oya mo oya da* evokes. Similarly, **T** in

(6-21) "the time at the point of utterance is past the time scheduled for the meeting to start" is an assumption about the referent of the subject *jikan* 'time', which the utterance *Jikan mo jikan da* evokes.

On the basis of the above discussion, this thesis proposes (6-23) as the encoded meaning of *A mo A da*.

(6-23)   The Meaning of *A mo A da* :
A mo A da must be processed in such a way as to evoke an assumption (**T**) about the referent of the subject *A* that provides one of several explanations for the state of affairs (**P**) that is under discussion at the point of utterance.

That is, by producing an utterance *A mo A da*, the speaker encourages the hearer to retrieve from her encyclopedic information about the referent of the subject *A*, an assumption that is understood as providing one of several explanations for the state of affairs that is under discussion at the point of utterance. Note that the assumption **T** communicated by the *A mo A da* utterance is not an explicature, but rather an implicature.

Before embarking on the discussion, let us examine my hypothesis about the meaning of *A mo A da* provided in (6-23) above. See (6-24). In the scenario where a boss is talking to his subordinate in a meeting room, (6-24a) the boss's utterance *Purojekutâ mo purojekutâ da* followed by *Shall we put off the meeting?* is acceptable, while (6-24b) the boss's utterance *Purojekutâ mo purojekutâ da* followed by *Shall we start the meeting?* would be unacceptable or odd. The meaning of *A mo A da* shown in (6-23) explains the difference in their acceptability.

(6-24)   [A boss is talking to his subordinate in a meeting room.]
   Boss : a.   ***Purojekutâ   mo   purojekutâ   da.***   Kaigi   wo
               projector   also   projector   COP   meeting   ACC
               enkishiyô.
               shall we put off
               '(lit.) <u>The projector is also the projector.</u> Shall we put off the meeting?'
         b. # ***Purojekutâ   mo   purojekutâ   da.***   Kaigi   wo
               projector   also   projector   COP   meeting   ACC
               hajiimeyô.

shall we start
'(lit.) The projector is also the projector. Shall we start the meeting?'

(6-24a) is acceptable since we can access an assumption (**T**) providing one of several explanations for the state of affairs (**P**) that is under discussion at the point of utterance "'we' shall postpone the meeting" (e.g. the projector in the meeting room does not work well). On the other hand, (6-24b) is not acceptable since it is difficult to access an assumption (**T**) providing one of several explanations for the state of affairs (**P**) that is under discussion at the point of utterance "'we' shall start the meeting". That is, the interpreters retrieve no appropriate assumption for starting the meeting from their encyclopedic information about projector since they usually experience smooth-running equipment in their daily routines and cannot therefore access any obvious assumption that might be interpreted as providing any one of several explanations for "'we' start the meeting". This strongly supports the meaning of *A mo A da* stipulated in (6-23).

Here, we return to the discussion about whether or not the assumption (**T**) communicated by the *A mo A da* utterance is an implicature. The discussion leads to the resolution of the following question: as briefly mentioned at the beginning of this chapter, from the husband's utterance *oya mo oya da* in (6-1) (=(6-19)), we gain the intuitive interpretation that "Taro's father is also responsible for the fight". How is such an interpretation associated with the meaning of *A mo A da* in (6-23)? To answer this question, I shall introduce the technical terms *implicated premise* and *implicated conclusion*. An implicature is an "ostensively communicated assumption which is not an explicature; that is, a communicated assumption which is derived solely via processes of pragmatic inference" (Carston 2002: 377). Implicatures fall into two categories: implicated premises and implicated conclusions. The former is "a subset of its contextual assumptions used in processing the utterance", while the latter is "a subset of its contextual implications" (ibid.: 135).

With this brief review in hand, consider again the following example:

(6-19) [A couple is talking about a boy named Taro and his father. The father is a notorious troublemaker.]
Wife : *Taro ga mata kurasumeito to kenkashitan datte.*
Taro SM again classmate with got into a fight HEAR
Hontoni yanchana ko yo ne.

| | really | (he is) a naughty boy | SFP | SFP |

'Taro got into a fight with a classmate again. He is really a naughty boy.'

Husband : *Mâ,   oya   mo   oya   da.   Taro   ga   gakkô   de*
well   parent also parent COP Taro   SM   school   P
mondai bakari okosu   no   mo   murimonai   yo.
(Taro) often gets into trouble   P   P   no wonder   SFP

'Well, (lit.) <u>the parent is also the parent</u>. No wonder Taro often gets into trouble at school.'

As we have discussed above, the husband's utterance *oya mo oya da* instructs the wife to retrieve from her encyclopedic information about Taro's father, an assumption that is interpreted as providing one of several explanations for the state of affairs (**P**) that is under discussion at the point of utterance. Let us suppose that (6-25) is included in the information:

(6-25)   Taro's father is a notorious troublemaker.

This would correspond to **T** (that is, an assumption that the utterance *oya mo oya da* evokes) in (6-19). If processed in a context containing assumption (6-25), the husband's utterance would derive the implicated conclusion (6-26e), constructing (6-26b)–(6-26d) as an implicated premise, and achieve relevance.

(6-26) a. Oya mo oya da.   (6-19) the husband's utterance
   b. Taro's father is a notorious troublemaker.   (6-25) evoked assumption
                                                                (implicated premise)
   c. If Taro's father is a notorious troublemaker, he brings about a bad influence on his child, Taro.   (implicated premise)
   d. The bad influence of Taro's father leads to Taro's bad behavior.
                                                                <u>(implicated premise)</u>
   e. Taro's father is responsible for the fight.   (implicated conclusion)

(6-26b)–(6-26d) are assumptions communicated by the speaker (that is, the husband), but do not follow deductively from the basic explicature of the husband's utterance (6-26a). It is concluded that these assumptions required for understanding utterance (6-26a) should be regarded as implicatures.

Here, recall the information that was implied by the wife, namely, that "Taro is responsible for the fight". On the other hand, as mentioned in (6-26e), the implicated conclusion, implicitly communicated by the husband, is that "Taro's father is responsible for the fight". Given this point, it is now recognized that there is a possibility that the husband intends to add some information. To put it another way, the husband intends the wife to derive parallel implications such as "Taro's father is also responsible for the fight" (which is exactly the intuitive interpretation descried at the beginning of this chapter). However, this is not the result of the information encoded in *A mo A da*, as evidenced by (6-17) and (6-18). These examples demonstrate that (the isolated) *A mo A da* cannot be characterized as meaning a juxtaposition of persons or things with negative features. (It seems to me that the notion of "parallel implications" can be regarded as being similar to the idea presented in previous studies, namely that *A mo A da* means a juxtaposition of persons or things with negative features. So I consider "parallel" and "juxtaposition" to be identical.)

6.5 Validating the Hypothesis that *A mo A da* Has a Specific Meaning

The previous section stipulated the meaning of *A mo A da*. If *A mo A da* itself encodes procedural information involved in deriving an implicature, as stipulated in (6-23), its meaning cannot be fully predicted on the basis of the meanings of the constituent parts of the sentence. This section will (i) hypothesize that the expressional form *A mo A da* has a specific meaning, (ii) present some counterarguments to the hypothesis, and (iii) reveal that the meaning of *A mo A da* cannot be explained in terms of the principle of compositionality.

In response to those who criticize my hypothesis, it might be argued that the meaning of *A mo A da* is the result of integrating the meanings of the components of the sentence. The constituents of the sentence *A mo A da* are the subject *A*, the particle *mo*, the predicate *A*, and the copular predication *da*. Critics might present counterarguments based on the following: counterarguments based on the uses of the particle *mo*, counterarguments based on formal similarities between *A mo A da* and *A mo B da*, and counterarguments from relevance theoretic perspectives.[6]

Counterarguments Based on the Uses of the Particle Mo

First, let us discuss counterarguments based on the uses of the particle *mo*.

There have been various previous studies of *mo*. The particle is classified as *kakari joshi* 'binding particle' (that is, a particle that specifies a certain expression later in the sentence) or *toritate (jo)shi* 'restrictive particle' (that is, a particle that specifically mentions a certain expression), in the Japanese grammatical category. It has generally been argued that *mo* has several meanings and usages; for example, it is used to add something and to express the speaker's high evaluation of something (cf. Teramura 1991; Numata 1986, 1995, 2009).[7] Consider the following example:

(6-27)   *Taro*   *mo*   *gakusei*   *da.*
         Taro   also   student   COP
         'Taro is also a student.'

Following the general approach, the sentence is used in a context in which there is another student. It implies that Taro and someone other than Taro (e.g. Jiro) are students. This analysis shows that the use of *mo* indicates some additional information. However, no one has yet successfully provided a systematic explanation of what kind of information is added in a context where *mo* is used. The analysis is defective. As illustrated in the next section, even if we focus on the uses and functions of *mo*, we cannot fully understand the meaning of the expressional form *A mo A da*.[8] This is because what is communicated by the expressional form *A mo A da* is complicated and varied. The analyses of *mo* cannot deal with the interpretation process of *A mo A da*.

***Counterarguments Based on Formal Similarities between* A mo A da *and* A mo B da**
     Next, critics might mention a similar form to *A mo A da*, and develop their arguments. The counterargument is that the form *A mo A da* is analogous to the form *A mo B da*, and so the meaning of *A mo A da* could be predicted by combining the meanings of the words in the sentence in the same way as that of *A mo B da*. We can respond to this objection as follows. As a first step, let us observe how *A mo B da* is understood. Consider, for example, (6-28):

(6-28)   *Haruko*   *mo*   *pianisuto*   *da.*
         Haruko   also   pianist   COP
         'Haruko is also a pianist.'

This example would be interpreted as communicating that the person referred to by the word *Haruko* is also a member of the class of *pianist*, and has the stereotypical characteristics exhibited by people in the class (e.g. a person whose occupation involves playing the piano). Then it would follow that by analogy with the similarity in the form, *A mo A da* would also be interpreted as communicating that the referent of the subject *A* is also a member of the class referred to by the predicate *A*, and has the stereotypical characteristics of people in the class. However, this view is insupportable. For instance, if the utterance *oya mo oya da* in (6-19) is interpreted in the same way as *A mo B da*, it would be interpreted as communicating that the referent of the subject *oya* (that is, Taro's father) is also a member of the class referred to by the predicate *oya*, and has the stereotypical characteristics of people in the class (e.g. bringing up children, being sober, complaining about children). In fact, as we have seen above, the utterance communicates "Taro's father is a notorious troublemaker" in the context described above. The communicated content is different from the interpretation based on the same approach as that of *A mo B da*. The same analysis can be applied to the other examples (6-20)–(6-22). Thus, it can be said that *A mo A da* is not interpreted in the same way as *A mo B da*.

A second counterargument is that, like *A mo B da*, the meaning of *A mo A da* stipulated in (6-23) implies someone or something other than the referent of the subject *A*, so its meaning can be (partly) predicted from the meaning of the particle *mo* 'also' included in the expression in question. However, this criticism is also incorrect. Here, let us again compare (6-19) *oya mo oya da* with (6-28) *Haruko mo pianisuto da*. (6-19) communicates "Taro is naughty" as well as "Taro's father is a notorious troublemaker". Each of these assumptions is interpreted as providing one of several explanations for the state of affairs (**P**) that is under discussion at the point of utterance "Taro got into a fight with a classmate". On the other hand, (6-28) implies someone other than *Haruko,* who I shall call *Natsuko* for the sake convenience. An interpreter can infer that "Natsuko is a pianist" from the utterance *Haruko mo pianisuto da*. However, the interpreter is not expected to understand the utterance to infer that "Natsuko is a pianist" and "Haruko is a pianist" must be interpreted as providing one of several explanations for the state of affairs in question. To put it simply, this utterance does not instruct a hearer to interpret it in the same way as with *A mo A da*. As we have seen, *A mo A da* is characterized in terms of inference as providing one of several explanations, while *A mo B da* is not. Therefore, the meaning of *A mo A da* can be predicted based on the expressional form itself rather than the meaning of *mo* included in the expression in question.

On the basis of the above observations, it can be said that the expressional form *A mo A da* is not interpreted in the same way as the similar expressional form *A mo B da*, which is to say that the meaning of *A mo A da* cannot be predicted by integrating the meanings of the words in the sentence in the same way as that of *A mo B da*. This conclusion corroborates the validation of the hypothesis that the expressional form *A mo A da* has a specific meaning.

Counterarguments from Relevance Theoretic Perspectives

The two counterarguments above to be disproved are based on the analogy between *A mo A da* and *A mo B da*. Furthermore, from a relevance theoretic perspective, there are two possible counterarguments for the hypothesis that *A mo A da* has a specific meaning. If I argue that the expressional form *A mo A da* itself encodes the meaning proposed in (6-23) and imposes a constraint on implicatures, I should demonstrate that the interpretation of *A mo A da* cannot be determined through the pragmatic processes involved in explicature derivation such as free enrichment and *ad hoc* concept construction, which are required in the derivation of explicature.

First, let us discuss the possibility of interpreting the expressional form via free enrichment. As outlined in 4.4.2, free enrichment is the process of adding further conceptual materials to the logical form without any linguistic mandate. For someone arguing the interpretation process of free enrichment, the predicate *A* in the utterance *A mo A da* might be understood by the addition of a constituent. For example, as shown in (6-19′), if the predicate *oya* in (6-19) would be interpreted via the process of free enrichment, the concept [who is a notorious troublemaker] would be provided contextually for purely pragmatic reasons, without being linguistically mandated.

(6-19′)   Oya mo oya [who is a notorious troublemaker] da.[9]
          'Taro's father is also a parent who is a notorious troublemaker.'

This expresses that Taro's father is a notorious troublemaker. Of course, such an interpretation shows that Taro's father makes trouble. It also implies that there is another parent who has the same character. However, the utterance *A mo A da* does not encourage us to draw such an interpretation. If it is assumed that the utterance in question gave rise to such a reading, something other than intended interpretations would be obtained. This analysis cannot account for the intended interpretations to be observed. The same thing should apply to the other examples.

Next, let us move on to the possibility of interpreting the expressional form via *ad hoc* concept construction. As we have seen in 4.4.2, *ad hoc* concept construction is the process of replacing an encoded lexical concept appearing in the logical form with a contextually adjusted one. For someone arguing the interpretation through a pragmatic process, the predicate *A* in examples (6-19)–(6-22) above can be interpreted as *ad hoc* concepts represented with an asterisk *. For instance, with the utterance *oya mo oya da* in (6-19), one might argue that the speaker uses the word *oya* to communicate a concept, which is not the lexically encoded concept, but rather something much more specific, for instance OYA* 'PARENT*'. The *ad hoc* concept would be something like "troublemaking parents". However, this apparently contextually adjusted concept should not be regarded as an *ad hoc* concept, since the range of possible interpretation provided by an *ad hoc* concept construction is severely limited by the hearer's lexical and encyclopedic knowledge regarding the original encoded concept in question. Quite clearly, in (6-19)–(6-22), the predicate *A* does not communicate a lexical meaning. Nor does it communicate encyclopedic knowledge concerning the original encoded concept *A*. As observed in the counterargument based on the analogy between *A mo A da* and *A mo B da*, for example, the encyclopedic information about *oya* 'parent' includes: bringing up children, being sober, and complaining about children. However, such a concept as "troublemaking parents" is far removed from the above encyclopedic information. The reason for this stems from the fact that assumptions communicated by the utterance *oya mo oya da* are regarded not as assumptions communicating contextually adjusted concepts of the lexical concept OYA, but as assumptions communicating information derived from the encyclopedic information of the referent of the subject *oya* (that is, Taro's father). The speaker of (6-19) intends the hearer to derive an assumption about the referent of the subject *oya*, Taro's father. The assumption (**T**) that the utterance *oya mo oya da* evokes "Taro's father is a notorious troublemaker" is not derived until the utterance itself instructs the hearer to access her encyclopedic information about the referent of the subject *oya*, which is regarded as providing one of several explanations for the state of affairs that is under discussion at the point of utterance. The same characterization can be applied to the other examples. In the course of interpreting the utterance *A mo A da*, the expressional form the speaker uses is just a hint or a clue that would help the hearer to pick out the assumption about the referent of the subject *A* that can be interpreted as one of several explanations in the fact-explanation relation. Thus, the possibility of interpretation via *ad hoc* concept construction is rejected.

As we observed above, *A mo A da* cannot be understood through the pragmatic process of free enrichment and *ad hoc* concept construction involved in explicature derivation. This strongly supports my hypothesis that *A mo A da* is an expressional form with the encoded procedural information involved in implicature derivation.

In the course of research designed to stipulate the meaning of *A mo A da*, we found that the interpretation of *A mo A da* is not fully predictable on the basis of the meanings of the constituent parts of the form. This reveals that the expressional form *A mo A da* itself encodes a procedural meaning such as (6-23).

6.6 Summary

This chapter discussed the encoded meaning of *A mo A da*. Moriyama (1989) and Okamoto (1993) argue that the meaning of *A mo A da* with a subordinate clause is a juxtaposition of persons or things with negative features such as *unusual* (*anomalous*) or *undesirable*. However, they dealt with only a small part of the *A mo A da* data, so their proposals are not considered to constitute a comprehensive theory of *A mo A da*. This chapter focused on *A mo A da*, which is not embedded in other sentences and occurs in isolation, and stipulated the following meaning: *A mo A da* must be processed in such a way as to evoke an assumption (**T**) about the referent of the subject *A* that provides one of several explanations for the state of affairs (**P**) that is under discussion at the point of utterance.

In the next chapter, I will generalize the characteristics of nominal tautologies in Japanese and English based on the research reported in this and the previous two chapters.

Notes

1 This chapter concentrates on examples of *A mo A da* involved only in the form of nominal tautology (i.e. *A mo A da*, which is not embedded in other sentences and occurs in isolation, and *A mo A da*, which is followed by *kara* 'because' and whose consequent part is not verbalized). *A* in *A mo A da* represents a noun or a noun phrase. *A mo A da* is directly translated into *A is also A*. Whether *A* in the English translation is singular or plural and whether or

not *A* in the English translation takes an article are context dependent.

As discussed in 6.2.3.1, this chapter's research target is different from Moriyama's (1989) and Okamoto's (1993). As for the difference in research target, if following the idea that a form associates with meaning, it might be concluded that the use of *A mo A da* with a subordinate clause differs from that of the isolated *A mo A da*. However, I adopt the Modified Occam's Razor principle, "senses are not to be multiplied beyond necessary" unless there is an arbitrary reason: for example, a word coincidentally encodes two or more distinct concepts (*bank*: (i) an organization that provides various financial services and (ii) the side of a river). For further discussion of Modified Occam's Razor, see Grice (1989).

2 As mentioned in chapter 5, Moriyama (1989) employs the term *futsû-dewanai* 'unusual' in two ways. Following his analysis, *A mo A da* means *futsû-dewanai* 'unusual', which is paraphrased as *ijôna* 'anomalous'.

3 Although clearly beyond the scope of the present study, Okamoto (1993) mentions that *A mo A da* is used as an adverb phrase in (i):

(i) "... *tonikaku,   kakko ii   kuruma o   te ni ireru no da*"
       at any rate, nice-looking car   (I) will get
     to honki de omotte simau no da.   Ori   mo   ori,   yuuzin no hitori
     (I) started thinking seriously that occasion also occasion one of (my) friends
     ga makka na   arufa romeo o   kawanai ka   to moti-kakete kita.
          bright red   Alfa Romeo   won't (you) buy? came to suggest that
     "'At any rate, I will get a nice-looking car," I started thinking seriously. That very moment, one of my friends came to suggest, "Won't you buy a bright red Alfa Romeo."'
                                                                                    (Okamoto 1993: 452)

Okamoto (1993) observes that *ori mo ori* in (i) intensifies the quality associated with *ori* 'occasion', and communicates the aptness of the timing. I will not argue this usage any further here.

4 Examples (6-3)–(6-5) are quoted from Okamoto (1993), so the transcription methods and conventions used for the example follow her rules.
5 Okamoto regards *Anata mo anata yo* in (6-4) as a set phrase. It can be said from this that she believes that the example has a fixed meaning and can be understood without a given context.
6 *A* and *B* in *A mo B da* represent a noun or a noun phrase.
7 Many past studies have been proposed, but there is little consensus on how many types of *mo* there are and how several types of *mo* are classified. Most Japanese linguistic researchers accept polysemous analyses with *mo*. However, I will not argue this point any further here.
8 Numata (2009) mentions the need for discussion of examples such as *Oya mo oya nara, ko mo ko da* 'If the parent is also the parent, the child is also the child', but she has provided no concrete claim.
9 It is assumed that the referent of the subject in (6-19′) has already been identified via reference assignment.

Chapter 7

The Phenomenon of Nominal Tautology in Japanese

In the previous three chapters, I have proposed a procedural encoding analysis that properly explains a wide variety of Japanese nominal tautological expressional forms. With this proposal in mind, in this chapter, I attempt to generalize the characteristics of Japanese nominal tautologies. Finally, I employ extensive English data to pin down what is common to Japanese and English nominal tautologies and pursue the possibility that nominal tautology in natural languages is an expressional form encoding procedural information.

7.1 Introduction

The previous three chapters have proposed that Japanese is a language with three kinds of expressional form of nominal tautology, each of which encodes a specific meaning. Their encoded meanings are stipulated as follows:

(7-1) **The Meaning of *A wa A da* :**
A wa A da must be processed in such a way as to communicate an assumption (**R**) that contradicts and eliminates another assumption (**Q**) about the referent of the subject *A*, attributed to someone other than the speaker at the point of utterance. (= (4-52))

(7-2) **The Meaning of *A ga A da* :**
A ga A da must be processed in such a way as to evoke an assumption (**S**) about the referent of the subject *A* that provides an explanation for the state of affairs (**P**) that is under discussion at the point of utterance. (= (5-20))

(7-3)   The Meaning of *A mo A da*:
A *mo A da* must be processed in such a way as to evoke an assumption (**T**) about the referent of the subject *A* that provides one of several explanations for the state of affairs (**P**) that is under discussion at the point of utterance.   (= (6-23))

My aim is to reveal more specifically the meaning of these three types of Japanese nominal tautology. In this chapter, using the above three stipulations as a basis, I discuss the differences between *A wa A da*, *A ga A da* and *A mo A da*, and generalize the characteristics of Japanese nominal tautology. I also propose a characteristic common to Japanese and English.

7.2   Characteristics of Japanese Nominal Tautology

I have focused on the fact that Japanese has a variety of nominal tautological forms and proposed that each of them encodes a specific meaning. Here, a question arises: how can we generalize the linguistic phenomenon of Japanese nominal tautology?

As already mentioned in chapter 4, it is generally accepted that nominal tautology can be explained in terms of negation, whose meaning varies from one researcher to another. However, in the course of research designed to determine the phenomenon of tautology in Japanese, according to (7-1), the Japanese nominal tautology *A wa A da* must be processed in such a way as to communicate an assumption (**R**) that contradicts and eliminates another assumption (**Q**) about the referent of the subject *A*, attributed to someone other than the speaker at the point of utterance. On this basis, it is concluded that the essence of negation in the phenomenon of Japanese nominal tautologies is to identify and resolve a contradiction.

I shall set aside the meaning of negation for the time being. The general view I have presented above is mainly based on data for the English nominal tautology *A is A* and data for the Japanese nominal tautology *A wa A da*. No one has yet given careful consideration to the point that there are various different expressional forms that are language dependent. The Japanese language has another two nominal tautological expressional forms: *A ga A da* and *A mo A da*. Is it really true that *negation* is a factor common to all types of Japanese nominal tautology? The answer is 'No'. According to (7-2) and (7-3), *A ga A da* and *A mo A da* have no connection with negation. In fact, they are specifically used to provide some sort of explanation for the state of affairs that is under discussion at the point of utterance. In brief, there are two factors involved in the process of interpreting Japanese nominal tautology: (i) identifying and resolving a contradiction and (ii) providing some sort of explanation for the state of affairs in question. In the next two subsections, I will describe the characteristics of the nominal tautology in Japanese.

7.2.1 Contradiction or not?

As we have already observed, *A wa A da* is specifically used for identifying and resolving a contradiction. Recall the following example:

(7-4)   [A couple is talking about their son Taro's academic record. Taro scored poorly on an exam again.]
Wife   : *Watashi mo   sonnani yoku   dekinakattashi   ne.*
          I   too very well   did not do   SFP
          Taro   bakkari   semerarenai   wa.
          Taro   only   (I will) not put a blame SFP
          'I didn't do very well, either. I won't put all the blame on him.'
Husband : *Sonnakoto   iuna   yo.*
          that   do not say   SFP
          Oya   wa oya   da*. Boku ga   hanashitemiru   yo.*
          parent TM parent COP   I   SM   try to talk (to him)   SFP
          'Don't say anything like that. (lit.) <u>Parents are parents</u>. I'll talk to him.'   (= (4-44))

In (7-4), the wife thinks that **Q** [she blames herself for Taro's poor score]. On the other hand, by uttering *Oya wa oya da*, the husband communicates that **R** [she is not blamed for Taro's poor score]. In this situation, the husband's utterance *Oya wa oya da* is interpreted as objecting to his wife. **Q** is contrary to **R**. This contradiction is resolved by eliminating **Q**. The hearer is expected to identify and resolve a contradiction. Based on this observation, it can be said that a characteristic of Japanese nominal tautology is to identify and resolve a contradiction. The characteristic applies to all cases of *A wa A da*.

Then, does the feature also apply to *A ga A da* and *A mo A da*? First, let us focus on the cases of *A ga A da*. Certainly, in contexts such as (7-5) and (7-6), the hearer might be expected to identify and resolve a contradiction.

(7-5) [X and Y are talking about an actress Haruko. She is a big-name actor's daughter.]

X : *Saikin,   Haruko   wo terebi   de   yoku mikakeru yo   ne.*
these days Haruko ACC television on often see SFP SFP
Rukkusu mo i   shi,   engi mo umaishi.
(she) looks so good and (she) performs well
'These days, we often see Haruko on television. She looks so good and performs well.'

Y : *Dakedo, oya   ga   oya   da   kara   ne.*
but   parent SM parent COP because SFP
But, because (lit.) <u>the parent is the parent</u>.'   (= (5-14))

(7-6) "*Gomennasai. — Â,   onaka ga suita.*"
sorry   ah   (I am) hungry.
Fuseijitsuna ayamarikata   da   ga,   honne   dearu.
insincere   the way of apologizing COP but real feeling COP
Pan   mo tabeteinai.   Inokori   no nakama to
bread even (I) have not eaten staying after school of group with
Fanta orenji   wo   nonda   dake da. Hontôni, pekopeko.
Fanta orange ACC (I) drank just COP really   (I am) starving
"*Jikan ga   jikan   da   kara   ne,*
time   SM   time   COP because SFP
oyatsu   nanka   tabenai   de   gohan ni shinasai."
snack   such like do not eat P   have dinner
'"Sorry, but I'm hungry." That's an insincere apology but my real feeling. I haven't even eaten any bread. I only drank Fanta orange with friends. I'm starving. "Because (lit.) <u>the time is the time</u>. Have dinner instead of eating snacks."'   (= (5-19))

In (7-5), X implies that Haruko frequently appears on television because she looks good and is a talented actress. On the other hand, Y implies that Haruko frequently appears on television because her father is a famous actor. They disagree with each other. Y's utterance *oya ga oya da* is interpreted as an objection to X. The same applies to the snack-or-dinner example (7-6). The daughter wants to eat something because she is hungry, while the mother does not want her daughter to eat snacks because dinnertime is approaching. The utterance *Jikan ga jikan da* is interpreted as expressing an objection to the daughter. Someone might argue that the expressional form *A ga A da* is specifically used for identifying and resolving a contradiction.

However, in the following example, the hearer is not expected to identify and resolve a contradiction:

(7-7)   [A couple is talking about their son Taro's academic record. Taro scored poorly on an exam again.]
Husband : *Omae, seiseki dôdatta?*
you   how were (your) grades?
'How were your grades?'
Wife   : *Un, mâ mâ. Dakara ne, Taro no seiseki ga*
well so-so   so   SFP Taro of grade SM
yokunainomo murimonai wa. Tokorode,
not very smart understandable SFP by the way
anata wa dôdatta?
how were (your grades)?
'Well, they were so-so. So it is understandable that Taro is not very smart. By the way, how were your grades?'
Husband : *Mâ mâ. Oya ga oya da.*
so-so   parent SM parent COP
Dôshiyômonai yo na.
there is nothing that can be done (about his grades) SFP SFP
'So-so. (lit.) <u>The parents are the parents</u>. There's nothing that can be done about his grades.'   (= (5-16))

As we have seen, in (7-7), the wife implies that it is understandable that Taro is not very smart. The husband's utterance *Oya ga oya da* is interpreted as agreeing with her. This example has nothing to do with the characteristic of identifying and resolving a contradiction. Based on these observations, it can be said that *A ga A da* is not solely used for identifying and resolving a contradiction.

Next, let us move on to *A mo A da*. As with the cases of *A ga A da*, the expressional form *A mo A da* is not simply used for identifying and resolving a contradiction. Recall the following examples:

(7-8)　[A couple is talking about a boy named Taro and his father. The father is a notorious troublemaker.]

Wife : *Taro ga mata kurasumeito to kenkashitan datte.*
Taro SM again classmate with got into a fight HEAR
Hontoni, yanchana ko yo ne.
really (he is) a naughty boy SFP SFP
'Taro got into a fight with a classmate again. He is a really naughty boy.'

Husband : *Mâ, oya mo oya da. Taro ga gakkô de*
well parent also parent COP Taro SM school P
mondai bakari okosu no mo murimonai yo.
(Taro) often gets into trouble P P no wonder SFP
'Well, (lit.) <u>the parent is also the parent</u>. No wonder Taro often gets into trouble at school.' (= (6-19))

(7-9)　[There are two men in a meeting room.]

Boss : [looking at the wall clock] *Jikan mo jikan da.*
　　　　　　　　　　　　　　　　　　　time also time COP
Sorosoro hajimeyôka.
soon let us start (the meeting)
'(lit.) <u>The time is also the time</u>. Let's start the meeting soon.'

Subordinate : *Sô desu ne.*
oh right COP SFP
'Oh, right. Boss.' (= (6-21))

For example, in a context such as (7-8), where the wife implies that Taro is responsible for the fight, the husband's utterance *oya mo oya da* is interpreted as agreeing with her. This example cannot be explained in terms of identifying and resolving a contradiction. In the meeting example (7-9), the utterance *Jikan mo jikan da* is used to describe a situation where the scheduled time has passed. From the above observations, it follows that *A mo A da* is not just for identifying and resolving a contradiction.

The above observations show that the expressional form *A wa A da* is specifically for identifying and resolving a contradiction, while the expressional forms *A ga A da* and *A mo A da* are not. This result reveals that *A ga A da* and *A mo A da* have a different characteristic from *A wa A da*. Then, how should *A ga A da* and *A mo A da* be characterized? I deal with this issue below.

7.2.2 Explanation or not?

Based on the meaning of *A ga A da* and *A mo A da* cited at the beginning of this chapter, I argue that their characteristic is to provide some sort of explanation for the state of affairs that is under discussion at the point of utterance. It applies to the cases of *A ga A da* and *A mo A da*. Here, recall the following example:

(7-10) [A couple is talking about a boy named Taro and his father. The father is a notorious troublemaker.]

    Wife : *Taro ga mata kurasumeito to kenkashitan datte.*
              Taro SM again classmate with got into a fight HEAR
           Hontoni yanchana ko yo ne.
           really (he is) a naughty boy SFP SFP
           'Taro got into a fight with a classmate again. He is really a naughty boy.'

    Husband : a. *Mâ, oya ga oya da. Taro ga gakkô de*
                well parent SM parent COP Taro SM school P
            mondai bakari okosu no mo murimonai yo.
            (Taro) often gets into trouble P P no wonder SFP
            'Well, (lit.) <u>the parent is the parent</u>. No wonder Taro often gets into trouble at school.' (= (5-17))

         b. *Mâ, oya mo oya da. Taro ga gakkô de*
            well parent also parent COP Taro SM school P
            mondai bakari okosu no mo murimonai yo.
            (Taro) often gets into trouble P P no wonder SFP
            'Well, (lit.) <u>the parent is also the parent</u>. No wonder Taro often gets into trouble at school.' (= (7-8))

As already observed in the other chapters, with (7-10a) the hearer would construct the following interpretation: **P** [Taro got into a fight with a classmate] because **S** [his father is a notorious troublemaker]. On the other hand, with (7-10b) the hearer would construct the following interpretation: **P** [Taro got into a fight with a classmate] because **Q** [Taro is naughty] and **T** [his father is a notorious troublemaker]. The former interpretation overlaps the latter. The reason for this is that they have something in common. What the expressional forms *A ga A da* and *A mo A da* have in common is that what each of the expressional forms evokes is interpreted as providing some sort of explanation for the state of affairs that is under discussion at the point of utterance. However, the expressional form *A wa A da* is not interpreted in the way outlined above.

Then, what are differences between the expressional forms *A ga A da* and *A mo A da*? The answer lies in whether what the expressional form in question evokes is interpreted as providing *an explanation* or *one of several explanations* for the state of affairs that is under discussion at the point of utterance.

First, let us describe the characteristic of *A ga A da*. According to (7-2), the expressional form in question must be processed in such a way as to evoke an assumption (S) about the referent of the subject *A* that provides an explanation for the state of affairs (P) that is under discussion at the point of utterance. To put it simply, what *A ga A da* evokes (S) is interpreted as providing *an explanation* for the state of affairs (P) that is under discussion at the point of utterance. As we found above, for instance, in a context such as (7-10a), the hearer would construct the following interpretation: (P) Taro got into a fight with a classmate because (S) Taro's father is a notorious troublemaker. In simple terms, what the utterance *oya ga oya da* evokes (S) is interpreted as providing *an explanation* for the state of affairs (P) that is discussion at the point of utterance. As we have discussed, the same characteristic applies to all the examples with *A ga A da* that were focused on in chapter 5.

Next, let us concentrate on *A mo A da*. According to (7-3), the expressional form *A mo A da* must be processed in such a way as to evoke an assumption (T) about the referent of the subject *A* that provides one of several explanations for the state of affairs (P) that is under discussion at the point of utterance. In short, what *A mo A da* evokes (T) is interpreted as providing *one of several explanations* for the state of affairs (P) that is under discussion at the point of utterance. In (7-10b), the hearer would construct the following interpretation: (P) Taro got into a fight with a classmate, because (Q) Taro is naughty and (T) his father is a notorious troublemaker. To put it concisely, what the utterance *oya mo oya da* evokes (T) is interpreted as providing *one of several explanations* for the state of affairs (P) that is under discussion at the point of utterance.

It can be said from this that both *A ga A da* and *A mo A da* are interpreted as providing some sort of explanation for the state of affairs that is under discussion at the point of utterance. However, there is a difference between *A ga A da* and *A mo A da* in that the former is interpreted as *an explanation* for the state of affairs in question, while the latter is interpreted as *one of several explanations* for the state of affairs in question.

The above observations show that there are two factors involved in the process of interpreting Japanese nominal tautology: (7-11(i)) identifying and resolving a contradiction and (7-11(ii)) providing some sort of explanation for the state of affairs that is under discussion at the point of utterance. The second factor is further divided into two: (7-11(iia)) what a nominal tautology evokes is interpreted as providing an explanation for the state of affairs in question, and (7-11(iib)) what a nominal tautology evokes is interpreted as providing one of several explanations for the state of affairs in question. This can be summarized as follows:

(7-11) Factors Involved in the Interpretation Process of Japanese Nominal Tautology
(i) identifying and resolving a contradiction
(ii) providing some sort of explanation for the state of affairs that is under discussion at the point of utterance
   a. what a nominal tautology evokes is interpreted as providing an explanation for the state of affairs in question
   b. what a nominal tautology evokes is interpreted as providing one of several explanations for the state of affairs in question

In past studies, little attention has been devoted to the formal variety of Japanese nominal tautologies so the clear characteristics of the formal variety have yet to be determined. In this section, I generalize the characteristics of nominal tautologies in Japanese. This result sheds new light on a discussion about the way in which really similar nominal tautological expressional forms resemble and differ from each other.

Throughout this book, I have shown that we can analyze three types of Japanese nominal tautologies as expressional forms encoding procedural information. This reveals that a procedural encoding account explains the data of Japanese nominal tautologies from a unified viewpoint. At the same time, this new approach to Japanese nominal tautologies yields a clue to understanding the universal nature of the linguistic phenomenon of nominal tautology. Finally, I shall observe the English nominal tautology *A is A*, which cannot be avoided in future research, and suggest the likelihood that this new line of research covers a wide area.

7.3 Characteristics of English Nominal Tautology

As we have already observed in chapter 1, an English nominal tautology is represented by the single form *A is A*. Japanese has three kinds of nominal tautologies: *A wa A da, A ga A da* and *A mo A da*, and these expressional forms convey different meanings. So it is hard in the English language to distinguish between these complicated meanings based only on its nominal tautological forms. It seems that this places great emphasis only on the abundance of Japanese expressional forms, or in other words, the specificity of Japanese nominal tautologies. However, after discussing only three types of Japanese nominal tautologies from a unified perspective, we can determine what direction we should take in the study of nominal tautology.

Finally, in relation to this point, I shall introduce example utterances to show how *A is A* is used and understood, and isolate what they all have in common.[1] To clarify the interpretation process, the following informal notations are used: **Q** is a pre-existing assumption, and **R** is an assumption held by the speaker. First, consider (7-12)–(7-14):

(7-12) 'What is this?' the pilot demanded.
'A ten-thousand-euro bearer bond drawn on the Vatican Bank.'
The pilot looked dubious.
'It's the same as cash.'
'Only *cash is cash*,' the pilot said, handing the bond back.
(Dan Brown, *The Da Vinci Code*, p. 340)

(7-13) 'Speedy!' shouted Powell into his radio. 'Come here!'
Speedy looked up and saw them. He stopped suddenly and remained standing for a moment. Then he turned and ran away, kicking up dust behind him. Over their radios, Donovan and Powell heard him singing a song. Donovan said weakly, 'Greg, he's crazy.'
'He's not crazy,' Powell said. '*A robot's only a robot*. There's something wrong with him that's confusing his brain patterns. Once we find out what it is, then we can fix it.'   (= (3-13))

(7-14) Secretary : [receiving a call from Mr. Burke] Mr. Burke wants to know if you've done anything on his advertising campaign.

Darrin : I haven't done a thing. You'd better tell him I have the chicken pox or something. [answering the phone] Hello, Mr. Burke. How are you? [Mr. Burke says something] No, I haven't. Not a darn thing. Well, no, Mr. Burke, I haven't forgotten about you. Just I've been snowed under with other things. [A spell is cast on Darrin.] To tell you the truth, I haven't been able to work up any enthusiasm for your product. Now look! We have a lot more important clients than you and ... The same to you, buddy.
Larry : Am I mistaken, or did you just throw an account out of the window?
Darrin : Yeah, I did. And it's about time to!
Larry : What's the matter with you? *An account's an account.*
Darrin : But there are some that just aren't worth it. And this is one of 'em. And what's more, you knew it when you gave it to me.
(*Bewitched*, Episode 48)

In (7-12), quoted from the novel *The Da Vinci Code*, the main character Langdon is trying to hand the pilot a bearer bond, but the pilot doubts that it is genuine and refuses to accept it. In this situation, Langdon thinks that Q [the bond is the same as cash]. On the other hand, by uttering *cash is cash*, the pilot communicates that R [the bond is not the same as cash]. In (7-13), two mechanics Donovan and Powell were looking for the lost robot Speedy and they finally found it out of order. In this situation, Donovan thinks that Q [Speedy is crazy]. On the other hand, by uttering *A robot's only a robot*, Powell communicates that R [Speedy is not crazy (but something is wrong)]. In (7-14) cited from an American situation comedy *Bewitched*, Darrin expresses his personal feelings on business with Mr. Burke because of his wife Samantha's witchcraft. In this situation, Darrin thinks that Q [an account with Mr. Burke should be thrown out of the window]. On the other hand, by uttering *An account's an account*, Larry communicates that R [an account with Mr. Burke should not be thrown out of the window]. In (7-12)–(7-14), Q is what is communicated by the previous speaker's (i.e. the hearer's) utterance.

Next, consider the following example. A tautological utterance is used as a response to a question.

(7-15)   Cheri Brush: He's taking a lot of ribbing from the guys in the neighborhood. I will tell you they're calling him Larry Poppins.
Dan Harris : And do you … you don't care when you hear that?
Larry Brush : *A job is a job*. I don't care about it, you know. You know, 'cuz nothing … female/ male, it doesn't matter. It's work.
(*ABC World News*, May 4, 2009)

In (7-15), on a news program discussing new gender roles, a man named Larry Brush, who works as a nurse after being laid off, gives an interview. People in general (including his neighbors) tease him since a male nurse falls outside traditional gender roles. In this situation, people in general (including his neighbors) think that **Q** [a job as a nurse is only for women]. On the other hand, by uttering *A job is a job*, Larry Brush communicates that **R** [a job as a nurse is not only for women]. Here, I would like to add that **Q** is the thought of people in general, or in other words, is attributed not to a certain kind of person (e.g. a hearer) but to people in general.

Furthermore, a tautological utterance does not always include a previous speaker's utterance. Consider (7-16):

(7-16)   Janet and Mike were really generous; they treated us to an elaborate dinner. I had a boiled lobster… I'd never had my food look at me before I was going to eat it … It was quite intimidating. However, *food is food*, and eventually I figured out how to eat the little guy.
(Kuno and Takami 2004: 5–6)

In (7-16), at a restaurant, a woman was scared of a whole boiled lobster staring her and yet finally managed to eat the lobster. In this situation, the woman (that is, the speaker of *food is food*) previously thought that **Q** [the lobster was a living creature]. On the other hand, she currently thinks that **R** [the lobster is not a living creature (that is, the lobster is an edible thing)]. This example has no previous speaker's utterance but we regard it as well-formed and we understand what the speaker intends to communicate. **Q** is a past thought of the speaker herself.

Finally, consider the following example:

(7-17)   Jake   : Nice! Good job, Nance. Good job, man.
Senior : Nance. 5′04″. You're four seconds over.

>   Jake   : Sir, give him another chance. He can make it.
>   Senior : *5'04" is 5'04"*.
>   Jake   : It's four seconds. You know how far he's come?   (= (3-17))

In (7-17), naval school students have to complete a race within five minutes. However, one of them could not finish the race within the required time. A student named Jake therefore asks his senior to allow the disqualified person Nance to pass the test. The senior rejects his request by saying *5'04" is 5'04"*. In this situation, Jake thinks **Q** [he wants his senior to give Nance another chance]. On the other hand, by uttering *5'04" is 5'04"*, the senior communicates **R** [he will not give Nance another chance].

What is common to all the examples with *A is A* from (7-12) to (7-17) is that the contradiction between **Q** and **R** is resolved by abandoning **Q**. A second common feature is that they are used to express an objection to or a rejection of an utterance or a thought attributed to someone other than the speaker at the point of utterance. For example, the utterance *cash is cash* in (7-12) is interpreted as expressing an objection to an utterance attributed to the hearer (that is, Langdon). The same characterization can be applied to the other examples (7-13) and (7-14). The utterance *A job is a job* in (7-15) is interpreted as expressing an objection to a thought attributed to people in general. The utterance *food is food* in (7-16) is interpreted as expressing an objection to a previous thought attributed to the speaker herself. The utterance *5'04" is 5'04"* in (7-17) is interpreted as expressing a rejection of an utterance attributed to the hearer (that is, Jake).

This observation shows that all of the above six examples with *A is A* are processed in a context that has a contrastive assumption, in the same way as *A wa A da*. Thus, restating this generalization in our analysis, there is at least one factor involved in the process of interpreting English nominal tautology: (i) identifying and resolving a contradiction.

(7-18)   Factors Involved in the Interpretation Process of English Nominal Tautology
(i) identifying and resolving a contradiction

This conclusion establishes a clear connection between *A is A* and *A wa A da*. Based on this connection, it is appropriate that the English nominal tautology *A is A*, which corresponds to *A wa A da*, is analyzed as an expressional form encoding procedural information. This suggests that a procedural encoding analysis generally applies to nominal tautologies in natural languages including English. I hope to have shown that an approach along these lines open up new possibilities for future research.

The account I have just proposed is far from complete; I have ignored a discussion of whether or not the meaning of *A is A* can be fully predicted on the basis of the meanings of the constituent parts of the sentences. However, previous analyses have focused on data obtained from a certain language, and in many cases on English data. As a result, a comparative study is lacking. Previous analyses have discussed English and Japanese nominal tautologies separately, but none has systematically provided an account of their similarities. This section reveals that the behavior of *A is A* and *A wa A da* converge on one basic concept in relevance theoretic terms.

7.4 Summary

My discussion, which was related to the observation of the characteristics of the phenomenon of Japanese nominal tautology, led to the conclusion that there are two factors involved in the process of interpreting Japanese nominal tautology as shown in (7-11):

(7-11) Factors Involved in the Interpretation Process of Japanese Nominal Tautology
    (i) identifying and resolving a contradiction
    (ii) providing some sort of explanation for the state of affairs that is under discussion at the point of utterance
        a. what a nominal tautology evokes is interpreted as providing an explanation for the state of affairs in question
        b. what a nominal tautology evokes is interpreted as providing one of several explanations for the state of affairs in question

On the other hand, it is concluded that there is at least one factor involved in the process of interpreting English nominal tautology as shown in (7-18):

(7-18)   Factors Involved in the Interpretation Process of English Nominal Tautology
(i) identifying and resolving a contradiction

    It is premature to talk about the characteristics common to Japanese and English nominal tautology, but from the above observations, I might propose the following. As summarized in (7-11) and (7-18), both Japanese and English have a tautological expressional form that is characterized as identifying and resolving a contradiction. On the other hand, Japanese has other tautological expressional forms that are characterized as providing some sort of explanation for the state of affairs that is under discussion at the point of utterance. The culmination of this long discussion is that the picture of the phenomenon of nominal tautology in Japanese has at last become clear.

Notes
1 This chapter focuses on *A is A*, which is not embedded in other sentences. *A* in *A is A* represents a noun or a noun phrase.

Chapter 8

Conclusion

This study has attempted to clarify the mechanism involved in interpreting nominal tautologies by focusing on *A wa A da*, *A ga A da* and *A mo A da* in Japanese and *A is A* in English. The expressional form of nominal tautology exists in most languages, yet the way it is expressed varies from one language to another. For instance, an English nominal tautology is generally expressed in the single form *A is A* since in English there is no lexical difference with the linking verb *be*. On the other hand, a Japanese nominal tautology is expressed in three different forms: *A wa A da*, *A ga A da* and *A mo A da* since in Japanese there are three particles: *wa* (topic marker), *ga* (subject marker) and *mo* (Eng. 'also'/'too').

These three expressional forms have different meanings as shown in (8-1)–(8-3):

(8-1) [A couple is talking about their son Taro's academic record. Taro scored poorly on an exam again.]
Wife : *Watashi mo sonnani yoku dekinakattashi ne. Taro bakkari*
I too very well did not do SFP Taro only
semerarenai wa.
(I will) not put a blame SFP
'I didn't do very well, either. I won't put all the blame on him.'
Husband : *Sonnakoto iuna yo.*
that do not say SFP
Oya wa oya da. Boku ga hanashitemiru yo.
parent TM parent COP I SM try to talk (to him) SFP
'Don't say anything like that. (lit.) <u>Parents are parents</u>. I try

to talk to him.'　　　　　　　　　　　　　(= (1-2), (4-44))

(8-2) [A couple is talking about their son Taro's academic record. Taro scored poorly on an exam again.]

Husband : *Omae, seiseki dôdatta?*
you　　how were (your) grades?
'How were your grades?'

Wife : *Un, mâ mâ. Dakara ne, Taro no seiseki ga*
well　so-so　so　SFP　Taro of　grade　SM
yokunainomo murimonai wa. Tokorode,
not very smart　understandable　SFP　by the way
anata wa dôdatta?
how were (your grades)?
'Well, they were so-so. So it is understandable that Taro is not very smart. By the way, how were your grades?'

Husband : *Mâ mâ. Oya ga oya da.*
so-so　parent　SM　parent　COP
Dôshiyômonai　　　　　　　　　yo na.
there is nothing that can be done (about his grades) SFP SFP
'So-so. (lit.) <u>The parents are the parents.</u> There's nothing that can be done about his grades.'　　　(= (1-3), (5-16))

(8-3) [A couple is talking about a boy named Taro and his father. The father is a notorious troublemaker.]

Wife : *Taro ga mata kurasumeito to kenkashitan datte.*
Taro SM again classmate with got into a fight HEAR
Hontoni yanchana ko　　yo ne.
really　(he is) a naughty boy　SFP SFP
'Taro got into a fight with a classmate again. He is really a naughty boy.'

Husband : *Mâ, oya mo oya da. Taro ga gakkô de*
well parent also parent COP Taro SM school P
mondai bakari okosu　　　no mo murimonai yo.
(Taro) often gets into trouble P P no wonder SFP
'Well, (lit.) <u>the parent is also the parent.</u> No wonder Taro often gets into trouble at school.'　　(= (1-4), (6-19))

However, in English it is difficult to distinguish between the three meanings based on the expressional form *A is A*, such as *Parents are parents*. This fact has interested me and has prompted two questions: how does the expressional form of nominal tautology work?; and if there is a common feature in Japanese and English nominal tautologies, what is it?

The starting point of this study was the above two simple questions about the facts of nominal tautology. To solve these two questions, I aimed (i) to stipulate the meaning of *A wa A da*, *A ga A da* and *A mo A da*, (ii) to show that each of the three expressional forms encodes a specific meaning and (iii) to generalize characteristics of Japanese and English nominal tautology and to propose their common characteristics. Further, I undertook this study as outlined below.

Chapter 2 provided general views of the concept of *tautology*. The word *tautology* has been roughly used in four ways. Two of these uses are related to this study: logical and linguistic tautology. In this study, it was important to understand the difference between them since logical tautologies ignore empirical facts but linguistic tautologies convey further information. As Ward and Hirschberg (1991: 508) state, when adopting the most straightforward definition based on propositional logic, only utterances such as *Either John will come or he won't* and *If he does it, he does it* are regarded as tautologies, but many researchers have traditionally discussed tautological utterances such as *War is war* and *Boys will be boys*. Thus, in this study, a tautology is defined as follows: *tautology* is an expression with a syntactic structure in which two nouns or noun phrases *A* are identical in form and are meaningfully linked with a certain word (i.e. the particles *wa*, *ga* and *mo* in Japanese; the linking verb *be* in English), as shown in (2-8).

Chapter 3 critically discussed previous nominal tautology studies, which have taken five approaches: radical pragmatic approaches (traditional pragmatics), radical semantic approaches, non-radical approaches, cognitive linguistic approaches and relevance theoretic approaches (cognitive pragmatics). However, all these fail to explain the process of interpreting nominal tautology. In this chapter, I presented appropriate counterexamples and refuted their claims.

In the next three chapters, I attempted to achieve goals (i) and (ii) by observing some examples in detail. First, chapter 4 focused on the Japanese expressional form *A wa A da*. It is generally accepted that a nominal tautological utterance can be accounted for in terms of negation (cf. Tsujimoto 1996; Nakamura 2000) but the use of negation varies depending on the researchers. I examined the data for *A wa A da*, and found that a speaker produces *A wa A da* to object and reject requests from others; these uses led to the conclusion that *A wa A da*, which includes no explicit negative words such as *nai* 'not', can be regarded as negation. Furthermore, introducing the notion of the *Cognitive Structure of Negation* (CSN) proposed by Yoshimura (1992, 1994, 1999), I stipulated the meaning of *A wa A da* as follows: *A wa A da* must be processed in such a way as to communicate an assumption (**R**) that contradicts and eliminates another assumption (**Q**) about the referent of the subject *A*, attributed to someone other than the speaker at the point of utterance. Then I demonstrated that the meaning cannot be expected based on the sentence's constituent parts, and proposed that the expressional form *A wa A da* encodes a specific meaning.

Chapter 5 focused on the expressional form *A ga A da*. There has been little research on *A ga A da*. As for the few previous studies, for example, Moriyama (1989) and Okamoto (1993), a detailed observation showed their claims to be incorrect. After investigating the data of *A ga A da* in the given contexts, I concluded that the expressional form encodes the following meaning: *A ga A da* must be processed in such a way as to evoke an assumption (**S**) about the referent of the subject *A* that provides an explanation for the state of affairs (**P**) that is under discussion at the point of utterance. The encoded meaning is not the result of combining the sentence's lexical items.

Chapter 6 focused on the expressional form *A mo A da*, which has attracted little attention in linguistic literature. There have been only two previous studies by Moriyama (1989) and Okamoto (1993), who claim that *A mo A da* has such a negative meaning as *unusual* (or *anomalous*) and *undesirable*. On the basis of detailed observations, I demonstrated that their claims should be rejected. The meaning is stipulated as follows: *A mo A da* must be processed in such a way as to evoke an assumption (**T**) about the referent of the subject *A* that provides one of several explanations for the state of affairs (**P**) that is under discussion at the point of utterance. This shows that the expressional form *A mo A da* itself has a specific meaning independent of the sentence's lexical items.

To achieve goal (iii), chapter 7 first identified the difference between *A wa A da*, *A ga A da* and *A mo A da*, based on the research described in the previous three chapters and generalized the characteristics of Japanese and English nominal tautologies. There are two factors involved in the process of interpreting Japanese nominal tautology: identifying and resolving a contradiction; and providing some sort of explanation for the state of affairs that is under discussion at the point of utterance. Furthermore, the second factor is divided as follows: what a nominal tautology evokes is interpreted as providing an explanation for the state of affairs in question and one of several explanations for the state of affairs in question. On the other hand, there is at least one factor involved in the interpretation process of English nominal tautology: identifying and resolving a contradiction. On this basis, it is appropriate that the English nominal tautology *A is A*, which corresponds to *A wa A da*, is regarded as an expressional form encoding a specific meaning. This suggests that a procedural encoding analysis provides nominal tautologies in natural languages including English with a unified characterization.

The discussion in this study clarified the following: (i) the meaning of three types of Japanese nominal tautologies is stipulated from a unified viewpoint, (ii) a nominal tautology encodes a specific meaning as a construction and (iii) Japanese and English have a tautological expressional form that is characterized as identifying and resolving a contradiction. The third point establishes a clear connection between *A wa A da* and *A is A*. Here, I can finally answer the two aforementioned questions. The answer to "how does the expressional form of nominal tautology work?" is that the expressional form of nominal tautology works as a construction encoding a specific meaning. The answer to "if there is a common feature in Japanese and English nominal tautologies, what is it?" is that yes, there is, and the feature is that in Japanese and English, there is a tautological expressional form that is characterized as identifying and resolving a contradiction.

The linguistic phenomenon of nominal tautology has been discussed mainly based on English data. However, the analyses cannot successfully explain the various forms of Japanese nominal tautologies, and they cannot be regarded as a promising theory. During the course of the discussion, I provide a clear picture of the mechanism involved in interpreting nominal tautologies. I hope this study will help explain a part of the world of nominal tautology.

References

Abe, Hiroshi. (2008) Tootorojii to Shukansei ni tsuite (On Tautologies and Subjectivity). *Nihonninchigengogakkaironbunshu* (*Proceedings of the 8th Annual Meeting of the Japanese Cognitive Linguistics Association*) 8: pp. 212–222.

Allwood, Jens, Lars-Gunnar Andersson and Östen Dahl. (1977) *Logic in Linguistics*. Cambridge: Cambridge University Press.

Ando, Sadao. (1986) *Eigo no Ronri, Nihongo no Ronri* (*The Logic of the English Language, the Logic of the Japanese Language*). Tokyo: Taishukan.

Araki, Kazuo and Minoru Yasui. (eds.) (1992) *Gendai Eibunpo Jiten* (*Sanseido's New Dictionary of English Grammar*). Tokyo: Sanseido.

Austin, John Langshaw. (1962) *How to Do Things with Words*. Oxford: Clarendon Press.

Blakemore, Diane. (1987) *Semantic Constraints on Relevance*. Oxford: Blackwell.

Blakemore, Diane. (1988) 'So' as a Constraint on Relevance. In Ruth Kempson. (ed.) *Mental Representation: The Interface between Language and Reality*, pp. 183–195. Cambridge: Cambridge University Press.

Blakemore, Diane. (1992) *Understanding Utterances: An Introduction to Pragmatics*. Oxford: Blackwell.

Blakemore, Diane. (1997) Restatement and Exemplification: A Relevance Theoretic Reassessment of Elaboration. *Pragmatics and Cognition* 5: pp. 1–19.

Blakemore, Diane. (2000) Indicators and Procedures: 'Nevertheless' and 'But'. *Journal of Linguistics* 36: pp. 463–486.

Blakemore, Diane. (2002) *Relevance and Linguistic Meaning: The Semantics and Pragmatics of Discourse Markers*. Cambridge: Cambridge University Press.

Blass, Regina. (1989) Pragmatic Effects of Co-ordination: The Case of 'And' in Sissala. *UCL Working Papers in Linguistics* 1: pp. 32–51. University College London.

Bulhof, Johannse and Steven Gimbel. (2001) Deep Tautologies. *Pragmatics and Cognition* 9: pp. 279–291.

Bulhof, Johannse and Steven Gimbel. (2004) A Tautology is a Tautology (or is it?). *Journal of Pragmatics* 36: pp. 1003–1005.

Carston, Robyn. (1988) Implicature, Explicature and Truth–Theoretical Semantics. In Ruth Kempson. (ed.) *Mental Representations: The Interface between Language and Reality*, pp. 151–181. Cambridge: Cambridge University Press.

Carston, Robyn. (1995) Quantity Maxims and Generalized Implicature. *Lingua* 96: pp. 213–244.

Carston, Robyn. (1996a) Metalingustic Negation and Echoic Use. *Journal of Pragmatics* 25: pp. 309–330.

Carston, Robyn. (1996b) Enrichment and Loosening: Complementary Processes in Deriving the Proposition Expressed. *UCL Working Papers in Linguistics* 8: pp. 61–88. University College London.

Carston, Robyn. (2002) *Thoughts and Utterances: The Pragmatics of Verbal Communication*. Oxford: Blackwell.

Carston, Robyn. (2004a) Explicature and Semantics. In Stephen Davis and Brendan S. Gillon. (eds.) *Semantics: A Reader*, pp. 817–845. Oxford: Oxford University Press.

Carston, Robyn. (2004b) Relevance Theory and the Saying/Implicating Distinction. In Laurence R. Horn and Gregory L. Ward. (eds.) *The Handbook of Pragmatics*, pp. 633–656. Oxford: Blackwell.

Farghal, Mohammed. (1992) Colloquial Jordanian Arabic Tautologies. *Journal of Pragmatics* 17: pp. 223–240.

Fauconnier, Gilles. (1994) *Mental Spaces: Aspects of Meaning Construction in Natural Language*. Cambridge: Cambridge University Press.

Fauconnier, Gilles. (1997) *Mappings in Thought and Language*. Cambridge: Cambridge University Press.

Fraser, Bruce. (1988) Motor Oil is Motor Oil: An Account of English Nominal Tautologies. *Journal of Pragmatics* 12: pp. 215–220.

Fujita, Tomoko. (1988) 'Une femmes est une femme': X ÊTRE X koobun Kaishaku no Kokoromi ('Une femmes est une femme': A Proposal for the Interpretation of the X ÊTRE X Construction). *Furansugogakukenkyu* (*Studies in French Linguistics*) 22: pp. 15–34.

Fujita, Tomoko. (1990) X ÊTRE X koobun Saikoo (Revisiting the X ÊTRE X Construction). *Kandagaigodaigakukiyo* (*The Journal of Kanda University of International Studies*) 2: pp. 115–133. Kanda University of International Studies.

Fujita, Tomoko. (1993) X ÊTRE X-gata koobun Daisankoo: Purototaipuriron to Sooshoobun (A Third Investigation on the X ÊTRE X Construction: Prototype Theory and Generic Sentences). *Kandagaigodaigakukiyo* (*The Journal of Kanda University of International Studies*) 5: pp. 91–109. Kanda University of International Studies.

Fukuchi, Hajime. (1985) *Danwa no Koozoo* (*The Structures of Discourse*). Tokyo: Taishukan.

Furumaki, Hisanori. (2009a) Tootorojii koobun kara Mita Dooshitsusei ni kansuru Koosatsu (A Study of Homogenization in Japanese Tautological Constructions). *KLS* 29: pp. 34–44.

Furumaki, Hisanori. (2009b) Tootorojii kara Mita Chishikikoozoo to Danwakoozoo (Understanding Japanese Tautological Constructions in Discourse). *Nihonninchigengogakkai ronbunshu* (*Proceedings of the 9th Annual Meeting of the Japanese Cognitive Linguistics Association*) 9: pp. 236–246.

Gazder, Gerald. (1979) *Pragmatics: Implicature, Presupposition and Logical Form*. New York: Academic Press.

Geurts, Bart. (1998) The Mechanisms of Denial. *Language* 74: pp. 274–307.

Gibbs, Jr. Raymond W. (1994) *The Poetics of Mind: Figurative Thought, Language and Understanding*. Cambridge: Cambridge University Press.

Gibbs, Jr. Raymond W. and Nancy S. McCarrell. (1990) Why Boys will be Boys and Girls will be Girls: Understanding Colloquial Tautologies. *Journal of Psycholinguistics Research* 19: pp. 125–145.

Givón, Talmy. (1978) Negation in Language: Pragmatics, Function, Ontology. In Peter Cole. (ed.) *Syntax and Semantics* 9, pp. 69–112. New York: Academic Press.

Glucksberg, Sam and Boaz Keysar. (1990) Understanding Metaphorical Comparisons: Beyond Similarity. *Psychological Review* 97: pp. 3–18.

Goldberg, Adele E. (1995) *Constructions: A Construction Grammar Approach to Argument Structure*. Chicago: University of Chicago Press.

Grice, Paul H. (1975) Logic and Conversation. In Peter Cole and Jerry Morgan. (eds.) *Syntax and Semantics* 3, pp. 41–58. New York: Academic Press.

Grice, Paul H. (1989) *Studies in the Way of Words*. Cambridge, MA.: Harvard University Press.

Higashimori, Isao and Akiko Yoshimura. (2003) *Kanrensei no Shintenkai* (*A New Development of Relevance Theory*). Tokyo: Kenkyusha.

Higashimori, Isao and Deirdre Wilson. (1996) Questions on Relevance. *UCL Working Papers in Linguistics* 8: pp. 111–124. University College London.

Higuchi, Mariko. (1988) Tootorojii no Imirikai (Understanding Tautology). *Kwassuironbunshu* (*Kwassui Bulletin*) 31: pp. 167–186. Kwassui Women's University.

Hirai, Akinori. (1992) On English Nominal Tautologies. *Shimanedaigakuhoobungakubukiyo* (*Memoirs of the Faculty of Law and Literature*) 17 (2): pp. 11–34. Shimane University.

Hirai, Akinori. (1995) Eigo no Meishiku Tootorojii no Hatsuwajookyoo ni tsuite (On Discourse Situations of English Nominal Tautologies). *Shimanedaigakuhoobungakubukiyo* (*Memoirs of the Faculty of Law and Literature*) 24: pp. 139–167. Shimane University.

Hirai, Akinori. (1997) Nichi-eigo no Meishiku Tootorojii ni kansuru Ichikoosatsu (A Study of Japanese and English Nominal Tautologies). *Shimadaigengobunka* (*Studies in Language and Culture*) 3: pp. 15–41. Shimane University.

Hirai, Akinori. (1998) Meishiku Tootorojii no Koozoo (The Structures of Nominal Tautologies). *Shimadaigengobunka* (*Studies in Language and Culture*) 6: pp. 29–63. [reprinted in Takahiro Otsu, Nobuaki Nishioka and Kenji Matsuse. (eds.) (2005) *Kotoba no Shirube: Hirai Akinori-kun Tsuitoo Ronbunshu* (*An Invitation of Language: The Memorial Collection of Papers for Akinori Hirai*), pp. 1–24. Fukuoka: Kyushu University Press.]

Horn, Laurence R. (2001^2) *A Natural History of Negation*. Chicago: University of Chicago Press.

Huang, Yan. (2007) *Pragmatics*. New York: Oxford University Press.

Ifantidou-Trouki, Elly. (1993) Sentential Adverbs and Relevance. *Lingua* 90: pp. 69–90.

Imai, Kunihiko and Yuji Nishiyama. (2012) *Kotoba no Imi towa Nandaroo: Imiron to Goyooron no Yakuwari* (*What is a Meaning of Language?: Functions of Semantics and Pragmatics*). Tokyo: Iwanami Shoten.

Kawakami, Seisaku. (1996) *Ninchigengogaku no Kiso* (*An Introduction to Cognitive Linguistics*). Tokyo: Kenkyusha.

Kay, Paul and Charles Fillmore. (1999) Grammatical Constructions and Linguistic Generalization: The 'What's X doing Y?'. *Language* 75: pp. 1–33.

Koizumi, Tamotsu. (1997) *Jooku to Retorikku no Goyooron* (Pragmatics of Jokes and Rhetorics). Tokyo: Taishukan.

Koya, Itsuki. (1993) Kanjootooei no 'Mo': sono Toogoteki Imiteki Tokuchoo ('Mo' as a Marker of Emotive Projections: its Syntactic and Semantic Features). *Kyoyoronso* 94: pp. 49–63. Keio University.

Koya, Itsuki. (1997) Kopyurabun to Shuujibun (Copular and Rhetorical Sentences). *Japanese Language Education in Europe* 2: pp. 35–46.

Koya, Itsuki. (2002) Tootorojii to Ryoogisei (Tautologies and Ambiguity). *Keiogijukudaigakugengobunkakenkyushokiyo* (*Reports of the Keio Institute of Cultural and Linguistic*

Studies) 34: pp. 1–25. The Keio Institute of Cultural and Linguistic Studies.
Koya, Itsuki. (2003) Shugo to Shugohogo no Imironkoo (Semantics of Subjects and Predicate Nominals). *Kyoyoronso* 120: pp. 1–30. Keio University.
Kubo, Tomoyuki. (1992) Nihongo no Doogohanpukukopyurabun ni kansuru Oboegaki: 'Jikan wa jikan da' to 'Jikan ga Jikan da' (A Note of Tautological Copular Sentences in Japanese: 'Jikan wa jikan da' and 'Jikan ga Jikan da'). *Fukuokakyoikudaigakukokugokakenkyuronshu* (*Bulletin of the Department of Japanese Language of Fukuoka University of Education*) 33: pp. 44–56. Fukuoka University of Education.
Kumamoto, Chiaki. (1992) Nichi-eigo no Kopyurabun ni kansuru Ichikoosatsu (A Study of Copular Sentences in English and Japanese). *Sagadaigakueibungakukenkyu* (*The University of Saga Studies in English*) 20: pp. 49–67. University of Saga.
Kuno, Susumu. (1973a) *Nihon Bunpo Kenkyu* (*A Study of Japanese Grammar*). Tokyo: Taishukan.
Kuno, Susumu. (1973b) *The Structure of the Japanese Language*. Cambridge, MA.: The MIT Press.
Kuno, Susumu and Ken-ichi Takami. (2004) *Nazotoki no Eibunpo: Kanshi to Meishi* (*A Solution to English Grammar: Articles and Nouns*). Tokyo: Kurosio Publishers.
Kuroda, Shige-yuki. (1979) *Generative Grammatical Studies in the Japanese Language*. New York: Garland.
Lakoff, George. (1987) *Women, Fire, and Dangerous Things: What Categories Reveal about the Mind*. Chicago: University of Chicago Press.
Levinson, Stephen C. (1983) *Pragmatics*. Cambridge: Cambridge University Press.
Lyons, John. (1977a) *Semantics* I. Cambridge: Cambridge University Press.
Lyons, John. (1977b) *Semantics* II. Cambridge: Cambridge University Press.
Masuoka, Takashi. (1990) Toritate no Shooten (Focuses of Restrictive Particles). *Nihongogaku* (*Japanese Linguistics*) 9 (5): pp. 4–15.
Matsui, Tomoko. (2002) Semantics and Pragmatics of a Japanese Discourse Marker 'Dakara' ('So'/ 'In other words'): A Unitary Account. *Journal of Pragmatics* 34: pp. 867–891.
Meibauer, Jörg. (2005) Lying and Falsely Implicating. *Journal of Pragmatics* 37: pp. 1373–1399.
Mikami, Akira. (1960) *Zoo wa Hana ga Nagai* (*The Elephant has a Long Trunk*). Tokyo: Kurosio Publishers.
Mikami, Akira. (1963) *Nihongo no Ronri* (*The Logic of the Japanese Language*). Tokyo: Kurosio Publishers.
Miki, Etsuzo. (1996) Evocation and Tautologies. *Journal of Pragmatics* 25: 635–648.
Mizuta, Yoko. (1995) Tootorojii ga Imi wo Motsu Toki (When Tautologies Have Meaning). *Gengo* (*Language*) 24 (13): pp. 52–55.
Mizuta, Yoko. (1996) Nominal-Predicate Sentence of Rhetorical Nature. *Osaka University Journal of Language and Culture* 5: pp. 75–90. Osaka University.
Mori, Sadashi. (1993) Tootorojii ni kansuru Ninchigengotekikoosatsu (A Cognitive Linguistic Analysis of Tautologies). *KLS* 13: pp. 13–22.
Moriyama, Takuro. (1989) Jidoo Hyoogen wo Megutte (On Japanese Nominal Tautologies). *Machikaneyamaronso Nihongakuhen* (*Machikaneyama Ronso Japanology*) 23: pp. 1–13. Osaka University.
Morimoto, Toshiyuki. (1999) Tootorojii ni okeru Kaishakutekihyoogen ni tsuite (On Interpretive Representation in Tautology). *Nagoyadaigakugengogakuronshu* (*Nagoya Working Papers in Linguistics*) 15: pp. 23–35. Nagoya University.

Murao, Haruhiko. (1991) Eigo Tootorojii no Imi to Kinoo (Meanings and Functions of English Tautologies). *Kyudaieibungaku* (*Kyushu University English Review*) 34: pp. 187–204. Kyushu University.

Nakajima, Satoshi. (2007) *Ronrigaku* (*Logic*). Okayama: Fukuro Publishers.

Nakamura, Yoshihisa. (2000) 'Kachi wa Kachi' 'Make wa Make': Tootorojii ni Hisomu Ninchitekihitei ('Victory is Victory' 'Defeat is Defeat': Cognitive Negation Hidden in Tautologies). *Gengo* (*Language*) 29 (11): pp. 71–76.

Nakamura, Yoshihisa. (2010) Hitei to (Kan-)Shukansei: Ninchibunpo ni okeru Hitei (Negation and (Inter-)Subjectivity: Negation in Cognitive Grammar). In Yasuhiko Kato, Akiko Yoshimura and Ikumi Imai. (eds.) *Hitei to Gengorikai* (*Negation and Understanding Language*), pp. 424–442. Tokyo: Kaitakusha.

Nakatsuji, Toshiaki. (2007) Tootorojii ni tsuite no Ichikoosatsu (A Study of Tautologies). *Oitadaigakukeizaironshu* (*Oita University Economic Review*) 58: pp. 79–100. Oita University.

Nishikawa, Mayumi. (2003) Tootorojii no Koosatsu: Ad hoc Gainen no Kanten kara (Tautology from the Perspective of Ad hoc Concept). *Goyooronkenkyu* (*Studies in Pragmatics*) 5: pp. 45–58.

Nishiyama, Yuji. (2001) Kanrensei Riron (Relevance Theory). In Yukio Tsuji. (ed.) *Kotoba no Ninchikagaku Jiten* (*A Dictionary of Cognitive Science of Language*), pp. 294–303. Tokyo: Taishukan.

Nishiyama, Yuji. (2003) *Nihongo Meishiku no Imiron to Goyooron: Shijiteki Meishiku to Hi-shijiteki Meishiku* (*Semantics and Pragmatics of Noun Phrases in Japanese: Referential Noun Phrases and Non-referential Noun Phrases*). Tokyo: Hituzi Syobo.

Nishiyama, Yuji and Koji Mineshima. (2005) Semantic Constraints on Free Enrichment. A manuscript of delivered at the 9th International Pragmatics Conference.

Nishiyama, Yuji and Koji Mineshima. (2006) Jojutsu Meishiku to Goyoorontekikaishaku (Predicate Nominals and Pragmatic Interpretation). In Takashi Iida. (ed.) *Language, Culture and European Tradition III: Tradition and Innovation*, pp. 21–50. The Keio Institute of Cultural and Linguistic Studies.

Nishiyama, Yuji and Koji Mineshima. (2007) Property Expressions and the Semantics-Pragmatics Interface. In Piotr Cap and Joanna Nijakowska. (eds.) *Current Trends in Pragmatics*, pp. 130–151. Cambridge: Cambridge Scholars Publishing.

Noda, Hisashi. (1996) *'Wa' to 'Ga'* (*'Wa' and 'Ga'*). Tokyo: Kurosio Publishers.

Numata, Yoshiko. (1986) Toritateshi (Restrictive Particles). In Kei-ichiro Okutsu, Yoshiko Numata and Takeshi Sugimoto. (eds.) *Iwayuru Nihongojoshi no Kenkyu* (*A Study of So-called Japanese Particles*), pp.105–391. Tokyo: Bonjinsha.

Numata, Yoshiko. (1995) Gendai Nihongo no 'Mo': Toritateshi to sono Shuuhen ('Mo' in Modern Japanese: Restrictive Particles and Related Issues). *'Mo' no Gengogaku* (*Linguistics of 'Mo'*), pp. 13–76. Tokyo: Hituzi Syobo.

Numata, Yoshiko. (2009) *Gendai Nihongo Toritashi no Kenkyu* (*A Study of Restrictive Particles in Modern Japanese*). Tokyo: Hituzi Syobo.

Ogata, Takafumi. (2006a) Sooshoobun to Kategorii (Generic Sentences and Category). *Kokusaibunkakenkyusyoronso* (*Bulletin of the International Cultural Research*) 17: pp. 39–55. Chikushi Jogakuen University and Junior College.

Ogata, Takafumi. (2006b) Tootorojii: Haikeika niyoru Kyoochoo (Tautologies: Emphasis through Grounding). *Chikushijogakuendaigaku·chikushijogakuentankidaigakubukiyo* (*Journal of Chikushi Jogakuen University and Junior College*) 1: pp. 31–47. Chikushi Jogakuen University and Junior College.

Ogata, Takafumi. (2007) Sooshoomeishi kara Mita Tootorojii (Generic Nouns in Nominal Tautologies). *Chikushijogakuendaigaku·chikushijogakuentankidaigakubukiyo* (*Journal of Chikushi Jogakuen University and Junior College*) 2: pp. 11–26. Chikushi Jogakuen University and Junior College.

Okamoto, Shigeko. (1993) Nominal Repetitive Constructions in Japanese: The 'Tautology' Controversy Revisited. *Journal of Pragmatics* 20: pp. 433–466.

Okubo, Tomonori. (1999) 'X wa X da' 'Kono X wa X dewanai' no Gengonaironshooriron ni motozuku Koosatsu (A Study of 'X wa X da' 'Kono X wa X dewanai' based on the Theory of Argumentations in Language). *Osakadaigakugengobunkagaku* (*Osaka University Journal of Language and Culture*) 8: pp. 77–91. Osaka University.

Okubo, Tomonori. (2000) Gijidoogohanpuku to Gijimujunbun (Pseudotautologies and Pseudocontradictions). *Bungakuronshu* (*Essays and Studies*) 49 (4): pp. 23–40. Kansai University.

Ohno, Susumu. (1987) *Nihongo no Bunpo wo Kangaeru* (*Thinking about Japanese Grammar*). Tokyo: Iwanami Shoten.

Ota, Akira. (1980) *Hitei no Imi* (*Meaning of Negation*). Tokyo: Taishukan.

Partee, Barbara H., Alice ter Meulen and Robert E. Wall. (1990) *Mathematical Methods in Linguistics*. Dordrecht: Kluwer Academic.

Pilkington, Adrian. (2010) Metaphor Comprehension: Some Questions for Current Accounts in Relevance Theory. In Belén Soria and Esther Romero. (eds.) *Explicit Communication: Robyn Carston's Pragmatics*, pp. 156–172. New York: Palgrave Macmillan.

Prince, Ellen F. (1978) A Comparison of Wh-clefts and It-clefts in Discourse. *Language* 54: pp. 883–906.

Recanati, François. (1993) *Direct Reference: Form Language to Thought*. Oxford: Blackwell.

Recanati, François. (2004) *Literal Meaning*. Cambridge: Cambridge University Press.

Sakahara, Shigeru. (1985) *Nichijoogengo no Suiron* (*Inference in Natural Language, Cognitive Science Series* 2) [reprinted in 2007 as *Cognitive Science Series* 4]. Tokyo: University of Tokyo Press.

Sakahara, Shigeru. (1990) Yakuwari, 'Ga' / 'Wa', Unagibun (Roles, the Particles 'Ga' / 'Wa', 'Eel' sentences). *Ninchikagaku no Hatten* (*A Development of Cognitive Science*) 3, pp. 29–66. Tokyo: Kodansha.

Sakahara, Shigeru. (1993) Tootorojii ni tsuite (On Tautologies). *Tokyodaigakukyooyoogakubugaikokugokakenkyukiyo* (*Proceedings of the Foreign Language Sections, Graduate School of Arts and Sciences, College of Arts and Sciences, the University of Tokyo*) 40 (2): pp. 57–83. College of General Education, University of Tokyo.

Sakahara, Shigeru. (2001) Mental Supeesu Riron (Mental Space Theory). In Yukio Tsuji. (ed.) *Kotoba no Ninchikagaku Jiten* (*A Dictionary of Cognitive Science of Language*), pp. 316–332. Tokyo: Taishukan.

Sakahara, Shigeru. (2002) Tootorojii to Kategorika no Dainamizumu (Tautologies and Dynamism of Categorization). In Yoshio Ohori. (ed.) *Ninchigengogaku 2: Kategoriika* (*Cognitive Linguistics* 2: *Categorization*), pp. 105–134. Tokyo: University of Tokyo Press.

Sakahara, Shigeru. (2006) Tootorojii to Kategorisaihensei no Dainamizumu (Tautologies and Dynamism of Reorganizing Category). A handout presented at the 31st Annual Conference of Kansai Linguistic Society.
Sakai, Tomohiro. (2005) On Tautologies of the Type *Hitchcock is Hitchcock* in Japanese. *KLS* 25: pp. 359–369.
Sakai, Tomohiro. (2006a) Kotaikan no Dooitsusei wo Danteisuru Tootorojii (Tautologies to Assert Homogeneity between Individuals). *Résonances* 4: pp. 75–80. University of Tokyo.
Sakai, Tomohiro. (2006b) Saihitei-gata Tootorojii (Difference Denying Tautologies). *Ninchigengogakuronkoo* (*Studies in Cognitive Linguistics*) 5: pp. 119–144. Tokyo: Hituzi Syobo.
Sakai, Tomohiro. (2007a) Nihongo ni okeru Buntekitootorojii to Jutsugotekitootorojii (Sentential and Predicative Tautologies in Japanese). *Meiseidaigakukenkyukiyo* (*Bulletin of Meisei University*) 15: pp. 162(79)–152(89). Meisei University.
Sakai, Tomohiro. (2007b) Heiretsu-gata Tootorojii no Kaishaku Sukiima (An Interpretive Schema of Parallel Tautologies). *KLS* 32: pp. 87–97.
Sakai, Tomohiro. (2008a) Heiretsu-gata Tootorojii to Retorikku (Parallel Tautologies and Rhetoric). In Yu-ichi Mori, Yoshiki Nishimura, Susumu Yamada and Mitsuaki Yoneyama. (eds.) *Kotoba no Dainamizumu* (*Dynamisms in Language*). Tokyo: Kurosio Publishers.
Sakai, Tomohiro. (2008b) Macchingu to Tootorojii no Dentatsujoohoo (Matching and Information Conveyed by Tautologies). *Nihonninchigengogakkaironbunshu* (*Proceedings of the 8th Annual Meeting of the Japanese Cognitive Linguistics Association*) 8: pp. 483–493.
Sakai, Tomohiro. (2009a) Tootorojii to Zenshoomeidai (Tautologies and Universal Propositions). *Nihonninchigengogakkaironbunshu* (*Proceedings of the 9th Annual Meeting of the Japanese Cognitive Linguistics Association*) 9: pp. 225–235.
Sakai, Tomohiro. (2009b) Tootorojii no Gengotekiimi to Daiichijigoyoorontekipurosesu (The Linguistic Meaning of Tautologies and Primary Pragmatic Processes). *Nihongoyoorongakkai daijuuikkaitaikaihappyouronbunshu* (*Proceedings of the 11th Conference of the Pragmatics Society of Japan*) 4: pp. 47–54.
Sakai, Tomohiro. (2010) Tootorojii no Shukansei no Gensen denai Mono (What is not the Source of Subjectivity in Tautology). *Tokyodaigakugengogakuronshu* (*Tokyo University Linguistic Papers*) 30: pp. 195–214. University of Tokyo.
Sakai, Tomohiro. (2012a) Contextualizing Tautologies: From Radical Pragmatics to Meaning Eliminativism. *English Linguistics* 29 (1): pp. 38–68.
Sakai, Tomohiro. (2012b) *Tootorojii no Imi wo Koochikusuru: 'Iminonai' Nichijoogengo no Imiron* (*Constructing Meanings of Tautologies: Semantics of 'Meaningless' Daily Language*). Tokyo: Kurosio Publishers.
Sasamoto, Ryoko. (2012) Silence in Ostensive Communication. In Akiko Yoshimura, Ayumi Suga and Naoko Yamamoto. (eds.) *Kotoba wo Mitsumete: Uchida Seiji Kyooju Taikan Kinen Ronbunshu* (*Observing Linguistic Phenomena: A Festschrift for Professor Seiji Uchida on the Occasion of His Retirement from Nara Women's University*), pp. 437–449. Tokyo: Eihōsha.
Sato, Nobuo. (1987) *Retorikku no Shoosoku* (*Movements of Rhetoric*). Tokyo: Hakusuisha.
Sato, Nobuo. (1992) *Retorikku Ninshiki* (*Rhetoric Recognition*). Tokyo: Kodansha.
Sato, Nobuo. (1993) *Retorikku no Kigooron* (*Semiotics of Rhetoric*). Tokyo: Kodansha.
Sawada, Nobushige. (1962) *Gendai Ronrigaku Nyuumon* (*An Introduction to Modern Logic*). Tokyo: Iwanami Shoten.

Seto, Ken-ichi. (1997) *Ninshiki no Retorikku (Rhetoric of Recognition)*. Tokyo: Kaimeisha.
Seto, Ken-ichi. (2002) *Nihongo no Retorikku (Rhetoric of the Japanese Language)*. Tokyo: Iwanami Shoten.
Sohmiya, Kiyoko. (2001) *Lewis Carroll no Imiron (Lewis Carroll's Semantics)*. Tokyo: Taishukan.
Sperber, Dan. (1994) Understanding Verbal Understanding. In Jean Khalfa. (ed.) *What is Intelligence?*, pp. 179–198. Cambridge: Cambridge University Press.
Sperber, Dan. (ed.) (2000) *Metarepresentation: A Multidisciplinary Perspective*. Oxford: Oxford University Press.
Sperber, Dan and Deirdre Wilson. (1986, 1995^2) *Relevance: Communication and Cognition*. Oxford: Blackwell.
Sperber, Dan and Deirdre Wilson. (1998) Irony and Relevance: A Replay to Seto, Hamamoto and Yamanashi. In Robyn Carston and Seiji Uchida. (eds.) *Relevance Theory: Applications and Implications*, pp. 283–293. Amsterdam: John Benjamins.
Takizawa, Osamu. (1996) Nihongo Shuujihyoogen no Koogakutekikaiseki (A Technological Analysis of Japanese Rhetorical Expressions). Unpublished Ph. D. dissertation, Osaka University.
Takizawa, Osamu and Hitoshi Isahara. (1997) A Computational Model for Understanding Rhetorical Tautologies. *International Journal of Psycholinguistics* 13: pp. 55–65.
Tanaka, Keiko. (1988) 'Wa' & 'Ga': A Pragmatic Approach to Japanese Particles. Unpublished manuscript.
Taylor, John R. (2003^3) *Linguistic Categorization*. Oxford: Oxford University Press.
Taylor, John R. and Ken-ichi Seto. (2008) *Ninchibunpo no Essensu* (The Essence of Cognitive Grammar). Tokyo: Taishukan.
Teramura, Hideo. (1991) *Nihongo no Shinttakusu to Imi (Syntax and Meanings of the Japanese Language)* III. Tokyo: Kurosio Publishers.
Tsujimoto, Tomoko. (1996) Tautology in Discourse. In Committee for Publishing a Festschrift for Professor Yoseharu Ozaki and Professor Masahiko Onuma on the Occasion of Their Retirements from Nara Women's University. (ed.) *Ozaki Yoseharu, Onuma Masahiko Ryookyooju Taikan Kinen Ronbunshu (A Festschrift for Professor Yoseharu Ozaki and Professor Masahiko Onuma on the Occasion of Their Retirements from Nara Women's University)*, pp. 127–136. Kyoto: Aporonsha.
van der Sandt, Rob A. (1991) Denial. *Chicago Linguistic Society* 27: pp. 331–344.
Ward, Gregory and Julia Hirschberg. (1988) The Pragmatics of Tautology. *Northwestern University Working Papers in Linguistics* 2 (spring): pp. 1–15. Northwestern University.
Ward, Gregory and Julia Hirschberg. (1991) A Pragmatic Analysis of Tautological Utterances. *Journal of Pragmatics* 15: pp. 507–520.
Wierzbicka, Anna. (1987) Boys will be Boys: 'Radical Semantics' vs. 'Radical Pragmatics'. *Language* 63: pp. 95–114.
Wierzbicka, Anna. (1988) Boys will be Boys: A Rejoinder to Bruce Fraser. *Journal of Pragmatics* 12: pp. 221–224.
Wierzbicka, Anna. (2003^2) *Cross-Cultural Pragmatics*. Berlin: Mouton de Gruyter.
Wilson, Deirdre. (2000) Metarepresentation in Linguistic Communication. In Dan Sperber. (ed.) *Metarepresentations: A Multidisciplinary Perspective*, pp. 411–441. Oxford: Oxford University Press.

Wilson, Deirdre. (2010) Parallels and Differences in the Treatment of Metaphor in Relevance Theory and Cognitive Linguistics. *UCL Working Papers in Linguistics* 22: pp. 41–55. University College London.
Wilson, Deirdre and Dan Sperber. (1988) Representation and Relevance. In Ruth Kempson. (ed.) *Mental Representation: The Interface between Language and Reality*, pp. 133–153. Cambridge: Cambridge University Press.
Wilson, Deirdre and Dan Sperber. (1992) On Verbal Irony. *Lingua* 87: pp. 53–76.
Wilson, Deirdre and Dan Sperber. (1993) Linguistic Form and Relevance. *Lingua* 90: pp. 1–25.
Wilson, Deirdre and Dan Sperber. (2000) Truthfulness and Relevance. *UCL Working Papers in Linguistics* 12: pp. 215–254. University College London.
Wilson, Deirdre and Dan Sperber. (2004) Relevance Theory. In Laurence R. Horn and Gregory L. Ward. (eds.) *The Handbook of Pragmatics*, pp. 607–632. Oxford: Blackwell.
Wittgenstein, Ludwing. (1922) *Tractatus Logico-Philosophicus*. London: Routledge and Kegan Paul.
Yamamoto, Naoko. (2007a) Tootorojii no Hatsuwakaishaku wo Megutte (On Tautological Utterances). *Ningenbunkakenkyukakiyo* (*Annual Reports of Graduate School of Humanities and Sciences*) 22: pp. 145–157. Nara Women's University.
Yamamoto, Naoko. (2007b) Suushi wo Tomonau Tootorojii (Nominal Tautologies with Number Terms). *Nihongoyoorongakkaidaikyukaitaikaihappyouronbunshu* (*Proceedings of the 9th Conference of Pragmatics Society of Japan*) 2: pp. 143–150.
Yamamoto, Naoko. (2008a) Cognitive Aspects of Tautology. *JELS* 25: pp. 265–274.
Yamamoto, Naoko. (2008b) Tootorojii ga Mochiirareru Bunmyaku ni kansuru Ichikoosatsu (The Usage of Tautology). *Ningenbunkakenkyukakiyo* (*Annual Reports of Graduate School of Humanities and Sciences*) 23: pp. 105–116. Nara Women's University.
Yamamoto, Naoko. (2009) 'Shosen' ni kansuru Ichikoosatsu (On the Procedural Meaning of 'Shosen'). *Nihongoyoorongakkaidaijuuikkaitaikaihappyouronbunshu* (*Proceedings of the 11th Conference of Pragmatics Society of Japan*) 4: pp. 143–150.
Yamamoto, Naoko. (2010) 'A ga A da' koobun ni kansuru Kisotekikoosatsu (On the 'A ga A da' Construction). *JELS* 27: pp. 307–316.
Yamamoto, Naoko. (2011) 'A mo A da' koobun no Imikaishaku (An Interpretation of 'A mo A da' in Japanese). *Nihongoyoorongakkaidaijuusankaitaikaihappyouronbunshu* (*Proceedings of the 13th Conference of Pragmatics Society of Japan*) 6: pp. 137–144.
Yamamoto, Naoko. (2012) 'A ga A da' ga Imisurumono. In Akiko Yoshimura, Ayumi Suga and Naoko Yamamoto. (eds.) *Kotoba wo Mitsumete: Uchida Seiji Kyooju Taikan Kinen Ronbunshu* (*Observing Linguistic Phenomena: A Festschrift for Professor Seiji Uchida on the Occasion of His Retirement from Nara Women's University*), pp. 503–510. Tokyo: Eihōsha.
Yamamoto, Naoko. (2013a) An Examination of the Controversy over English Nominal Tautologies. *Annual Reports of Graduate School of Humanities and Sciences* 28: pp. 13–28. Nara Women's University.
Yamamoto, Naoko. (2013b) Nihongo Meishiku Tootorojii 'A mo A da' no Ninchigoyooronteki kenkyu (A Cognitive Pragmatic Study of the Japanese Nominal Tautology 'A mo A da'). *Goyooronkenkyu* (*Studies in Pragmatics*) 14: pp. 20–36.
Yamamoto, Naoko. (2013c) Nihongo Meishiku Tootorojii Saikoo: 'A wa A da' (Revisiting Japanese Nominal Tautologies: 'A wa A da').

Nihongoyoorongakkaidaijuugokaihappyouronbunshu (*Proceedings of the 15th Conference of Pragmatics Society of Japan*) 8: pp. 269–272.

Yasui, Minoru. (2007) *Shinpan Gengai no Imi 1* (*A New Edition Connotative Meaning* 1). Tokyo: Kaitakusha.

Yasui, Minoru. (2007) *Shinpan Gengai no Imi 2* (*A New Edition Connotative Meaning* 2). Tokyo: Kaitakusha.

Yasui, Sen. (1980) Eigo no 'Be' dooshi no Tagisei: Yottsu no 'Be' no Toositsusei to Ishitsusei (Ambiguity of the English 'Be' verb: Homogeneity and Heterogeneity of Four types of the 'Be' verb). *Eigogaku* (*English Linguistics*) 23: pp. 40–67.

Yoshimura, Akiko. (1992) The Cognitive Structure of Negation as an NPI-Licensing Condition. *English Linguistics* 9: pp. 244–264.

Yoshimura, Akiko. (1994) A Cognitive Constraint on Negative Polarity Phenomena. *Proceedings of the 20th Annual Meeting of the Berkeley Linguistics Society* 20: pp. 599–610.

Yoshimura, Akiko. (1999) *Hitei Kyokusei Gensho* (*Negative Polarity Phenomena*). Tokyo: Eihōsha.

Yoshimura, Akiko. (2000) The Target of Metalinguistic Use of Negation: A Unified Characterization from the Cognitive Processing Point of View. *Bulletin of the Language Institute of Gakushuin University* 24: pp. 109–118.

Yoshimura, Akiko. (2010) Nihongo no Metagengohitei to 'Wake dewa nai' (Metalinguistic Negation and 'Wake de wa nai' in Japanese). *Ningenbunkakenkyukakiyo* (*Annual Reports of Graduate School of Humanities and Sciences*) 25: pp. 1–11. Nara Women's University.

Cited Works

[Novels]

Asimov, Isaac. (1950) *I, Robot*. [the 2008 Retold Version as Oxford Bookworms Library. Oxford: Oxford University Press.]

Brown, Dan. (2003) *The Da Vinci Code*. New York: Doubleday.

Carroll, Lewis. (1865) *Alice's Adventures in Wonderland*. [the 1994 Reissued Version as Puffin Classics. London: the Penguin Group.]

Kitamura, Kaoru. (1999) *Sukippu* (*Skip*). Tokyo: Shinchosha.

Koike, Mariko. (1985) Kanojo wo Aishita Ore to Inu (I and the Dog who Love Her). *Daisan Suiyoobi no Jooji* (*Love Affairs on the Third Wednesday*). Tokyo: Kadokawa Shoten.

[TV]

ABC World News. American Broadcasting Company.

[DVD]

Annapolis. Buena Vista Home Entertainment Inc.

Bewitched. Sony Pictures Home Entertainment Inc.

Dictionaries

Daijisen. Tokyo: Shogakukan. 2012.

Kojien. Tokyo: Iwanami Shoten. 2008.

Longman Dictionary of Contemporary English. London: Longman. 2009.

日本語の読者のための内容紹介

1. はじめに

　英語の名詞句トートロジーに関する先行研究は豊富にあるが、日本語の多様な名詞句トートロジー表現形式を包括的に説明できるものはこれまでになかった。本書は、日本語の名詞句トートロジー発話の解釈メカニズムについて、認知語用論の視点から分析を行い、名詞句トートロジーが手続き的情報をコード化している表現形式であることを提案する。そしてそれに基づき、多くの言語に普遍的に存在する名詞句トートロジー発話解釈の全体像を解明することを目指す。

　ここでは、日本語の読者のために、トートロジーにまつわる主要な分析を簡潔に概説し、日本語の名詞句トートロジー研究の意義を示す。そして、本書の概要を述べる。

2.「tautology（トートロジー）」の概念

　日本語の「仕事は仕事だ」や英語のBusiness is businessといった名詞句トートロジーは、一見すると無意味なもののように思われるが、実際の発話文脈においては有意味なものと解釈される。それはなぜ、どのようにして可能となるのか。このような問題提起は、トートロジー研究の出発点となることが多く、その問いに対する答えを導き出すことが、トートロジー研究の中心となるのは言うまでもない。しかしながら、従来の研究ではほとんど言及されることはなかったが、「tautology（トートロジー）」という語は、さまざまな分野で用いられる、多様な概念を示す語である。そのため、トートロジーの分析を始める前に、その語が示す概念を正確に認識することが、最初の第一歩であり、その議論の正確さを左右すると思われる。本書第2章で述べているように、tautologyには主に四つの意味がある。その中でも特に、論理

学のトートロジーと自然言語のトートロジーの違いを確認しなければならない。まず、命題論理学におけるトートロジーは、「論理式の要素がいかなる値をとっても、全体が常に真である論理式」と定義される（荒木・安井(1992: 1469)）。要するに、論理学のトートロジーは、形式的な真偽を問うことはできたとしても、経験的事実については何も語らない情報量がゼロの文である。それに対して、自然言語におけるトートロジーは、（命題）論理学のトートロジーと同じ論理形式を有する、つまり、見た目は（命題）論理学のトートロジーと同じであるが、情報量が豊かな文（発話）であるといえる。本書は、自然言語のトートロジーを研究対象とし、聴者が、トートロジー発話の情報量が豊かであると解釈するプロセスを探る。

3. トートロジーに関する先行研究

言語学における、トートロジーに関する最初の記述は、Grice (1975) によるものである。それ以来、トートロジー研究は、主に3領域で行われてきた。

一つ目は、ラディカルな語用論（従来の語用論）である。これは、Grice の協調の原則と四つの格率に基づくものである。Levinson (1983: 111) は、トートロジーは量の第一格率違反の事例であるとする Grice の分析に従い、トートロジーが伝達する具体的な含意を提案する。例えば、War is war は、"terrible thing always happens in war, that's its nature and it's no good lamenting that particular disaster" という含意を含むと分析する。また Ward and Hirschberg (1991) は、名詞句トートロジー A is A は、意図的に避けられた A is B という発話を文脈から想定し、A is B が無関係であることを伝達するために用いられると主張する。この領域の分析は、文脈情報の重要性を理解しているが、トートロジーの解釈に文脈情報がどのように関わっているかに関する一般化は十分ではない。

二つ目は、ラディカルな意味論である。Wierzbicka (1987: 105) は、トートロジーの解釈は言語特有であり、英語の場合は、(ART) N^i be (ART) N^i という一般式で表される統語構造に依存していると述べる。例えば、War is war や Business is business のような N_{abstr} is N_{abstr} は、"a sober attitude toward complex human activities"を意味する。彼女の分析は、解釈プロセスから語用論的貢献を過度に排除しようとするあまり、トートロジーの豊かな伝達内容を適切に説明できない。

　最後は、前者二つの折衷的アプローチである。Fraser (1988)は、英語名詞句トートロジー NP_i-be-NP_i の慣習的意味を次のように定義している。

（１）　An English nominal tautology signals that the speaker intends that the hearer recognize:
　　　（i）　that the speaker holds some view towards all objects referenced by the NP;
　　　（ii）　that the speaker believes that the hearer can recognize this particular view;
　　　（iii）　that this view is relevant to the conversation
　　　　　　　　　　　　　　　　　　　　　　　　（Fraser 1988: 217–218）

だが、このような定義は、NP_i-be-NP_i 以外にも該当し、名詞句トートロジーの特性を示しているとは言い難い。

　以上のように、トートロジーに関する従来の研究は、主に3領域で議論されてきたが、近年、認知言語学や関連性理論の枠組みを用いた新たな分析が提案されている。

　まず認知言語学では、Mizuta (1995)のフレームモデルに基づく分析が提示されたのち、坂原 (2002)によるトートロジー用法の4分類（記述トートロジー、同定トートロジー、記述拒否トートロジー、同定拒否トートロジー）の中の一つである、記述トートロジーの解釈をめぐる論争が起こっている。坂原 (1993, 2002) は、カテゴリー化の概念を用いて、記述トートロジー「XはXだ」には、「すべてのXはXだ」と解釈する同質化トートロジーと、「Xを、それと類似したYとはっきり区別せよ」と解釈する異質化トートロジーがあると述べている。両者の解釈は以下のようにまとめられる。（両者が示すカテゴリー構成については、本書3.5.2.1を参照されたい。）

（2）a.　同質化トートロジー：
　　　　「XはXだ」は、カテゴリーX内部のメンバー間の同質性を焦点化する。このときは、カテゴリーXとそのメンバーを考えている。
　　b.　異質化トートロジー：
　　　　「XはXだ」は、カテゴリーW内部のメンバー間の異質性を焦点化する。このときは、XをカテゴリーWのメンバーとして捉え、かつWの別のメンバーYと対比している。（坂原2002: 110–111）
　　　　　　　　　　　　　　（一貫性を保つために表記法を一部変更）

また小屋（2002, 2003）は、坂原の分析を踏まえ、トートロジーは、「差異否定の意味（どのようなXもXには変わりがない）」と「差異強調の意味（XはYではない）」という両義性を有し、トートロジーが一義的にしか解釈できない場合は、「差異強調の意味」しか表さないと主張する。古牧（2009a, 2009b）は、坂原の同質化トートロジーを、「決定的側面用法」「多側面的用法」「非特定的用法」の3タイプの用法に分類し、その解釈の多義性を説明している。酒井（2006b, 2008a）は、拡大メンタルスペース理論の枠組みを用いて、坂原の同質化トートロジー、異質化トートロジーの解釈を図式化することを試みている。（これまで、酒井は認知言語学的見地に基づく分析を次々と提案していたが、酒井（2012a）では、Recanati（2004）の「contextualism（文脈主義）」に基づく分析を提案している。）

以上、認知言語学における分析をごく簡単にまとめた。これらの提案は、坂原による分類に端を発するものであり、（特に、同質化）トートロジーの用法を整理・分類することに主眼を置いている。

一方、関連性理論のアドホック概念を用いた西川（2003）は、A is A という発話の解釈プロセスを以下のように示している。

（3）a.　Utterance: *A is A*.
　　b.　Explicature: *A is A**.
　　c.　Higher-level explicature:
　　　　The speaker intends the hearer to know that *A is A**.

d.　Implicatures: (They depend on the contexts.)　　（Nishikawa 2003: 53）

　要するに、A is A という発話の聞き手は、二つ目の A を、A に言語的にコード化された概念がその語の百科事典的知識などに基づき語用論的に調整されたその場限りのアドホック概念に取って代わられた A* だと解釈する、と考えているのである。
　関連性理論では、メタファーやアイロニーに関する研究は盛んに行われてきたが、それらと同じように、字義的な意味と話者の意味とのギャップが大きい言語現象であるトートロジーについては、西川（2003）による英語の分析以来ほとんど行われることはなかった。そのため、アドホック概念を用いた分析はトートロジー発話の包括的解釈理論と見なすことが可能であるのか、日本語のトートロジーは関連性理論でどのように分析されるのか、といった点が議論されず、手つかずのところがたくさん残されていた。そこで、本書は、関連性理論の枠組みを用いて、比較的議論の多い「A は A だ」だけではなく、「A が A だ」「A も A だ」も取り上げ、今まで統一的な視点から議論されることのなかった、日本語名詞句トートロジーを、表現形式（構文）の観点から検証し、従来の分析とは異なった分析を提示している。（具体的な分析は、本書第 4、5、6 章を参照されたい。）

4. 日本語のトートロジー研究の意義

　前節では、トートロジーの意味解釈の問題を議論する際に依拠する領域ごとに、トートロジーに関する先行研究を概説した。このような議論の広がりは、トートロジーに関する関心の高まりを示しているように思われるが、その広がりは研究対象となる言語間によって異なる。先に示した、各領域の中心的な主張を、研究対象言語という観点から再検討すると、英語の事例を扱うものが大半を占め、日本語の事例を扱うものが極端に少ないことに気づく。その大きな理由は、日本語が有するトートロジー形式の豊かさや、トートロジー発話解釈メカニズムの普遍性を解明する必要性が認識されてこなかったからだと筆者は考える。もちろん、英語の分析が、トートロジー研究

において重要な役割を担ってきたことは言うまでもない。だが、一つの言語のみを考察するだけでは見えてこないこともある。

　本書で焦点を当てた日本語名詞句トートロジーには、「AはAだ」「AがAだ」「AもAだ」という三つの表現形式がある。このような表現形式の多様性は、英語のように、A is A という単一の名詞句トートロジー表現形式しか有さない言語には見られない特徴である。したがって、日本語名詞句トートロジーの研究は、トートロジー発話の解釈メカニズムの全体像を解明する上できわめて有意義な材料を提供してくれるように思われる。英語の知見を踏まえながら、日本語の具体例を考察すると、両者の共通点や相違点が見えてくる。この段階になって初めて、トートロジー発話解釈メカニズムの普遍的な側面を探ることが可能となるのである。これまでの研究の中で、複数言語の比較検討がほとんど行われなかったことを考えれば、普遍性を解明する必要性が意識されてこなかったことは当然である。しかし、ほとんどの言語にトートロジー表現形式が存在するという事実は、それらの形式に共通する何らかの普遍性があるのではないかという推測をもたらすのである。

　ではここで、日本語名詞句トートロジーの三つの表現形式に関する研究の現状を把握しておきたい。これまでの日本語名詞句トートロジー研究において、「AはAだ」「AがAだ」「AもAだ」を統一的な視点から扱おうとしたものは、ほぼ皆無である。また、その三つの表現形式に対する言語学者の注目度もまちまちであり、研究が比較的進んでいるものもあれば、そうではないものもある。以下、各表現形式に関する主要な考え方を概略する。

　まず、「AはAだ」についてである。「AはAだ」に関する分析は、他の二つの表現形式に関するものよりも（比較的）多い。ここで注目すべきものは、「AはAだ」の解釈プロセスは、「否定」という点から説明可能であるという考え方である。もちろん、「否定」が意味するものは、それを主張する者によって異なるが、「否定」という概念は、「AはAだ」の意味を説明する上で重要な役割を果たすものである。辻本（1996）は、聴者が、X is not A と定式化されるような、話者に対する反対意見を持っている状況で、話者が、X is A を再度強く主張するために、A is A を発話する、と述べる。X は、その時点でトピックになっている事物・事象、A は、A is A で用いられる A

を指す。辻本の「否定」は、話者に対する反対意見を定式化したX is not Aの中に表れている。また中村（2000: 72）は、「「AはAである」というトートロジーは、カテゴリーAと別のカテゴリーBとを連続的に捉えるカテゴリー観に対して、AとBの非連続的なカテゴリー観を提示し、連続的なカテゴリー観を否定する」と分析する。中村の「否定」は、連続的カテゴリー観の否定を指す。このように、「AはAだ」を分析する際、「否定」がキーワードとみなされるが、「AはAだ」の解釈プロセスにおける「否定」とは具体的に何か、それが何から生じるかについては明らかになっていない。

　一方、「AがAだ」「AもAだ」については、従来の日本語名詞句トートロジー研究においてさほど関心を向けられることがなかったために、体系的な記述そのものが乏しい。その中で、森山（1989）やOkamoto（1993）の分析は、大変興味深い。

　まず「AがAだ」についてである。森山（1989）は、文全体で「普通ではない（想定通りではない）」という意味を持つと主張する。またOkamoto（1993）は、「AがAだ」は、Aによって指示される対象が望ましくない（undesirable）特性や脅威的な（threatening）特性を持つことを示唆する、と述べる。一方、「AもAだ」について、森山（1989）は、「普通ではない（異常な）」事態の並列を意味するものだと考えているのに対して、Okamoto（1993）は、「望ましくない（undesirable）」ものの並列を意味するものだと考えている。もしこのような主張が正しければ、「AがAだ」「AもAだ」はそれぞれ、先に示したような意味を常に持っていなければならないが、本書の分析は、事実がそうではないことを示している。

　以上、日本語名詞句トートロジー研究の必要性を示し、日本語名詞句トートロジーの3つの表現形式をめぐる議論を概略した。本節の冒頭においても触れたように、従来の研究において英語以外の言語がさほど意識されることはなかった。しかし本書のように、英語の知見を踏まえた上で、日本語に目を向けることによって、名詞句トートロジーという言語現象をまったく新しい角度から考察することが可能となるのである。そして、この日英比較から、日本語名詞句トートロジーが豊かな表現形式を有すること、また、〈日本語名詞句トートロジーは表現形式（構文）として意味を持つ〉という本書の

主張が、名詞句トートロジー全体像を説明する上で重要な役割を果たすものであること、を知ることができる。(トートロジー発話解釈メカニズムの普遍性に関する具体的な分析は、本書第7章を参照されたい。)

5. 各章の概要

次に、本書の各章の概要を述べる。本書は、全8章からなる。

第1章 Introduction では、本研究の着想に至った経緯、目的及び論文構成の概略を示す。名詞句トートロジーという表現形式は、ほとんどの言語に存在するが、その表現方法は異なっている。一般的に、英語の名詞句トートロジーは、A is A という単一の形式で表される。一方、日本語では、「は」「が」「も」の区別があるため、名詞句トートロジーとして、「A は A だ」「A が A だ」「A も A だ」という三つの形式が存在し、かつ伝達する意味はまったく異なっている。本書の目的は、これら三つの表現形式の解釈の違いを生み出す要因を明らかにし、そのメカニズムを解明することである。

第2章 Concepts of Tautology では、「tautology(トートロジー)」という概念について概観する。そもそも、tautology という語は、古代ギリシャ語 ταυτολογία に由来し、同じことを2度繰り返す修辞表現を指して用いられていたが、その後新しい意味を獲得し、様々な分野で用いられるようになってきた。本章では、まず、主に論理学におけるトートロジーと自然言語におけるトートロジーに着目し、その違いを示す。この章の議論は、従来の研究では欠けていた、トートロジーとは何かという点を簡潔に示している。

第3章 Previous Studies of Tautology では、名詞句トートロジーに関する先行研究を検証する。先行研究には、ラディカルな語用論(従来の語用論)、ラディカルな意味論、両者折衷的アプローチ、認知言語学、関連性理論(認知語用論)という5領域がある。この章では、具体的な反例を示しながら、どの分析も名詞句トートロジーの包括的解釈理論として容認できないことを明らかにしている。

第4章から第6章では、関連性理論(Sperber and Wilson (1986, 1995[2]))に基づき、日本語名詞句トートロジー「A は A だ」「A が A だ」「A も A だ」

にコード化されている意味を明らかにし、これら三つの表現形式が、独自の意味をコード化していることを主張する。

まず、第 4 章 *A wa A da* では、「A は A だ」に焦点を当てる。第 3 章で吟味、検討したように、名詞句トートロジーに関する分析は、理論的背景・前提の異なる領域間で行われているため、一見するとそれらには共通点さえないように思われる。そのような中で、名詞句トートロジーは、「否定」という観点から分析可能であるという指摘がなされていることは注目に値する（辻本 (1996)、中村 (2000)）。だが、「ない」のような明示的な否定語を含まない名詞句トートロジーにおいて、「否定」とは明確には何であるか、なぜ「否定」と見なされるかについては未解決であった。本章は、「A は A だ」は、異議を唱えたり、他者の要求を拒絶したりする機能を果たし、その機能によって、明示的な否定語を伴わない「A は A だ」が「否定」と見なされるということを確認する。そして、広範な事例考察に基づき、「A は A」が、対比的な想定を持つ文脈、つまり、否定の認知構造（吉村 (1992, 1994, 1999)）で処理されることを示し、「A は A だ」は、それによって伝達される想定が、発話時点の話者以外の誰かに帰属する、主語 A の指示対象に関する想定と矛盾し、それを削除するように処理されることを要求する表現形式であると規定する。

第 5 章 *A ga A da* では、「A が A だ」を分析対象とする。まず「A が A だ」は、「普通ではない（想定通りではない）」「望ましくない」「脅威的である」といったことを意味するという森山 (1989) や Okamoto (1993) の主張に誤りがあることを示す。そして、具体例を示しながら、「A が A だ」は、発話時点で話題になっている事象に対してある説明を与えるものとなるような、主語 A の指示対象に関する想定を呼び出すように処理されることを要求する表現形式であるという規定を提案する。

第 6 章 *A mo A da* では、「A も A だ」について議論する。森山 (1989) や Okamoto (1993) は、従属節を伴う「A も A だ」の意味は、「普通ではない（異常な）」「望ましくない」といったマイナスの特性を持つものの並列であると述べている。だが彼らが扱うデータは、「A も A だ」という形式を持つデータの一部であるため、先に示した主張は、「A も A だ」の総合的な説明とし

て十分なものではない。本章は、具体的な文脈の中での事例考察を通して、「AもAだ」は、発話時点で話題になっている事象に対していくつかある説明のうちの一つを与えるものとなるような、主語Aの指示対象に関する想定を呼び出すように処理されることを要求する表現形式であると規定する。

第7章 The Phenomenon of Nominal Tautology in Japanese では、第4章から第6章の分析結果に基づき、日本語名詞句トートロジーの三つの表現形式の違いを明らかにした上で、日本語及び英語名詞句トートロジーの解釈プロセスに関わるファクターを一般化し、両者の共通点を探る。日本語名詞句トートロジーの解釈プロセスには、(i)矛盾を同定し、削除する、(ii)発話時点で話題になっている事象に対して何らかの説明を与える、というファクターが関わり、さらに、後者は、(a)当該名詞句トートロジーが呼び出す想定は、発話時点で話題になっている事象に対してある説明を与えるものとして解釈される、(b)当該名詞句トートロジーが呼び出す想定は、発話時点で話題になっている事象に対していくつかある説明のうちの一つを与えるものとして解釈される、に二分される。一方、英語名詞句トートロジーの解釈プロセスには、少なくとも(i)矛盾を同定し、削除するというファクターが関わる。このように、日本語及び英語の名詞句トートロジーの解釈プロセスを一般化できることを踏まえ、日本語と英語には、矛盾を同定し、削除する名詞句トートロジー表現形式(構文)が存在しているということを提案する。

第8章 Conclusion では、簡単に結論を述べる。

6. おわりに

本書は、今まで統一的な視点から議論されることのなかった、日本語名詞句トートロジーの三つの表現形式に焦点を当て、名詞句トートロジー発話の解釈プロセスを分析し、〈手続き的コード化という概念こそが、日本語の多様な名詞句トートロジー表現形式を正しく分析し、説明する上で有効である〉と主張する。このような主張は、名詞句トートロジー研究に新しい光を投げかけるものである。また、本書は、これまで語(句)以外のものに適用されることのなかった手続き的コード化という概念が、表現形式(構文)の分析

にも有効であることを初めて指摘し、関連性理論のさらなる発展の可能性をも示唆している。

　最後に、本稿の結びとして今後の展望を述べたい。名詞句トートロジーは、きわめて単純な形式であるがゆえに、メタファーやアイロニーといった、字義的な意味と話者の意味とのギャップが大きい他の現象と比べると、これまであまり注目されてこなかった。だが実際には、予想以上に複雑で興味深いものであることを、日本語の具体例を通して知ることができる。Aという語をAという語そのものを用いて表現する名詞句トートロジーは、それで一体何を伝達しているかについての手がかりが明示的に与えられていないため、メタファーやアイロニーよりも一層複雑な解釈プロセスを必要としているように思われる。この点を踏まえれば、本書の研究成果は、名詞句トートロジーの解釈メカニズムの全体像の把握だけではなく、今日活発に議論されているメタファーやアイロニーといった現象ともかかわりがある内容であり、伝統的レトリック研究への貢献も期待できるであろう。また、ほとんどの言語に存在するトートロジーという現象は、人間の言語認知における普遍的な機能の解明に大きくかかわっており、近年急速に研究が進んでいる、自然言語をコンピュータに処理させる自然言語解析への応用も考えられるであろう。

　以上、日本語の読者のために、現在の名詞句トートロジーにまつわる議論と本書の概要を簡潔に述べた。本書が、今後新たな展開が見込まれるトートロジー研究の一助となれば、筆者として、これに勝る喜びはない。

Index

a
ad hoc concept construction 41–42, 67–68, 84–85, 109–111, 138–139
assumption 81

c
categorization 12, 27, 32–33, 46, 56–58
category formation 31
cognitive effect (or contextual effect) 61
cognitive environment 61, 77, 81
Cognitive Principle of Relevance 63
cognitive structure 77
Cognitive Structure of Negation (CSN) 4, 76–78, 86, 87, 160
Communicative Principle of Relevance 63
compositionality 82, 106, 134
conceptual information 68
Cooperative Principle 16

e
encyclopedic information 109–111, 138
explicature 41, 42, 64–68
extended mental space theory 39–40, 48, 49

f
figure 77, 78
frame model 27–29, 46
free enrichment 66, 84, 109, 137

g
generalized conversational implicature 18, 20, 45
ground 77, 78

h
higher-level explicature 41, 42

i
implicated conclusion 42, 132–134
implicated premise 42, 132, 133
implicature 41, 42, 64, 132–134

l
logical form 8, 23, 64, 84, 109

m
manifest 61
mental space 27

p
particularized conversational implicature 20, 45
predicate logic 9, 13
Presumption of Optimal Relevance 63, 110
principle of relevance 63
procedural information 68–72
propositional logic 4, 7–11, 14
prototype 19

r
relevance 61
Relevance Theoretic Comprehension Strategy 63
relevance theory 61–64

s
scalar implicature 84, 87–88
shared knowledge 12, 27–30
stereotypical (or typical) 29–30, 36, 39, 41
structured database 81
syntactic structure 12, 21, 24–25, 159

t
translatability 22
truth table 9, 13
truth-value 7–9, 15

【著者紹介】

山本尚子（やまもと なおこ）

1981年鳥取生まれ。
2004年奈良女子大学文学部卒業。2009年奈良女子大学大学院人間文化研究科博士後期課程単位取得退学。2012年博士（文学）（奈良女子大学）。奈良女子大学大学院助教を経て、現在、奈良大学教養部講師。

〈主な論文〉
"Cognitive Aspects of Tautology," *JELS* 25 (2008)、「「しょせん」に関する一考察」『日本語用論学会第 11 回大会発表論文集』第 4 号(2009)、「日本語名詞句トートロジー「A も A だ」の認知語用論的研究」『語用論研究』第 14 号(2013) など。

Hituzi Linguistics in English No. 21

A Cognitive Pragmatic Analysis of Nominal Tautologies

発行	2014 年 2 月 14 日　初版 1 刷
定価	8800 円＋税
著者	© 山本尚子
発行者	松本功
印刷所	株式会社 ディグ
製本所	株式会社 中條製本工場
発行所	株式会社 ひつじ書房

〒 112-0011 東京都文京区千石 2-1-2 大和ビル 2F
Tel.03-5319-4916　Fax.03-5319-4917
郵便振替 00120-8-142852
toiawase@hituzi.co.jp　http://www.hituzi.co.jp/

ISBN 978-4-89476-684-6　C3080

造本には充分注意しておりますが、落丁・乱丁などがございましたら、小社かお買上げ書店におとりかえいたします。ご意見、ご感想など、小社までお寄せ下されば幸いです。